# RADIANCES

A volume in the series

## Medieval Societies, Religions, and Cultures

*Edited by M. Cecilia Gaposchkin and Anne E. Lester*

A list of titles in this series is available at cornellpress.cornell.edu

# RADIANCES

## UNPUBLISHED ESSAYS ON GODS, KINGSHIP, AND IMAGES OF THE STATE

ERNST KANTOROWICZ
EDITED BY ROBERT E. LERNER

FOREWORD BY M. CECILIA
GAPOSCHKIN AND
ANNE E. LESTER

CORNELL UNIVERSITY PRESS
*Ithaca and London*

First published 2025 by Cornell University Press

Library of Congress Cataloging-in-Publication Data

Names: Kantorowicz, Ernst H. (Ernst Hartwig), 1895–1963, author. | Lerner, Robert E., editor, writer of introduction.
Title: Radiances : unpublished essays on gods, kingship, and images of the state / Ernst Kantorowicz, edited by Robert E. Lerner.
Description: Ithaca : Cornell University Press, 2025. | Series: Medieval societies, religions, and cultures | Includes bibliographical references and index.
Identifiers: LCCN 2024048429 (print) | LCCN 2024048430 (ebook) | ISBN 9781501782503 (hardcover) | ISBN 9781501782510 (paperback) | ISBN 9781501782527 (pdf) | ISBN 9781501782534 (epub)
Subjects: LCSH: Middle Ages. | Civilization, Medieval. | LCGFT: Essays.
Classification: LCC CB351 .K296 2023 (print) | LCC CB351 (ebook) | DDC 909.07—dc23/eng/20241213
LC record available at https://lccn.loc.gov/2024048429
LC ebook record available at https://lccn.loc.gov/2024048430

*For Eckhart Grünewald*

transformations, implications, and radiations

# Contents

# Series Editors' Foreword

The posthumous publications of nine essays by Ernst Hartwig Kantorowicz (1895–1963), recovered, edited, and brilliantly introduced by the eminent medievalist and Kantorowicz biographer, Robert E. Lerner, is a major event for the field of medieval history. It is hard to overstate the importance of Kantorowicz's influence on the field of medieval history in the twentieth and twenty-first centuries. Given the continued and ongoing importance of Kantorowicz's scholarship, these essays bring Kantorowicz back into scholarly discussion and promise to inject the many subfields that continue to draw from and wrestle with Kantorowicz's writings a series of new ideas and inputs to animate our work.

A Jewish émigré from Germany who landed at Berkeley in 1939 and then (in 1951) at the Institute for Advanced Studies in Princeton, Kantorowicz completed his most influential scholarship while working in the US. He was the author of a stream of important studies written in both German and English but is best known for his book *The King's Two Bodies: A Study in Mediaeval Political Theology*. First published by Princeton University Press in 1957, *The King's Two Bodies* has been reissued in new editions several times (most recently in 2016), and, for its enormous importance, even possesses its own Wikipedia page. The masterpiece is still widely read, cited, and taught; and, having become influential beyond academic circles, the concept behind the book and its title has entered mainstream political vocabulary.

It is hard to exaggerate the enduring importance and influence of Kantorowicz's work in the field of medieval history, art history, and political theory, particularly in studies bearing on politics, ideology, intellectual history, international affairs, and religious ideas. Characteristic of his published work, and in evidence throughout the nine essays in this volume, Kantorowicz's learning was unparalleled, and his scholarly work ranged from the ancient and late antique periods deep into early modern history. Methodologically somewhat *sui generis* but rooted in the deep learning of his capacious German education, his ability to master the technicalities of liturgical, canonical, legal, and theological sources, and to read these sources together to produce new narrative and intellectual exposition, remains an astounding and revelatory achievement, which continues to influence our field profoundly. His main arguments aside, stunning insights can often be had from Kantorowicz's incidental, parenthetical observations, revealing of a deep mastery not merely of his sources but, in a way that seems to us a capacity of lost generations, of the texture of the past itself.

As Lerner explains in his introduction to the volume, Kantorowicz conceived of five of these nine essays together, and even imagined bringing them out together as a unit. The four others are salutary additions that round out our expanded portrait of his oeuvre and certainly deserve a place in the published corpus of his writings. As a group, the essays deal with the same core themes and questions that animated *The King's Two Bodies*, as well as his important *Laudes Regiae: A Study in Liturgical Acclamations and Mediaeval Ruler Worship* (published by the University of California Press in 1946), and also focus around ruler worship, political ideology, and the relationship of sovereignty to religious ideas and frameworks. The opening essay on Synthronos, which reaches far back into ancient history, explores the theme of "co-throning" (and co-rulership), linking it to the development of religious history and key ideals in Christian theology. His essay (chapter 3) on coronations east and west compares the development and underlying ideology of sacral rulership. Whereas the essay (chapter 4) on Charles the Bald presents a new analysis of the Carolingian Renaissance. The second and the fifth essays explore, in different ways, the relationship between Rome and Christianity. In the second, Kantorowicz uses the iconography of coins as an index for the transmission and transmutation of ideas. The fifth essay ("Roma and the Coal") engages the enduring question of how Christianity was shaped by, and then changed, Rome and Roman culture. The sixth essay explores the relationship between Roman law and the early modern imagery of the state; and the seventh essay treats the Burgundian Renaissance. In all, the essays range in time from antiquity up through early modernity—and, as reflected in his somewhat whimsical ninth essay, discussing the iconography of postage stamps, even into the modern period. The essay (chapter 8) on "Humanities and History" reminds us that the need to explain the value of our field both within the university and more broadly is a constant. The analysis throughout is extraordinary, demonstrating the author's enormous range and erudition, and his facility with both liturgical and legal sources that characterizes his foundational work. His insights astound, with incidental observations or formulations that make each page worth reading and rereading. We have absolutely no doubt that this collection of essays will be of enormous interest to a wide range of readers and scholars.

The essays gathered here are edited versions of unpublished works found among the materials of Kantorowicz's literary estate. Before his death Kantorowicz named Michael Cherniavsky and Ralph Giesey, his two most prominent graduate students from his Berkeley days, as his literary executors. Giesey had begun to compile materials from Kantorowicz's files and made some available online, but the site was not maintained after his death in 2011. With the exception of chapter 6, "Glosses on the Late-Medieval State Imagery," which Lerner rescued from obscurity, Kantorowicz's unpublished essays along with other materials (principally letters and notes) were collected and are now housed at the Leo Baeck Institute, where the digitized originals can be consulted online. The essays published here have been edited for clarity and coherence. We will note that the bibliographic citations have not been brought up to date, although in many cases a wide bibliography, often itself in great debt to Kantorowicz's earlier studies, would be relevant, and a good number of the primary sources that he consulted now exist in more recent editions. Lerner retained the footnotes as Kantorowicz had included them, which offers complete information albeit rendered in an archaic, now antiquated form. In his appendix to chapter 4 ("Charles the Bald and the *Natales* of the King"), Kantorowicz included only short parenthetical notations, the key to which are provided in a footnote. That same appendix included indicators for six footnotes that are now lost, which have been excised from the text. The whole has been retained as exemplary for Kantorowicz's sources and research practices, themselves of interest in regard to evolving modes and methods of historical scholarship in the twentieth century.

Finally, we wish to express our deep gratitude to Robert E. Lerner for bringing this project to our series. Lerner's recovery of these essays follows his masterful biography of Kantorowicz, *Ernst Kantorowicz: A Life*, published by Princeton University Press in 2017. In his short introduction to this volume, and in the illuminating frames he provides for each chapter, Lerner positions these essays in both a general and individual context. Lerner thus provides an easy way for the reader to enter again into the conversations that Kantorowicz was having with the field at the time he wrote. We are delighted that these rediscovered essays can now be added to Kantorowicz's intellectual legacy, joining *The King's Two Bodies*, *Laudes Reges*, and his other writings that continue to inspire scholars, students, and other readers for generations to come.

M. Cecilia Gaposchkin and Anne E. Lester

# PREFACE

A French critic has noted that the writings of Ernst Kantorowicz hold "a powerful and durable fascination for many generations of historians and intellectuals."[1] Readers have been fascinated primarily by Kantorowicz's two main books—his biography of Emperor Frederick II and his masterwork, *The King's Two Bodies*.[2] For some the fascination extends further to a number of impressive articles, most of them gathered in the volume *Selected Studies*.[3] And the bounty of the internet even provides two pages of Kantorowicz quotations.[4] Who might have thought then that there is still greater wealth? Yet nine contributions that have never been published appear here now.

The editor would like to thank M. Cecilia Gaposchkin for proposing the splendid title *Radiances* for the present book and for including it in the series Medieval Societies, Religions, and Cultures that she oversees for Cornell University Press with Anne E. Lester. Cecilia Gaposchkin was also blessedly indefatigable in locating appropriate illustrations. Mahinder Kingra, editorial director at Cornell University Press, also lent his invaluable support. Not least, Robert Lerner's debt to Karen Hwa, senior production editor at Cornell Press, is huge for overseeing the entire project with sovereign capabilty.

---

1. Florent Coste, review of *Ernst Kantorowicz, une vie d'historien*, by Robert E. Lerner, *Annales: Histoire, Sciences Sociales* 78 (2023): 640: "une fascination considérable et durable sur plusieurs générations d'historiens et d'intellectuels."

2. Ernst H. Kantorowicz, *Kaiser Friedrich der Zweite* (Berlin, 1927), translated by E. O. Lorimer as *Frederick the Second, 1194–1250* (London, 1931); *The King's Two Bodies* (Princeton, 1957).

3. Ernst H. Kantorowicz, *Selected Studies* (Locust Valley, NY, 1965).

4. Wikiquote, https://en.wikiquote.org/.

# Introduction

*Robert E. Lerner*

Writing to Leonardo Olschki, one of his closest scholarly colleagues, in June 1961, Ernst Kantorowicz lamented that he urgently needed to finish an article on which he had been working intermittently for sixteen years. He envied Olschki, who always finished what he had started, but as for himself: "I have files upon files of unfinished things, always three-quarters finished, but never entirely. [I am] always waiting to publish them all together but never doing that. [I] should of course have brought them right into print, but now it's a torture that yields nothing new but only staleness."[1]

The self-reproach was a constant. In 1951 he wrote "I hope to finish finally the manuscript of the *Synthronos* and *Epiphany and Coronation* papers. . . . Well, those are the dreams and we all know that they are made of a different stuff than the reality."[2] In 1955 while laboring over *The King's Two Bodies*, he joked mordantly about how long his "pregnancies" were, "with innumerable aborted articles coming in between."[3] In

---

1. Kantorowicz to Olschki, June 11, 1961, Leonardo Olschki Papers, Special Collections, Getty Research Institute, Los Angeles.

2. To Albert M. Friend, January 5, 1951, Kantorowicz papers, Dumbarton Oaks Archives, Washington, DC.

3. To Elise ("Lieschen") Peters, June 26, 1955, Lerner Archive.

the same year he admitted in a letter to Olschki that it was stupid for him to have accepted an invitation to lecture at a meeting of the College Art Association because he was still working on *The King's Two Bodies*: he had been working on that for eight years, and soon he really needed to complete two collections of articles for the Dumbarton Oaks research institute that he had so long promised.[4] But at the time of his death in 1963 he had not completed either.

In regard to scholarly articles, Kantorowicz of course had nothing to be ashamed of, for he published some forty over the course of his scholarly lifetime. With only a few exceptions these were not appendages to book projects but were independent works that owed their existence to the superabundance of their author's ideas and interests. A collection of twenty-five was published after his death in a stately folio-size volume that still remains relevant and fascinating to a wide range of readers.[5] Yet still, there are the unfinished ones. A perfectionist, Kantorowicz did not want to release anything that he did not consider absolutely ready. Thus, six articles in various states of near completion have lain to this day among his posthumous papers. He left instructions that nothing he had not overseen be brought into print, but after half a century his grandniece has acknowledged that it is time to put this injunction aside. Consequently the six mentioned articles, together with three apposite accompanying pieces, are here published for the first time. Some of the typescripts are full of handwritten emendations and jottings; one offers numbers for footnotes but not the notes themselves; one exists in two versions that need to be integrated. Nevertheless, the entirety can safely be said to rank with Kantorowicz's best work.

Five of the articles originated in different times and circumstances, but Kantorowicz later thought of them as a set. These are "Synthronos"; "Roman Coins and Christian Rites"; "Coronation Scenarios Eastern and Western"; "Charles the Bald and the *Natales* of the King"; and "Roma and the Coal." His Boswell, Ralph Giesey, reported that toward the end of his life Kantorowicz had intended these five to be published in a volume that was to be called *Studies Eastern and Western in the History of Late Classical and Mediaeval Ideas.*[6] Giesey did not mention a sixth article, "Glosses on Late-Mediaeval State Imagery," for unknown reasons. But it was as near to being finished as most of the others and is

---

4. To Olschki, December 8, 1955, Olschki Papers.
5. Ernst H. Kantorowicz, *Selected Studies* (Locust Valley, NY, 1965).
6. *Dumbarton Oaks Papers* 17 (1963): 118.

equally worthy. "The Dukes of Burgundy and the Italian Renaissance" was meant only as a lecture, but despite the lack of footnotes one can easily see that it is based on original archival research. Whether "Humanities and History" was meant for publication is uncertain, but it can be viewed as an important, hitherto neglected expression of the author's credo. Finally, a vivacious after-dinner talk, "Postage Stamps and the Historian," appropriately comes after the dinner that is served here.

Ernst Kantorowicz is customarily understood to have been a medieval historian; his Wikipedia entry (as last edited on May 26, 2024) describes him as "a German historian of medieval political and intellectual history and art." This characterization, however, fails to recognize his astounding chronological range. Seven articles range over a span of eighteen centuries: "Synthronos" refers mainly to the Hellenistic era, with a glance at Pharaonic Egypt and culminating with early Christianity; "Roman Coins" mainly to the Roman period; "Coronation Scenarios" mainly to early Byzance. After that "Charles the Bald" concentrates on a later Carolingian ruler; "Roma and the Coal" on an event in Rome that took place in the year 1000. "Late-Medieval State Imagery" deals mainly with the thirteenth and fourteenth centuries; and "The Dukes of Burgundy and the Italian Renaissance" treats the reign of Charles the Bold (1467–1477). Lest we think that Kantorowicz's range stopped in the fifteenth century, one might add that "Postage Stamps and the Historian" ventures to refer to the Napoleonic era and to postage stamps from the 1850s to the 1940s.

As the chronological range of the pieces offered here is astounding, so is the diverse range of source materials. In "Synthronos" alone we find Pharaonic sculptures, Cretan inscriptions, coins, sarcophagi, a Sophoclean tragedy, rabbinic exegesis, Origen, Tertullian, and correspondence of "Julian the Egyptian" from the time of Justinian. "Roman Coins" treats not only coins and medallions but moves into Latin Christian liturgy, while "Coronation Scenarios" builds primarily on the Greek Fathers and Greek liturgy. The piece on Charles the Bald features late-Carolingian charters, and "Roma and the Coal" revolves around a Latin poem. "Late-Medieval State Imagery" features a class of sources—legal glosses—that Kantorowicz turned to in the fifties; and "The Dukes of Burgundy" draws on both Renaissance medals and unpublished diplomatic dispatches. Could Kantorowicz possibly then have omitted postage stamps? Well, it turns out he did not.

As these essays show, Kantorowicz's place in the historiographical landscape of his day was unique. The dominant concern of American scholarship was English and French political and constitutional history, as exemplified by J. R. Strayer (Princeton), C. H. Taylor (Harvard), and their numerous students. In France, the Annales school was in full swing, but this meant the practice of quantitative economic and social history, entirely foreign to anything Kantorowicz did. Granted that a third topic featured in the subtitle of the journal *Annales* was "mentalities," in Kantorowicz's day students of this were lacking. As for the study of ritual, a few specialized scholars of Christian liturgy were at work in various countries, but they were not to be found in history departments. Later came an "anthropological turn" but only after Kantorowicz's death, and at any rate EKa would have had no patience for the social science implications associated with the school of Victor Turner and Clifford Geertz. Scholars of the history of ritual and symbolism without such implications could be found in Germany, but after Kantorowicz's departure from that country in 1938 he was not in close contact with any of them, and after the war he did not have any meaningful community with them. (His early friendship with and admiration for Germany's leading student of medieval symbolism, Percy Ernst Schramm, had worn thin: Schramm published a book in 1958 with the word "Reichsapfel" [i.e. "Orb"] in its title, but behind the author's back Kantorowicz mockingly called this "Pferdeapfel," or "horse dropping.")

Five of the six formal articles presented here (the exception is the earliest, "Charles the Bald and the *Natales* of the King") belong squarely in the realm of Kantorowicz's "second manner." The most obvious trait of this manner is its polymathic erudition. How did this man who never went to church know that "[the] *Triodion* [was] the chant sung at the morning service on Thursday of the second week in Lent"? How did he know that "Russian marriage rituals remember in the Dismissal not only Christ and Mary, but also Saint Constantine the Great and Saint Helen, the emperor's mother"? How did he know that a medallion of Henry VIII bore inscriptions in the three biblical languages—Hebrew, Greek, and Latin? How was it that he was as well-informed about "the tomb of Dexileos in the Athenian cemetery of the Kerameikos" as he was of the tomb of "Guillaume Filastre, the second Chancellor of the Order of the Golden Fleece, made in the workshop of the Della Robbia"? Discursive footnotes laden with recherché bibliographical references spanning languages and centuries abound. In 1959 Kantorowicz observed that he had "made about 10,000 footnotes in his life," adding, "one of my major pleasures."[7]

---

7. To Ernst Kitzinger, April 5, 1959, Kantorowicz papers, Dumbarton Oaks Archives.

Less obtrusive but crucial for understanding what the author was doing is the fact that Kantorowicz understood the term "historical problem" in his own fashion. Simply stated he did not equate it with "question" or something that needed to be solved but rather with "topic" or "subject matter." Thus the article on "Coronation Scenarios" opens with the words "The problem of the Byzantine coronation . . . is still a subject given to controversy," with the words "problem" and "subject" being used interchangeably. Examples could be multiplied. The usage also appears in *The King's Two Bodies*, as when the author refers to his work as a contribution to the greater "problem" of "The Myth of the State" (ix).

In treating "problems," Kantorowicz wished to explore their "radiations." He wrote in "Roma and the Coal" that he intended to pursue "the dogmatic, ritual, and archeological radiations" of the metaphor of coal as Eucharistic bread. Similarly, he used the term in the preface to *The King's Two Bodies*: he intended to pursue the fiction of the two bodies in its "transformations, implications, and radiations" (ix). His aim was not to cover a topic methodically but to limn its origins, shifting shapes, interrelations, and transferences. Christian "Epiphany," for example, had many epiphanies.

The reason for this approach is set out most clearly in a passage of *The King's Two Bodies*:

> Any effort to "explain" a historical phenomenon, even though one may hope to understand some factors by which it was conditioned and which it was interrelated, remains a hopeless task because there are too many layers of life effective at the same time and actively concatenated as to permit any straightforward explanation; and to answer the question why certain potentialities actualized in one way and why they did not crystallize in another will necessarily be an undertaking of limited and doubtful value. (447)

In keeping with this position, the author left blank the space on the Princeton University Press's publisher form that asked for his book's "thesis," and he refrained from offering "conclusions" for *The King's Two Bodies* itself, presenting instead an "Epilogue" that almost cheekily dealt with a period earlier than that covered in the book.

Similarly, five of the six formal articles presented here display "radiations" but are unconcerned with "coverage" or answering questions. (The exception is "Charles the Bald and the *Natales* of the King," which offers unique "coverage" of the Carolingian Renaissance and formulates a distinct proposition about Charles the Bald.) A problem for the present editor has been to decide whether "Synthronos" and "Roma and the Coal" intentionally ended where they did or were left incomplete because as they stand their endings seem abrupt. Perhaps it is this freedom that makes Kantorowicz's work so fascinating. Unexpected interrelations abound, and hazardous juxtapositions offer room for thought; watching the author leap from one hardly known datum to another is exhilarating.

The items presented here appear in chronological order of subject matter rather than date of composition. Even had one preferred the latter alternative it would have been very difficult to accomplish because dates of composition frequently cannot be pinned down. A disadvantage is that one is unable to observe closely any evolution in Kantorowicz's mastery of English other than to note that in the earliest of the pieces his English is often wobbly. (As late as the "State Imagery" article of the mid-1950s, he could still fall into a malapropism, using "equivocation" when he meant "equivalence.") Throughout, the editor has generally adhered to Kantorowicz's sometimes peculiar spellings except in cases of clear-cut errors. Numerous circumlocutory constructions and inconsistencies of comma usage have also been retained. Just as Kantorowicz's spoken intonation was notably eccentric, so he seems to have wished to have a distinctive voice on the printed page. Characteristically too, he never spared his readers arcane technical vocabulary: "teicheoskopia," "taurobulion," "trichonomastic." One winces, but it is the price of admission.

CHAPTER 1

# Synthronos

## *On Throne-Sharing of Gods and Men*

In a letter to Leonardo Olschki of June 1961 Ernst Kantorowicz characterized an article on which he was currently working as "tomfoolery" (the term he used was "Allotria").[1] He had been working on this article, "Synthronos," for a very long time, and now he was as much sick and tired of it as he was "of Bardot's pout." He only wanted to be finished with it. By the time of his death it was not yet entirely finished, but looking at what we have today leads one to say that, far from "tomfoolery," it must count as one of his most impressive pieces.

The earliest reference to "Synthronos" appears in the records of the Berkeley Colloquium Orientologicum. There we learn that Kantorowicz presented a paper, "Synthronos: Throne Sharing with the Deity," at a meeting of the Colloquium of December 6, 1945. Given the title, this was just the first part of the three-part work that Kantorowicz finished toward the end of his life. A few weeks earlier Kantorowicz had written to Fritz Saxl that he intended to publish the paper he was writing in a volume to be

---

1. Kantorowicz to Olschki, June 11, 1961, Leonardo Olschki Papers, Special Collections, Getty Research Institute, Los Angeles: "Du siehst, mein Lieber, es ist lauter Allotria was ich treibe, und die *Synthronoi* hängen mir zum Halse heraus, wie der (auf Deutsch:) 'Schmoll-mund' der Bardot."

called "Studies in Political Liturgy."[2] That plan, however, was vastly premature. Not only was the original "Synthronos" paper unfinished in 1945, but the same was true of the other two pieces Kantorowicz said were to be its companions, "Roma and the Coal" and "Epiphany and Coronation." And, in fact, all three were then postponed.

Kantorowicz brushed the dust off of the Berkeley "Synthronos" paper to give it again in April 1950 at a conference at Dumbarton Oaks.[3] In January of the following year he wrote to the Dumbarton Oaks director that it was unfinished, and in 1953 he referred in print to "Σγηθροπς: God and King as Throne Sharers" as a "forthcoming study."[4] Around that time it lay on his desk, for in *The King's Two Bodies*, finished for practical purposes in 1955, he included a passage (p. 501) that nearly duplicated one that was to appear in the article on "Synthronos." (In both he referred to Philip II of Macedon sitting in the theater while his throned effigy was paraded with those of the gods.) By 1959 or slightly later, the article had advanced: the surviving manuscript contains three parts and refers to Gerhart Ladner's *Idea of Reform*, published in 1959. But in his letter to Olschki of June 1961, Kantorowicz wrote that "the Synthronoi are weighing on me and if I don't get this done now it will never be done." In 1945 "Synthronos" had been meant for a volume to be called *Studies in Political Liturgy*; shortly before September 1963 Kantorowicz planned for it to be the opening chapter of a book to be called *Studies Eastern and Western in the History of Late Classical and Medieval Ideas.*[5]

The surviving manuscript is clean, and the author evidently took some trouble to prepare it for publication, for he availed himself of a Greek typewriter to type in Greek words. (Earlier he had penned in necessary Greek by hand.) Occasionally he also corrected in pencil passages containing some of the eccentric English of his earlier days. But although the text could have been handed to a printer, that was not true of the footnotes. Kantorowicz evidently recognized this himself by leaving large spaces between the typed text of each note. Sometimes he left blanks for details that he did not have to hand; more often he used abbreviated forms for longer titles. Thus it

---

2. Kantorowicz to Saxl, November 11, 1945, Fritz Saxl Papers, Warburg Institute Archives, London.

3. Kantorowicz papers, Dumbarton Oaks Archives: Program for Symposium "The Emperor and the Palace," April 27–29, 1950.

4. To Albert M. Friend, January 5, 1951, Dumbarton Oaks Archives. "ΣΥΝΘΡΟΝΟΣ ΔΙΚΗΙ" [Synthronos Dike], *American Journal of Archeology* 57 (1953): 65–70, at n. 12; reprinted in Kantorowicz, *Selected Studies* (Locust Valley, NY 1965), 1–6.

5. This according to a statement by Ralph Giesey in *Dumbarton Oaks Papers* 17 (1963): 118.

was necessary to plug some holes and perform some unraveling for the present publication. (The present publication also omits long supporting quotations in Greek and a considerable number of notes that consist of superfluous cross-referencing.)

"Synthronos" might well be the most learned among all the author's other tolerably learned pieces. The chronological and geographical range is vast. It centers on Hellenistic and Roman episodes, but within that compass it roams to Pharaonic Egypt, the Persian Empire, and the kingdom of Commagene; then it moves to Christianity by means of the Old and New Testaments, the Greek Fathers, rabbinic literature, and abstruse Christological debates. It employs such phrases as "an Attic demos of the Hadrianic phyle," and words such as "hierothesion" and "synonymity." The author is a show-off in other ways. He refers to a "famous passage" in Tertullian and tells us that "we have to recall the philosopher Peregrinus-Proteus." All told, his repertoire is astounding: a predigital match for Professor Google.

Nevertheless, the greatest recommendation of the article is its progression of "throne-sharings." Rulers in the ancient world could be depicted as seated next to gods, thereby acquiring divine auras. Thus also could the dead be seen to be co-throned with gods in the afterlife. And from there we reach the Son who ascends to be seated next to the Father. (Kantorowicz informs us at the start that he is treating the theme of "seated next to" as opposed to "standing next to," thereby allowing him to keep up his sleeve until his third part the line from the ordinary of the Mass, "Qui sedes ad dexteram Patris.") The article is thus at once a fundamental study of an aspect of the cult of rulers in antiquity as well as a "radiation" of that into the theology of Christianity.

Antinous, the beautiful young Bithynian and beloved of Divus Hadrianus, died in or on the Nile in 130 A.D. Whatever the circumstances of his mysterious death may have been, accident or self-sacrifice, certain it is that Hadrian's grief was matched by his desire to exalt the victim of a tragic fate. Antinous became a god. Statues displaying his lovely features—soft, sad, sensual, the eyebrows closely drawn together—were set up all over the world.

Coins portraying him bore the legend ΘΕΟΣ ΑΝΤΙΝΟΟΣ.

Attic ephebes made him the god of their feasts. An Attic demos [suburb of Athens] of the Hadrianic phyle [clan] was named *Antinoeis*. A Roman funerary guild recognized him as patron. Some of the divine honors conferred upon him are recorded on the obelisk which Hadrian erected for his friend in Rome, now on the Pincio. In Egypt, where

**FIGURE 1.1**  Marble bust of Antinous, from Syria, after 130 CE. Wikimedia Commons, CC BY-SA 2.0. Photo: Carole Raddato.

Antinous died to rise again as a god, a city was named for him. Among the divine honors granted to him occurs the one which is to form the subject of this essay and which was announced in inscriptions set up for him: "To Antinous, the *synthronos*, the throne-sharer, of the gods" (Ἀντινόῳ συνθρόνῳ τῶν ἐν Αἰγύπτῳ θεῶν).[6]

Antinous therewith entered into the tradition of the kings of the Ptolemaic dynasty who, in their turn, had continued the tradition of Pharaonic Egypt. "Throne-sharer of the gods" was, by the time of Antinous's death, a title of cultual or semi-cultual honor closely connected with the Hellenistic cult of the ruler.[7] It had become almost a technical

---

6. For Antinous as Osiris, Franz J. Dölger, "Esietus: Der Ertrunkene oder der zum Osiris gewordene," *Antike und Christentum* 1 (1929), 174–83, at 183, n. 38. [The Greek that appears in this article was inserted by Kantorowicz in his typescript by hand and has generously been transcribed for me by Jeremy Thompson.]

7. The problem here to be discussed has not yet been treated, although a good start has been made long ago by George d'Arnaud, *De diis παρέδροις sive adsessoribus et coniunctis commentarius* (The Hague, 1732); but the closely related subject of "temple-sharing" in Antiquity has,

**FIGURE 1.2** Antinous bronze coin, his head in profile Ancyra, 138–161 CE American Numismatic Society, 1944.100.62226.

term enjoying popularity, not only in Egypt whence some of our evidence comes, but all over the Hellenistic world.

Though a relatively late word, *synthronos* was always a solemn expression, used mostly when things sacred or dignified were under discussion. The throne, of course, was itself a seat of distinction and honor of gods and kings. "Throne-sharer," therefore, was by its very nature a lofty designation for any person, even within the purely human political sphere when, for example, the Sassanian king invested the commander of the guards his *synthronos*.[8] The one called upon to share the throne with a king appeared as the king's equal, or at least as the king's vice-gerent, *a rege secundus*. And the man called upon to share the throne with the gods became in some respects their co-equal and fellow-god, or at least a *diis secundus*.

Gods themselves, in art and literature, were often introduced as having other divinities—often minor ones—for their throne-companions. "Zeus, in all that he does, has Aidos for co-partner of his throne," says

---

with characteristic brilliance, been dealt with by Arthur Darby Nock, "Σύνναος θεός," *Harvard Studies in Classical Philology* 41 (1930), 1–62, a study without which I would have been lost and to which I feel greatly indebted.

8. Edward Bratke, *Das sogennante Religionsgespräch am Hofe der Sassaniden* (Berlin, 1893), 3, lines 6–15. For other Persian examples, Hans Volkmann, "Der Zweite nach den König," *Philologus* 92 (1937), 285–316.

Sophocles;[9] and Pan, in the Orphic Hymns, is called "throne-sharer of the Horae."[10] At the very end of the dying Greco-Roman world, Nonnos of Panopolis, in his heroic epic of the savior Dionysos, visualizes the comforter god of the vine and redeemer of mankind, after the god's ascension as "*synthronos* of Apollo and one sharing the hearth with Hermes."[11] Furthermore, the emperor Julian mentions that according to ancient belief Athens Pronoia was a *synthronos* of Apollo, whereas Julian himself worshipped Helios as "*synthronos* of the Mother," while styling the Great Mother one "sharing the seat and sharing the throne with great Zeus,"[12] thus venerating a throne-sharing trinity which governed the universe. As the notion gained currency in the vocabulary of the Hellenistic world, *synthronos* was used also in a figurative and poetical sense without forfeiting its solemn character. To Philo, for example, the Virtues appeared as "*synthroni* of the soul."[13] And Origen mentions the Virtues as *synthroni* of Eusebia, Piety.[14] The Virtues, or Personifications, were also *synthroni* of each other, for example, Bia, the Force, the throne-sharer of Dikē, Right. And in the Vienna Dioskorides manuscript we find a miniature showing Megalopsychia, Sophia, and Phronesis seated on one throne.[15]

In a figurative sense, man could be called a throne-sharer of certain Virtues. Meleager, for example, ends his cycle of poems by claiming that now he was seated as "a throne-sharer with Wit who marks the goal of Docility (Eumathia)." Just as the regal virtues Dikē and Themis were said to be seated at sides of Zeus, so had, according to Dio of Prusa,

---

9. Sophocles, *Oedipus at Colonus*, 1267–68.

10. *Orphica*, ed. Eugenius Abel (Leipzig, 1885), XI, 4, p. 64. Leonardus van Liempt, *De vocabulario hymnorum Orphicorum atque aetate* (Utrecht, diss., 1930), 19. *Synthronismoi* of deities, of course, are suggested by numerous double-thrones; see, e.g., Wolfgang Reichel, *Über vorhellenische Götterculte* (Vienna, 1897), 30–31, fig. 8. But it is not the intention here to broach the problem of throne-sharing gods such as the Capitoline triad and other similar groups of deities.

11. Nonnos, *Dionysiaca*, 48, 974 [for 978], ed. W. H. D. Rouse (3 vols., Cambridge, 1940–1955), 3, 492.

12. Julian, *Oratio IV*, 149C; *Oratio V*, 167B, ed. W. C. Wright (2 vols., New York, 1913, 1923), 1, 408, 500.

13. Philo, *Legum allegoriae*, III, 247, c. 88, ed. Leopold Cohn and Paul Wendland, *Philo Alexandrini, Opera quae supersunt* (2 vols., Berlin, 1896–1930), 1, 168; see also the related passage in Cicero, *Ad Quintum fratrem*, I, 1. 31; see Nock, "Σύνναος θεός," 57, n. 2.

14. Origen, *Contra Celsum*, III, 50.

15. Joseph von Karabač, ed., *Dioskorides: Codex Aniciae Julianae picturis illustratis . . . phototypice editus* (Leiden, 1906), fol. 6ᵛ.

Kingship at her right side Dikē and Eunomia, and at her left, Eirene.[16] What was valid for Kingship at large, was valid also for the individual king whom, for example, Themistius visualized seated with Nomos and Budikia (Righteous Judgment).[17] Actually the ruler was quite often represented, even in mediaeval and early Renaissance art, as a throne-sharer of various Virtues.[18]

Provincial governors were treated similarly. In Didyma, for example, several inscriptions were dedicated to the Proconsul Festus who, in or around 263, accomplished some public works and obliged the citizens by a new setting of a fountain which Apollo had caused to gush forth when Barbarians besieged the city. An inscription announces that the waters once were sacred to the god—"now, however, this has become the fountain of Festus, *synthronos* of golden Dikē."[19] Julian the Egyptian, under Justinian, praised the provisional governor Tetianus, calling him "an amazing man" because "Justice as [your] throne-sharer knows that you loath to touch wealth won from those that you rule." It is not impossible, however, that the figurative speech of "throne-sharer of Dikē," or one of its equivalents, had a slightly more realistic meaning because the statues of governors might be flanked by statues of Dikē and any other personified Virtue, or because their statues were placed in the τέμενος Δίκης, that is, in the Praetorium, the *Palais de Justice*.

The notion of "throne-sharer of the gods," however, acquired a political rather than a poetical meaning ever since it became fashionable to visualize and worship Hellenistic kings as "gods manifest." In a technical sense the designation of "*synthronos* of a god" or "of gods" implied that to the images of gods ceremoniously seated on their thrones there was added, equal in material and often equal in size, the statue of the monarch, an honor by which the king became almost *isotheos*.

---

16. Dio Chrysostom, *Oratio I*, 73ff. See Vladimir Valdenberg, "La théorie monarchique de Dion Chrysostome," *Revue des études grecques* 40 (1927), 142–62, at 159. See, in general, Rudolf Hirzel, *Themis, Dike und Verwandtes* (Leipzig, 1907).

17. Themistius, *Oratio XV*, ed. Wilhelm Dindorf (Leipzig, 1832, p. 230, 19, and 233, 13). See also *Oratio XXV*, ed. Dindorf, 375, 16.

18. Ambrogio Lorenzetti's fresco of the Buon Governo (Siena, Palazzo Pubblico) likens a paraphrase of *Basileia* surrounded by the Virtues sharing her throne; see Nicolai Rubinstein, "Political Ideas in Sienese Art: The Frescoes by Ambrogio Lorenzetti and Taddeo di Bartolo in the Palazzo Pubblico," *Journal of the Warburg and Courtauld Institutes* 21 (1958), 179–207. See also my remarks in "ΣΥΝΘΡΟΝΟΣ ΔΙΚΗΙ," *American Journal of Archeology* 57 (1953), 65–70.

19. *Supplementum epigraphicum graecum*, ed. J. J. E. Hondius, 4 (1929), no. 467. See Louis Robert, *Hellenica* 4 (1948), 25–26, 68–69, 98–99, for this epigram and related material collected from governor inscriptions.

Moreover, since the cult statue of a prince, when allocated to those of the gods, would be placed in a sanctuary, a shrine or a sacred district, the royal *synthronos* might be, at the same time, a "temple-sharer" or an "altar-sharer" of the god or gods in whose sanctuary his statue had been placed. "Throne-sharing," therefore, might amount to some kind of "temple-sharing," and in essence the privilege of being a *synthronos* would not differ greatly from the related, and much more frequently mentioned, honor of being a *synnaos*, an honor lavishly bestowed upon the Ptolemaic dynasts of Egypt and more sparingly upon other Hellenistic kings or upon Roman princes. The relative rarity of *synthronos* as compared to *synnaos* may be explained by the fact that the epithet "throne-sharer" could be applied only if the deities whose dignity the king's statuary likeness was to share, were themselves represented seated on their thrones. If the effigies of the gods were standing upright, the statue of the monarch was not likely to be a representative of a seated ruler. *Synthronos*, therefore, suggested the statue of a throned ruler being added to the statues of enthroned gods; and it remains to be seen whether the "sitting" as opposed to the "standing" had a specific meaning.

## 1. Kings as Throne-sharers of Gods

Our evidence for a king's throne-partnership with the gods starts in the Hellenistic period and, if we may believe Diodorus, it begins with Philip II of Macedonia.[20] When this king celebrated at Aigai, in 336 B.C., the marriage of his daughter Cleopatra, the images of the Twelve Gods, seated on the thrones, were carried as customary into the theatre. In that solemn *pompē* [procession], however, there was added to the images of the Twelve the image of King Philip as that of a throne-sharing thirteenth. His image was equal in form and material to those of the gods. In other words, the king's throned effigy was paraded with those of the gods, and while the king *in natura* presided over the show, the king *in effigie*—so to say, his *numen*—was seated in the midst of the gods to watch the performance as a throne-sharing thirteenth.[21]

The report of Diodorus foreshadows several interesting features of the later cult of rulers: it is our earliest evidence for a royal *sellisternium*,

---

20. Diodorus Siculus, *Bibliotheca historica*, XVI, 92, 5; XVI, 95.
21. See, for this feature, E. H. Kantorowicz, *The King's Two Bodies* (Princeton, 1957), 501.

the custom of exposing together with the couches or thrones of the gods the draped throne of the monarch, with or without his effigy; and it is also an evidence for the ruler as the *triskaidekatos*, the thirteenth god, a feature that was to play a considerable role in later times.[22] For these reasons doubts have been cast on the reliability of Diodorus's report concerning Philip, which has been labeled anachronistic. This skepticism, however, has not been generally accepted. Besides, the alleged anachronism does not exceed perfectly reliable evidence for royal *synthronismoi* by more than some fifty years. It is true, of course, that a throne-sharing with gods is not recorded with regard to Alexander the Great. Only in Pseudo-Callisthenes's *Alexander Novel* does the term appear several times. According to this source Alexander was offered to become the *synthronos* of Zeus.[23] Moreover, Dareios appropriated for himself in his royal style the title "*synthronos* of Mithras," or of Helios, or of the gods.[24] But even so this royal style, well attested in later times, reflects perhaps not more than the relative popularity of that term around 300 A.D. when the *Alexander Novel* was composed. Nor is there any other reference to Alexander as throne-sharer of a divinity, although according to Clement of Alexandria he had been elevated to the rank of a thirteenth god.

The story was different with regard to Alexander's successors in Egypt. Ptolemy I Soter died and was deified in 283 B.C. His statue showing the king enthroned was put up in the temple of Zeus where, according to Theocritus, Alexander, himself a god "was seated friendly beside him," while "over against him was set the adamantine throne of Hercules."[25] The first Ptolemaic ruler thus had been recognized, after his death, as a *synthronos* of the gods and heroes of his country. Twelve years later, around 270, an inscription honors the still living

---

22. See, for the *sellisternia*, Lily Ross Taylor, "A Sellisternium on the Parthenon Frieze?" *Quantulacumque: Studies Presented to Kirsopp Lake* (London, 1937), 253–64; and for Rome, Kurt Latte, *Römische Religionsgeschichte* (Munich, 1960), 242ff. For the thirteenth god, see Otto Weinreich, *Lykische Zwölfgötter-Reliefs* (Sitzungsberichte der Heidelbergische Akademie der Wissenschaften, 1913, Abhandlung 5), and his article "*Zwölfgötter*" in W. H. Roscher, *Lexikon der griechischen und römischen Mythologie* (6 vols., Leipzig, 1884–1937), 6, 764–848.

23. Pseudo-Callisthenes, *Historia Alexandri Magni*, II, 22, 9, ed. Wilhelm Kroll (Berlin, 1926), 97, 15. Alexander himself calls Roxane his *synthronos*; ibid., 22, 6 and 10, ed. Kroll, 97, 3 and 16. Cf. W. W. Tarn, *Alexander the Great* (Cambridge, 1950), 2, 365.

24. See for the ironic discussion of the Persian royal title, Pseudo-Callisthenes, I, 36, 2, ed. Kroll, 40, 21: Dareios styled himself *synthronos* of Mithras; I, 38, 2–3, Kroll 42, 21, and 24. Alexander styling Dareios *synthronos* of Helios and of the gods; cf. I, 40, 2, Kroll, 45, 5, where Dareios refers to himself as *synthronos* of the gods.

25. Theocritus, *Encomium* (*Idylls*), XVII, 16ff.

royal couple, Ptolemy II Philadelphia and his sister-queen Arsinoe, the θεοὶ Ἀδελφοί, plainly as "*synthronoi* of the gods in Egypt." This, we recall, was verbatim the formula chosen to describe Antinous's cultual status. Moreover, the official cult for the Adelphian gods was established around 271–270; it included, from early times, a temple-sharing of the royal couple.[26] But even a few years before that date there are some significant features in connection with the festive *pompē* arranged by Ptolemy Philadelphia and described in great detail by Kallixenos. For in that procession the throne of the deceased and deified rulers of the dynasty were paraded with symbolic emblems placed on the seats, and to these there was added the throne of Philadelphos himself.[27] In other words, through the medium of the exposed thrones Philadelphos became the *synthronos* of the deified founders, Alexander and Ptolemy Soter, or vice versa, the deified predecessor king-gods appeared as the σύνθρονοι θεοί of the ruling king.

It is not quite by chance that some of our earliest evidence for throne-sharing refers to Ptolemaic practice; for the idea of the king's throne-partnership with gods has a Pharaonic tradition. At any rate, there are quite a number of monuments of the New Empire showing the king as the *synthronos* of a deity. In the cells of the temple at Medinet Habu several statues have been found showing Thutmose III (18th dynasty: 1501–1447) in the company of Amon, seated together with the god on one throne, twice on the right hand of the god, once on his left;[28] and a similar twin statue of king and god had its place in the temple of Amon at Karnak, where another group showed the king between two deities. Moreover, Seti I (19th dynasty) shared in Abydos not only the thrones of the deified dead kings, but also that of Amon who, in an inscription, made it known that he had placed his "great seat beside their majesties." An earlier king, Horemheb (last of the 18th dynasty) was seated next to

---

26. Nock, "Σύνναος θεός," 4ff. See also Ernst Kornemann, "Zur Geschichte der Antiken-herrscherkulte," *Klio* 1 (1901), 51–146, at 70ff. For the inscription θεοὶ ἀδελφοί distributed on both obverse and reverse on coins, see Walter Gieseke, *Das Ptolemäergeld* (Leipzig, 1930), 20 and pl. II, fig. 12.

27. Wilhelm Franzmayer, *Kallixenos' Bericht über das Prachtzeit und den Festung Ptolomaeus II* (Strasbourg, diss., 1904), 49. W. W. Tarn, "Two Notes on *Ptolemaic* History," *Journal of Hellenic Studies* 53 (1933), 57–68, assumes an earlier date and therefore comes to deny the divine character of the royal ancestors.

28. Jacques Vandier, *Manuel d'archéologie égyptienne* (Paris, 1958), III, 304, and pl. CI, fig. 6; Uvo Hölscher, *The Excavations of the Eighteenth Dynasty: The Excavations of Medinet Habu* 2 (Chicago, 1939), pl. III (facing p. 12), and figs. 43–44 (p. 51).

**FIGURE 1.3**   Ramses II (1303 BCE–1213 BCE) as *synthronos* of the Egyptian gods Horus, Ptah, and Amon. Wikimedia Commons, CC BY-SA 4.0. Photo: Diego Delso.

Horus, at the right hand of the god, and it was probably the same king who is shown between Osiris and Horus with Isis sitting next to Osiris. Of Seti's successor Ramses II there are very many sculptures known in which he is represented on one seat with gods and goddesses. On one occasion Ramses II appears as the *synthronos* of Ptah, Amon, and Horus in the temple at Abu-Simbel in Nubia and other divinities are allocated to him in other Nubian sanctuaries. These few examples, no doubt, could be multiplied considerably. They suffice, however, to understand that the Hellenistic kings of Egypt of the Ptolemaic dynasty continued a Pharaonic tradition when they assumed the honor not only of temple sharing with the gods, but also that of throne-sharing.

Throne-sharings between gods and kings may have been quite frequent in other Hellenistic kingdoms as well, but they are usually not readily recognizable. Did, for example, the sanctuary of the Twelve Gods in Delos harbor a statue of Demetrius Polloketes as well, and if so, was he a *synnaos* of the Twelve or also their *synthronos*? King Eumenes II of Pergamon was a *synnaos* in the port of Pergamon, Eleia; was he perhaps also a *synthronos*? Throne-sharing, at any rate was known in Pergamon. For in 37 or 39 A.D. Julia Livilla, the daughter of Germanicus, was officially styled a *Nea Nikephoros* and the *synthronos* of Athena Nikephoros, of the goddess whose image showed her seated, carrying on her right hand a small statuette of Victory.[29]

The most impressive example, and quite unambiguous testimony, of royal throne-partnership with the gods is the great monument and inscription of the sanctuary which Antiochus of Commagene established, in the thirties of the first century B.C. on the summit of Nemrud Dagh.[30] He has chosen, declared the king of that small kingdom straddling in Asia Minor the Hellenistic and Parthian orbits of culture, to consecrate the new temple as a sacred seat for the gods to share.

> Wherefore, as thou seest, I have established these godlike effigies of Zeus Oromazdos, and of Apollo Mithras Helios Hermes, and of Artagnos Heracles Ares, and of mine all nurturing country Commagene; and of the self-same stonework I have set up a copy of my own form as throne-sharer of the gods that hearken to prayers (δαίμοσιν ἐπηκόοις σύνθρονον), and have caused the ancient honor of great gods to become coeval with a great Tyche.[31]

The ruins of this *hierothesion* [royal mausoleum] on Nemrud Dagh show, in a truly stunning fashion, the colossal figures, each measuring some twenty feet, sitting side by side on their huge thrones. Zeus is the central figure with personified Commagene at his right and King Antiochus at his left, throne-sharers who in their turn are flanked by Apollo and Heracles respectively. The rigid frontality of the colossi increased the solemn monumentality of this "throne of the gods" (θεῶν ἐνθρόνισμα). To these "royal gods" (βασιλικοὶ δαίμονες) who were at the same time the kings' planetary divinities (Jupiter, Mars, Mercury), there were added slabs displaying the images of the "god kings" (θεοὶ βασιλεῖς) that is, the ancestors and deified predecessors of Antiochus back to that Dareios, adversary of Alexander the Great, who according to Pseudo-Callisthenes, proudly styled himself "*synthronos* of Mithras."

---

29. Max Fränkel, *Die Altertümer von Pergamon*, VIII: 2: *Die Inschriften von Pergamon* (Berlin, 1895), 330, no. 497. For the image of Athene Nikephoros on Pergamenian coins, see Hans von Fritze, *Die Münzen von Pergamon* (Abhandlungen der Preussischen Akademie der Wissenschaften, Berlin, 1910, Anhang zu Abhandlung 1), pl. IV, fig. 15, and pp. 58–59.

30. The Commagene inscriptions are published by Louis Jalabert and René Mouterde, *Inscriptions grecques et latines de la Syrie* (Paris, 1929) 1, nos. 1ff., where also the former publications are enumerated. The work in Commagene, carried on by Friedrich Karl Dörner and R. Naumann, *Forschungen in Kommagene* (Berlin 1939), and, with the latest bibliography, Dörner, "Die Entdeckung von Arsameia am Nymphenfluss und die Ausgrabungen in Hierothesion des Mithridates Kallinikos von Kommagene," *Neue deutsche Ausgrabungen im Mittelmeergebiet und im Vorderen Orient* (Berlin, 1939), 71–88. See also Nock, "Σύνναος θεός," 26–27.

31. See Jalabert and Mouterde for the Nemrud Dagh inscription, line 53ff.

**FIGURE 1.4**  Personified Commagene and King Antiochus, seated with Zeus, Apollo, and Heracles, on Nemrud Dagh, 62 BCE. Wikimedia Commons, CC BY-SA 3.0. Photo: Klaus-Peter Simon.

Here his descendent, Antiochus of Commagene, has adopted that very title. Visibly and, through the medium of the inscriptions, almost audibly, the King of Commagene placed himself in the newly established shrine as the *synthronos*, the throne-sharing equal of the great gods as well as of his ancestral divinities while expounding his own glory by means of the title, repeated over and over again, of the "Great King Antiochus, the just god manifest" (Βασιλεὺς μέγας Ἀντίοχος θεὸς Δίκαιος Ἐπιφανής).[32] At the same time he asserted in the inscription that he had

---

32. This title is constant in all the inscriptions on Nemrud Dagh as well as in those from Gerger, Samosata, and Arsameia on the river Nymphaeus; see, for the latter, Dörner, "Die Königsresidenz Arsameia am Nymphenfluss," *Das Altertum* 2 (1956), 71, and, for the inscriptions, Jalabert and Mouterde. For the *Dikaios Theos*, sometimes identified with Mithras, see Franz Cumont, "Dikaios," *Realencyclopädie der classischen Altertumswissenschaft* V: 1, 564 § 2; also Stig Wikander, *Feuerpriester in Kleinasien und Iran* (Lund, 1946), 4–5. For *Epiphanes* as *cognomen* or title, see Pfister, "Epiphanie," *Realencyclopädie, Suppl. IV*; A. D. Nock, "Notes on Ruler-Cult," *Journal of Hellenic Studies* 48 (1928), 21–43, at 38–41. It is interesting to find that also the hero became a ἥρως ἐπιφανής; see Louis Robert, "Hellenica," *Revue de Philologie* 13 (1939), 200–201, and 18 (1944), 36–37. It is remarkable that the throne-sharing colossi on Nemrud Dagh are, as it were, "preceded" by slabs depicting the Epiphany or *Adventus* of the king who shakes hands with each of the four deities; cf. Karl Humann and Otto Puchstein, *Reisen in Kleinasien und Nordsyrien* (Berlin, 1890), pls. XXXVIII, figs. 1–2, and XXXIX, figs. 1–2. These representations match by and large, unless verbatim, Roman imperial *Adventus* coinages, especially some specimens of Alexandria, where the emperor shakes hands with Osiris; cf. Jocelyn M. C. Toynbee, *The Hadrianic School* (Cambridge, 1934), 42–45, pls. II, figs. 20–21, XI figs. 1–3. I am inclined to think that the Nemrud Dagh monument was intended to represent two distinctly different scenes, (1) the *Adventus* of Antiochus, who is met by the divinities, and (2) his enthronization at the side of the supreme god as his *synthronos* and that of the others.

caused his Tyche (the Persian *Hvarenō*) to become manifest as equal in age with the gods themselves.

Moreover, the inscription perhaps allows us to make a guess at a more succinct meaning of *synthronos*. For Antiochus claimed he had become a *synthronos—ἐπήκοοι—*of the gods that "hearken to prayers." That is to say, Antiochus considered himself a throne-partner of those gods who in *ex voto* monuments are so often represented by a huge pair of ears per se; and it has been observed, by the archaeologists in the field, that the divinities on Nemrud Dagh were distinguished by unproportionately large ears. Also in the inscription of Samosata, Antiochus associated himself as *synthronos* with the ἐπήκοοι, the "celestial divinities that hearken to prayers." Now St. John Chrysostom remarks on one occasion that

> so long as the king is seated on his throne, he listens to the petitioners and they may achieve what they desire. Once, however, the king rises from his throne, all words on the part of the petitioners are futile.[33]

In other words, to sit or be enthroned means benevolence and benevolent listening. The royal *synthronos*, therefore, is one that hearkens together with the gods to prayers, acting perhaps as the advocate or intercessor of the people, and especially of those of his own country.

The monuments and inscriptions of the Kingdom of Commagene represent in more than one respect the apogee of the Hellenistic cults of rulers, and it seems as though Antiochus I had a definite plan to organize the ruler cult more or less uniformly throughout his kingdom.[34] Antiochus, however, had good reason for adding to his more divine titles also that of *Philorhomaios*, friend of the Romans. For in his days the star of Caesar had risen, and with the dictator Hellenistic concepts of kingship began to make their way into Rome—so far as they had not been received before—and there to be remolded according to Roman ideas of rulership.

To the Dictator C. Iulius Caesar the Romans voted, in addition to other divine honors, that his golden chair adorned with his crown be carried into the theatre and the circus in the very same manner as the

---

33. John Chrysostom, *In Acta Apostolorum*, XXI, n. 4⁰, PG 60, 170.
34. See, for this problem, Josef Keil, "Basaltstele des Königs Antiochus I. von Commagene," *Serta Hoffilleriana* (Zagreb, 1940), 129–34.

thrones of the gods. Later, after his death and consecration, there was added to throne and crown the effigy of Divus Iulius who, being himself a god became quite logically and legally the de facto throne-sharer of the other gods.[35] The technical term of *synthronos*, however, rarely appears in the language of the cult of emperors; and its Latin equivalent, *consessor*, which we know from Julius Valerius' translation of the *Alexander Novel*, has a very vague meaning and is hardly found in pre-Christian times.[36] The whole idea of throne-sharing was adventitious to Rome and remained, to say the least, without emphasis, even though poets visualized occasionally their emperor's future table-fellowship with the immortals.[37]

This does not imply that a throne-community of Roman emperors and princes with gods was beyond Roman imagination. We learn, for example, that the image of Augustus, seated on a couch, was placed— at least temporarily after the death of the *princeps*—in the temple of Mars.[38] It may be doubted whether this action really implied an *Augustus Marti consessor*. In one case, however, there certainly was a genuine throne-sharing of Augustus and a deity, which is well illustrated by the famous cameos in Vienna. Reclining in his throne of Sphinxes Augustus is shown, in the smaller gem, at the side of the goddess Roma.[39]

On earth, the *princeps* had shared temples, altars, and priests with this goddess, the numerous sanctuaries *Romae et Augusti*. It is therefore plausible enough that the exalted Augustus, as shown in the larger gem was represented once more as the *synthronos* of the goddess Roma who gratuitously made, as it were, his enemies his footstool while taming the proud.[40] Apart from Roma and Augustus, throne sharings were not too frequent in Rome, whereas it occurred in the Provinces. We recall the case of Antinous who became *synthronos* of the gods in Egypt, or

---

35. Andreas Alföldi, *Insignien und Tracht der römischen Kaiser* (Munich, 1935), pp. 41ff., 154–55.

36. For *consessor* as translation of σύνθρονος, Franz Cumont, *Textes et monuments figurés relatifs aux mystères de Mithra* (2 vols., Brussels, 1899), 2, 36–37.

37. For the table-fellowship of Augustus with the gods and heroes, see Anton Elter, *Donarem pateras* (Bonn, 1905), II, 43ff., cf. Franz Cumont, *Recherches sur le symbolisme funéraire des Romains* (Paris, 1942).

38. Nock, "Σύνναος θεός," 30, n. 3.

39. Adolf Furtwängler, *Die antiken Gemmen* (Leipzig, 1900), pl. LVI, and 251ff.; Alföldi, *Insignien*, pl. XIX. A blue glass cast of the Vienna cameo (Kunsthistorisches Museum) is in the Dumbarton Oaks Collection (no. 46.10); see *Handbook of the Dumbarton Oaks Collection* (Washington, DC, 1955), 131, No. 260, and the reproduction on p. 136.

40. Alföldi, *Insignien*, pl. XVIII and pp. 126ff.

**FIGURE 1.5**    Augustus seated next to Roma, ca. 15 CE. Detail from the Gemma Augustea. Wikimedia Commons, CC BY-SA 3.0. Photo: James Steakley.

Julia Livilla who, in Pergamon, became the *synthronos* of Athena Nikephoros. To these may be added Julia Domna, empress of Septimius Severus. For in 196–197 A.D. the Athenians voted to set up her statue in the temple of Athene to become the latter's *synthronos* and to be worshiped under the same roof with the goddess.[41] Moreover, in the age of the Tetrarchs, a coin displays the emperor Maximian, head of the so-called "Herculian" dynasty, as the *consessor* of Hercules, the emperor being in uniform and the god naked.

Finally, Servius in his commentary on *Aeneid*, I, 276 and 292, mentioned a strange mythical feature: in expiation for the death of Remus there should always be a *sella curalis* with scepter, crown, and other regal insignia placed next to that of Romulus-Quirinus so that the two brothers seemed to take all actions together in like manner.[42]

To summarize, throne-sharings of kings and gods were quite common in the Hellenistic kingdoms even though the evidence is not as rich as it is with regard to temple-sharing; and also in Rome, though to a lesser degree, this cultual honor of princes was not quite absent.

---

41. Anton von Premerstein, "Athenische Kultehren für Kaiserin Julia Domna," *Jahreshefte des Österreichischen Archäologischen Instituts in Wien* 16 (1913), 249–70, at 250, lines 19–20, see also 259–63. See also Nock, "Σύνναος θεός," 34–35.

42. Servius, *In Vergilii carmina comentaria*, ad Aen. I. 276. Professor Andreas Alföldi obligingly called my attention to this place.

**FIGURES 1.6A AND 1.6B**    Silver Antoninianus of Maximian, Lugdunum (today Lyon), 292 CE. Obverse: Bust of Maximian; reverse: Hercules holding a lion skin. American Numismatic Society, 1984.146.133.

## 2. The Dead as Throne-sharers of Gods

Most of the documents hitherto discussed referred to living princes as *synthronoi* of gods. We have to consider, however, numerous and manifold interrelations which prevail cultually between gods, kings, and dead. To that triangle of gods, kings, and dead—a common denominator may be the cult of heroes—and the similarities of their worship Tertullian, in a famous passage, called attention by objecting to the worship of the dead rather sarcastically. He asks:[43]

What then do you do to honor the gods that you might not offer to your dead as well? You build temples for the gods, and after

43. Tertullian, *Ad nationes*, I, 10, 26ff., ed. Reifferscheid-Wissowa (*Corpus scriptorum ecclesiasticorum latinorum*, 20), 77; ed. J. G. P. Borleffs (Corpus Christianorum, I:1), 26–27. Cf. Franz

the same fashion you build temples also for the dead. You erect altars for the gods, and after the same fashion altars for the dead. You write the same characters at the head of the inscriptions. You form the effigies of gods and dead in the same manner depending upon craft, trade, or age of the deceased . . . who can excuse the disgrace of non-distinguishing between god and dead? Moreover, in the rulers too there are attached colleges or priests and the requisites of sacred rites, chariots, and processional carts, preparations of thrones, festivals, and games.[44]

To this long list of agreements between the cults of the gods, and those of the dead and of rulers, the scandalized apologist might have added other items; and in fact he added them in other writings. He mentioned the identity of the sacrificial bowl and of the cup of libation to the dead. He devoted a whole treatise to the crown as an insignia and stressed correctly that the dead were crowned as a sign of their deification or, as he put it, "because they become idols as soon as they are dead both by their attire and by the service of consecration."[45] And he might have mentioned, unless this parallel was indicated by the remark concerning the *solisternia*, also the preparation of thrones: likened to gods and kings, the dead had their thrones too.

The purpose of these ceremonial chairs placed in the sepulchral chamber was to provide a seat for the dead at the ritual meal offered to them by mourners and friends; invisibly the deceased were supposed to be present in the vacant throne to share the offerings of their friends.[46] This idea, however, does not exclude another implication, to wit, that the dead were meant to be exalted by the throne, and that the throne became an insignia of his "heroization" or "deification" after death.[47] That is, he was to be received in the community of gods and

---

J. Dölger, *IXΘYC* (Münster, 1922), II, 1ff. Karl Baus, *Der Kranz in Antike und Christentum* (Bonn, 1940), 126. Alfred C. Rush, *Death and Burial in Christian Antiquity* (Washington, DC, 1941), 137ff.

44. The characters heading the inscriptions were *D.M.* (*Dis Manibus*) or *D.M.S.* (*Dis Manibus Sacrum*). Cf. Dölger, *IXΘYC*, II, 8; Baus, op. cit., 196–97. For *sellisternia* and *solisternia*, see above, n. 17. For the processional chariots (*tensae* and others), see Aline L. Abaecherli, "Fercula, Carpenta, and Tensae in the Roman Procession," *Bollettino dell'associazione internazionale degli Studi Mediterranei* 6 (1935–36), 7ff. In general, for the triangle of cults of heroes, kings, and dead, see Dölger, *IXΘYC*, II, 1–19.

45. Tertullian, *De corona*, 10; Baus, *Der Kranz*, 124.

46. Theodor Klauser, *Die Cathedra im Totenkult der heidnischen und christlichen Antike* (Münster, 1927), has discussed the problem brilliantly.

47. For the funerary throne as a sign of exaltation, see the careful remarks of Klauser, *Cathedra*, 58, also 44–45 for the θρόνωσις of the deas. The idea of heroic exaltation indicated by

heroes, not dissimilar to the heroized and apotheosized rulers. This hope of hero-like immortality was expressed in many another fashion as well—by the crown carved in the tombstone, by the *clipeata*, the portrait disk of the dead, or by the presence of Nike conferring the crown.[48] Whereas the transcendental banquet community of dead and heroes has been studied with reasonable thoroughness,[49] less attention has been paid to the dead's "throne-sharing" with the immortals, an idea which the "serene dwellings" of the gods, the *sedes quieta*, invite the dead to rest, was supplemented by a vision of a more ceremonious posture of the dead.

It is true, the concept of otherworldly table-fellowship with the gods and heroes was much more common in later pagan times than that of a stern and hieratic throne-partnership which grants less relaxation, though perhaps greater distraction. But the throne-partnership is nevertheless quite well known. In the earlier period, the king- or judge-like exaltation of the dead's enthronement referred to the realm of Hades. The exalted dead would be visualized as privileged "partners of the seats of the gods below" (πάρεδροι τοῖς κάτω θεοῖς). Instead of joining the crowd of almost nameless shadows, some elect, the χῶρος εὐσεβῶν, were granted seats near the throne of Hades and Persephone, or were allowed to share the seat of Minos, the paragon of the just and himself a judge in the kingdom below. It was perhaps the right of προεδρία of sitting in the first rows at the games and in the theatre which the seat-sharing dead would enjoy.[50] But by this very right of honor the distinguished dead might have become also associated with the heroes. An inscription from Cnossos glorifies a warrior, Thrasymachos, whose fame (it is said) will prevent him from vanishing among the shadows in the house of Hades. For "Hades, the glorious, will make you to sit down as a *synthronos* of Idomeneus, the possessor of cities."[51] That is to

---

the throne has been strongly stressed by Odo Casel, in his review of Klauser's book, in *Jahrbuch für Liturgiewissenschaft*, 8 (1928), 349.

48. For the crown, see Baus, *Der Kranz*, 126ff.; Cumont, *Symbolisme funéraire*, passim (see index, s.v. "Couronne"); Erwin R. Goodenough, "The Crown of Victory in Judaism," *Art Bulletin* 28 (1946), 142–43. For the round shield images, see Johannes Bolten, *Die imago clipeata* (Paderborn, 1937). For Nikai conferring crowns, see Cumont, op. cit., 464, fig. 99, and p. 466.

49. The standard works are, after Erwin Rohde, *Psyche* (9th ed., Tübingen, 1925), Mrs. [sic] Arthur Strong, *Apotheosis after Life* (New York, 1915), and Franz Cumont, *After Life in Roman Paganism* (New Haven, 1928), to which his most recent monumental works must be added, his *Symbolisme funéraire* and *Lux perpetua* (Paris, 1949).

50. Rohde, *Psyche*, 314, note; Cumont, *Symbolisme funéraire*, 49, n. 4.

51. Henri Lechat, "Inscriptions de Crète," *Bulletin de Correspondence Hellénique* 13 (1889), 60; art. "Paredroi," in Roscher, *Lexikon der griechischen und römischen Mythologie* 3:1 (1877).

say, Thrasymachos was to become the throne-sharer of the local Cretan hero Idomeneus.

The great metamorphosis of eschatological belief, however, was brought about when, in the beginning Hellenistic age, human mind was conquered by the doctrine according to which man's soul might ascend to the skies to become immortal among the stars or gods.[52] The "soul sharing the seat of the immortals" (ψυχὴ σύνεδρος ἀθανάτων) was a term suggesting that the privileged was to share like very few heroes, not the thrones of the "gods below," but those of the "gods above." The vulgarization of heroship by the new mystical and philosophical doctrines, as well as the mutual interpenetration of beliefs in the immortality of the soul and in the ascension to the gods of some heroes, are subjects representing the most complicated and complex phenomena of religious history. Suffice it here to say that the idea of a throne-partnership with the gods began to move away from the nether regions and to seek its materialization in the regions above.

The formal and official heroization by which Alexander supposedly honored his dead friend Hephaestion, has always attracted the attention of scholars, though it is not too well attested. Allegedly the king gave orders that in addition to other honors sacrifices were to be offered to Hephaestion as θεὸς πάρεδρος, a "seat-sharing god."[53] The dead as *paredroi* of the immortals was an honor not unheard of, but it went beyond custom to style the defunct himself a god sharing the seats of the other gods. At any event, a throne-sharing with the Olympians appears as a vehicle of deification and heroization. This is true to a certain extent also with regard to the ruler of Commagene. In the great inscription Antiochus, *synthronos* of the gods in this present world, gave vent to his hope that "after having expired his god-fearing soul into the infinite eternity," his body would rest in the cairn, which he had established, indelible by the stars of time, in greatest proximity of the celestial thrones, near the thrones of Zeus Oromasdes in heaven. That is to say Antiochus expected to continue his throne-partnership with the gods after his death—partly in effigy, and partly because the *hierothesion* on the summit of Nemrud Dagh, where his body would rest, was at least in greatest proximity of the celestial thrones.

---

52. Cumont, *After Life*, 95ff., 194ff.

53. Diodorus Siculus, *Bibliotheca historica*, XVII, 115, 6. See Kornemann, "Zur Geschichte der Antikenherrscherkulte," 59-60; Fritz Taeger, *Charisma: Studien zur Geschichte des antiken Herrscherkultes* (2 vols., Stuttgart, 1957), 1, 227, n. 8.

This lofty throne-sharing with the "gods above" was not only a privilege of heroized kings, but it was accessible to other mortals as well, in the first place to the wise men and the adepts of philosophy.[54] An inscription of the second century after Christ, from Ephesus, announces very assuredly: "I am dwelling in the sacred and most lovely place of the pious, a throne-sharer of the heroes on account of my self-control." In this epitaph inscription the throne-sharing with the heroes appeared as the reward of a philosophical virtue, self-control, or of a philosopher's life in general. The caricature of this heroic *synthronismos* is not missing. We have to recall the philosopher exhibitionist Peregrinus-Proteus who vaingloriously thrust himself like another Phoenix into the flames of a pyre with the intention to die and resurrect from the ashes as a god. Mockingly, a poet, Theagnes, described the ambitions of Peregrinus, and wrote: "Then all men shall worship that great hero, who wanders through the darkness of night, a throne-sharer of Hephaestus and of the Lord Heracles."[55] The boastful suicidal philosopher thus allegedly expected to share, after his resurrection and ascension, the thrones of the demiurge Hephaestus and of the savior Heracles, two gods who are found together also on a sarcophagus.[56]

The throne-partnership with the savior gods and their lower concomitants, for example, the Muses, was obviously a more desirable destiny in the life thereafter than sharing the seat of Minos in the bleak regions of the shadows. Not only the philosophical doctrines but also the mystery cult promised to their adherents a community with the gods in the life after death, that is, the heroization. Throne-sharing, it is true, seems to have been of no importance in the mystery religions, even though the ritual of initiation provides sometimes also for the θρόνωσις of the neophyte, the enthronement on the chair of the god. To certain gnostic symbols, however, whose teaching may well be called a Christianized equivalent of the mysteries, an other-worldly throne-sharing of the dead with secondary deities was known. In the *Stromata*, Clement of Alexandria gives an account of gnostic perfection according to which those having preserved a pure heart during their life on earth shall be taken up to the neighborhood of the Lord in the other world;

---

54. Cumont, *Symbolisme funéraire*, 246ff., 281ff., 507, and passim; also his *Lux perpetua*, 324–25. See also the passage from Philo discussed by Erwin R. Goodenough, "Philo on Immortality," *Harvard Theological Review* 39 (1946), 85–108, at 103.

55. Lucian, *De morte Peregrini*, 29.

56. Cumont, *Symbolisme funéraire*, 324.

and there "they shall be called gods and become throne-sharers of the other gods who rank first after the Savior."[57]

The ideas blended in this passage are interesting. First, there is the apotheosis of the dead: they shall be taken up to heaven and be called "gods."[58] Further, the apotheosis is combined not with the more customary *coronatio* but with an enthronement: the meritorious dead, after their ascent to heaven, become the "throne-sharers" of certain deities. Moreover, the future σύνθρονοι θεοί of the dead are the "gods ranking first after the savior." In the pagan orbit this would have meant probably the community with the companion gods of the greater gods: here the δεύτεροι may be recognized as *logoi* or *dynameis*—"angels" according to Christian terminology. Finally, the passage in the *Stromata* renders Christian thought; the virtuous dead shall be called to the proximity of the Savior to share the throne with the savior god's companion.

## 3. Christos *Synthronos*

When we survey the considerable number of places in the New Testament in which the throne-sharing of the glorified Son of man with God the Father is mentioned, it might appear that this metaphor sprang exclusively from the tradition of ancient Israelitic thought. No verse of the Old Testament has been quoted so often, and so significantly in the New as Psalm 109, the decisive passage announcing the royal or messianic throne-partnership with Jehovah: "The Lord said unto my Lord: Sit thou at my right hand, until I make thine enemies thy footstool."[59] This verse is referred to so authoritatively in the Gospels, and it is repeated or alluded to so often in the Apostolic writings that the celestial

---

57. Clement of Alexandria, *Stromata*, VII, 56, 6, ed. Otto Stählin (4 vols. Leipzig, 1905), 3, 41:24. See G. W. Butterworth, "The Deification of Man in Clement of Alexandria," *Journal of Theological Studies* 17 (1916), 157–69, at 161, n. 5, and Cuthbert Lattey, "The Deification of Man in Clement of Alexandria: Some Further Notes," *Journal of Theological Studies* 17 (1916), 257–62, at 261–62, who very emphatically argues that Clement's choice of the word *synthronos* was determined by the cultual language of Ptolemaic ruler worship.

58. See Psalms, 81, 6. Cf. Gerhart B. Ladner, *The Idea of Reform* (Cambridge, Mass., 1959), 89, n. 22, also 94–95 for this Psalm in the Christian doctrine of deification; see also Ernst H. Kantorowicz, "Deus per naturam, Deus per gratiam," *Harvard Theological Review* 45 (1952), 253–77.

59. The material has been sifted by Walter Grundmann in "δέξιος," *Theologisches Wörterbuch zum Neuen Testament* II (Stuttgart, 1935), 37–39. For the rabbinic interpretation of the Psalm, see Hermann L. Strack and Paul Billerbeck, *Kommentar zum Neuen Testament aus Talmud und Midrasch* (Munich 1928), IV, 452–65, Excursus 18: "Der 110. Psalm in der altrabbinischen Literatur." See further the monograph on the Psalms by Lorenz Dürr, *Psalm 110 im Lichte der neueren altorientalischen Forschung* (Münster, 1929).

throne-companionship of the Son of Man with God the Father is explained sufficiently by the Psalms alone. It may seem superfluous, therefore, to search for an influence of the Hellenistic tradition with regard to this metaphor.

The distinction, however, between Israelitic and Hellenistic tradition is not fortunate in this case. For the image of Israelitic kingship as reflected by the Psalter is inseparable from the concept of divine kingship in the ancient Near East; and this, in its turn, formed also the basis of Hellenistic ruler worship. The decisive factor is rather the difference between both Jewish and Hellenistic concepts of human-divine throne-partnership on the one hand and the image of Christ sharing the throne of the Father on the other. In the Psalm, no matter whether it be interpreted "historically" or "messianically,"[60] the throne-sharing of the Lord who is addressed with the Lord who speaks is, as it were, "absolute" and not determined by time—despite the promise of a future victory "until I make thine enemies thy footstool." The Israelitic throne-sharing has no recognizable cause nor, beyond the final victory, a conceivable consequence. The same is true with regard to the throne-sharings of the Hellenistic kings. The king's throne-fellowship with one or more gods is a mark of distinction or honor, but it is not bound to a definite moment in the life of the ruler and does not have any consequences in regard to other men.

The applications of Psalm 109 in the New Testament, however, deviate from both the Israelitic and the Hellenistic traditions in so far as the throne-sharing of the Messiah, the Son of Man, with God the Father is bound to a specific moment in the life of Jesus and the history of the human race, and it is integrated into a universal economy of salvation. For the sitting of the man Jesus on the right side of God the Father appears as an ultimate goal, as the last consequence of a tragedy, the last scene of a terrifying drama which began on earth by the incarnation and ended in the crucifixion, the resurrection, and the ascension to heaven. The ensuing *synthronismos*, therefore is meant to appear as the last station of a long journey, as the supreme exaltation and glorification of the one who asserted himself, also by his ἆθλα, his exploits, as

---

60. See Billerbeck, who discusses both the historical (Davidic) and the messianic interpretations of that Psalm in rabbinic literature. In Christian writings, the messianic interpretation predominated, especially since David himself was a messianic figure, both ancestor and prefiguration of Christ; see Kantorowicz, "The Quinity of Winchester," *Art Bulletin* 29 (1947), 73–85, at 75, n. 17.

the world savior. It is the apotheosis of the hero's *human* nature,[61] the triumph of the Son of man as the Son of God, a throne-sharing for the duration of this world and beyond it; it has a stage of finality, eclipsed and interrupted on by the Second Coming, that of the Judge, at the end of time. The throne-sharing in the New Testament thus has both an individual meaning and an eschatological meaning relevant to all men, which it did not have either in the Psalm or in the Hellenistic ruler cult. The evangelical throne-sharing, though itself timeless and beyond the world's time, is yet linked to Time.

Nothing illustrates so signally the linking to Time as the very first mention of Christ's celestial *synthronismos* in the Gospels. Jesus, when asked by Caiphas whether he really was the anointed and Son of God, answered "*from now* (Matth. 26:64: ἀπ' ἄρτι; Luke 26:69: ἀπὸ τοῦ νῦν) ye shall see the Son of man sitting on the right hand of the power of God and coming in the clouds of heaven." *From now*—these words indicate a definite historical moment in the history of mankind. Where the passion and the defeat on earth start, there the future triumph in heaven begins to take shape. The throne-sharing with the Father becomes part of the unfolding of the history of man, and it receives a fateful place within Time. It is *from now*, from that portentous historical moment fraught with density and foreshadowing the nearness of the passion, that the throne-sharing of the Messiah with God may be guessed at, though it will become manifest only after the crucifixion and the ascent to heaven. Moreover, ἀπὸ τοῦ νῦν foreshadows also the future throne-fellowship with the Savior of the martyrs and of every loyal believer, a throne-fellowship which, through the Son of man, is simultaneously one with God the Father on the throne of heaven.

Neither in the tradition of Israel nor in that of Hellenistic kingship has the element of Time been effective in the assertion of a throne-fellowship with a god. The Jewish apocalyptic ideas of throne-sharings

---

61. This fact may have been sometimes forgotten (see, e.g., Josef Andreas Jungmann, "Die Abwehr des germanischen Arianismus und der Umbruch der religiösen Kultur im frühen Mittelalter," *Zeitschrift für katholische Theologie* 69 [1947]: 39–99, 75, n. 8), but was normally emphasized. See, e.g., Athanasius, on Psalm 109, PG 27, 461; also his *Sermo maior de fide*, c. 28, PG 26, 1281C. See also John Chrysostom, *In Ascensionem*, 3, PG 50, 446, and Hieronymus, *Breviarium in Psalmos* CIX, PL 26, 1163–64: ". . . cui praecipitur ut sedeat, Deus non sedet, assumptio corporis sedet. Huic ergo praecipitur ut sedeat, qui homo est, qui assumptus est." And a late gloss on Psalm 109 gives as a summary of the Psalm the explanation: "Materia [huius Psalmi] est Christus secundum utramque naturam." Cf. Kantorowicz, "Quinity," 75–76.

were primarily messianic and beyond time;[62] the Hellenistic ideas were primarily individual and mythical, and without time. And neither one nor the other claimed to be consequential with regard to mankind. Contrariwise, the throne-sharing of the Son of man (and it was the human nature of Christ which was said to share the throne with the Father) eventually became the cornerstone of the new faith and the essence of the doctrine of salvation. That is to say, the enthronement of the Son of man as King of Glory includes the promise to all faithful that they themselves in the life after life will be summoned to share the throne with God's *synthronos*. "To him that shall overcome, I will give to sit with me in my throne, as I also have overcome and am set down with my Father in my throne" reads the decisive passage in the Apocalypse (3:21) expressing the idea of the *condominium* of the faithful with Christ in the life thereafter.

Despite this new evaluation of both the Jewish and the Hellenistic symbols the older tradition had not lost its power. In fact, the sitting of the Son at the right hand of the Father was back-translated, before long, in the current vocabulary of Hellenistic rule and hero worship. The word *synthronos* is not found in the New Testament, nor is it used in the Septuagint. Since, however, it was a technical term of the Hellenistic world for a ruler's or other person's equality with the gods, the word very soon made its appearance in the works of Christian theological and exegetical writers as well. Philo and Origen had used it in a figurative sense. Clement of Alexandria visualized a throne-sharing with the *deuteroi* in the life thereafter for those endowed with gnosis. Eusebius of Caesaria, however, used the term not only casually or figuratively, but transferred the Hellenistic title of honor almost systematically to Christ, especially in connection with Psalm 109. Christ, writes Eusebius is publicly proclaimed to be "the *synthronos* of the highest God" in accordance with Psalm 109.[63] He is "the priest of the God over all and *synthronos* of the uncreated power." He is "an eternal priest and son of the most highest God, so far as he is engendered by the most highest God and is a *synthronos* of his kingship." "He is the anointed God and the one that became the Anointed, the Beloved of God and his child, the

---

62. See Billerbeck, who shows that in the earlier times the Psalm was usually interpreted as a reference to Abraham, but without stress on the Time. For the role of Time in the Christian exegesis, Oscar Cullmann, *Christus und die Zeit* (2nd ed., Zürich, 1948).

63. Eusebius, *Demonstratio evangelica*, IV, 15, 33, ed. Ivar A. Heikel, *Eusebius Werke* (Leipzig, 1913), VI, 178, 17. References to the same work in the ensuing paragraph are: IV, 15, 39; IV, 15, 43; IV, 15, 64; V, 19, 3; V, 3, 2; V, 3, 5; V, 3, 6.

eternal priest and the publicly proclaimed *synthronos* of the Father." He is the "captain (ἀρχιστράτηγος) of the host of the Lord" (Joshua 5:14) ... and the "angel of the great counsel" (Isaiah 9:6), and the *synthronos* of the Father as well as the eternal great high priest. Moreover, in the paraphrase and exegesis of Psalm 109, to which Eusebius devotes a whole chapter of his *Demonstratio evangelica* (V, 3) he uses the term *synthronos* over and over again. Despite his inclinations toward Arianism, Eusebius does not use the term in a subordinating sense. "The Psalm styles him *Kyrios* and teaches that he is at once the *synthronos* and the Son of God over all and Lord of the universe." The prophetic spirit of the Psalmist "quite rightly demonstrates that the Lord is the only *synthronos* of the Father, through whom all has been created." "Right it is therefore that he, the Father's similitude (*homoiosis*), has the Lordship, just as he is also declared to be the *synthronos* of the Father." Finally, in his Commentary on Luke, Eusebius holds, in connection with the Transfiguration, that God the Father demonstrated on this occasion Christ as his σύνθρονος and συμβασιλεύς and constituted him above every power.[64] This is an important passage because it foreshadows the later parallelism or even synonymity of two notions of throne-sharer and co-emperor.

Few authors, it is true, have so consistently designated Christ as the *synthronos* of the Father as Eusebius, who thereby added a Hellenistic cultual-constitutional note to the fundamentals of the Christian faith. Eusebius, however, was in that respect not alone, since by the later fourth and early fifth centuries the expression was of fairly common usage. Gregory Nazianzen, in his diatribe against Emperor Julian, refers to Christ as the great Father's son and Logos and high priest and *synthronos*.[65] Saint Basil uses the term at least once,[66] and St. John Chrysostom uses it several times.[67] The term is found in the writings of Cyril of Alexandria and of Proclus of Constantinople, perhaps even on occasion in those of Athanasius.[68] And Nonnos, in the proem of his poetical paraphrase of the Fourth Gospel, styled Christ "the Light of

---

64. Eusebius, *Commentaria in Lucam*, IX, 28, PG 24, 549C. See for *symbasileia* in Eusebius, Ladner, *Idea of Reform* (as n. 52), 122, n. 41, and 132. See also Eusebius, *Contra Marcellum*, II, 3, PG 24, 909C.

65. Gregory Nazianzen, *Contra Julianum*, I, 78, PG 35, 604B.

66. Basil, *De spiritu sancto*, c. 6, PG 32, 93A, ed. Benoît Pruche (Paris, 1945), 131, who in his index interprets *synthronos* "peut-être équivalent de *homoousios*."

67. John Chrysostom, *In Ioannem* 64, 3, PG 59, 358; *In Epistolam ad Colossenses*, V, 1, PG 62, 332.

68. Cyril of Alexandria, *In Psalmos*, 40, 11, PG 69, 997B; Proclus of Constantinople, *De incarnatione*, II, 1, PG 65, 692C; Athanasius, [title of work left blank] ii, 414B.

Light, inseparable from the Father, and God's *synthronos* in the eternal throne."[69]

At one point, the cultual notion enters the orbit of what may be termed celestial politics. St. John Chrysostom indicates that the wicked, who were possessed by demons and did not know that there was a god, nevertheless desired to become the *synthronoi* of God.[70] This desire to be throne-sharer of God was, unless authorized by the devotion to Christ, *hubris* and as such sinful and evil. Therefore the serpent, in an apocryphal gnostic writing on Adam, persuades Eve to eat the fruit from the Tree of Knowledge because after eating it man would become *syndoxos* and *synthronos* of God, a sharer of God's glory and throne.[71] Contrariwise, Christ, in a paschal homily of the Syrian poet Cyrillonas, is made to say: "The throne expects me to ascend and sit on it, and allow to sit on it with me the humbled Adam who now again is exalted."[72] Similar ideas are found in the *Pistis Sophia* and other writings, for example when John Chrysostom, in an Ascension sermon, says: "Today the archangels are our [human] nature shining like lightning from the royal throne in glory and immortal beauty."[73]

The concept of "throne-sharing" on the basis of Psalm 109 had dogmatic bearings as well. This became manifest during the struggles of the Orthodox against the Arians' subordinating interpretation of Christ. The equality of the Son with the Father had been evidenced by the Orthodox also by indicating the throne-companionship of the first with the second person. These effort, however, were ridiculed by the Arians who claimed that the Son was inferior to the Father, and mockingly the Arians declared that the sitting of the Son at the right hand of the Father might as well be taken as an evidence for the superiority of the Son over the Father because *qui est ad dexteram, ipse est maior.*[74] Saint

---

69. Nonnos of Panopolis, *Paraphrasis S. evangelii Ioannis*, I, 4, PG 44, 749; cf. K. Kuiper, "De Nonno evangelii Ioannei interprete," *Mnemosyne*, N.S. 46 (1918), 225–70, at 235.

70. John Chrysostom, *In Epistolam ad Colossenses* (as n. 61).

71. See Erwin Preuschen, *Die apokryphen gnostischen Adamschriften aus dem Armenischen übersetzt und untersucht* (Giessen, 1900), p. 28, n. 2, and p. 35.

72. Cyrillonas, "Zweite Homilie über das Pascha Christi," tr. Simon Konrad Landersdorfer (Kempten, 1912), 41.

73. John Chrysostom, *In Ascensionem*, 3, PG 50, 446, esp. 448.

74. See, for the Arian arguments, Antonio Spagnolo and C. H. Turner, "An Arian Sermon from a Manuscript in the Chapter Library of Verona," *Journal of Theological Studies* 13 (1912), 19–28, at 23–28. The argument was quite common; see e.g. for the refutation of these and other Arian arguments, the controversy *contra Virimadum*, V, c. 37, PL 62, 376–77: "Filium ad dexteram Patris non alterius iussione sedisse, sed propria potestate." See, however, also Hieronymus.

Ambrose, of course, found it easy to parry this attack by maintaining: *Divinitas gradus nescit.*[75] But the Arians could deny the significance of throne-sharing altogether by indicating that according to Psalm 109 the Son shared the divine throne because he had been ordered to do so (*quia iussus sedet ad dexteram*), and accordingly they could argue that the Father who ordered was greater than the Son who obeyed.

---

75. Ambrose, *De fide*, II, 12, 102 and 103.

# CHAPTER 2

# Roman Coins and Christian Rites

Kantorowicz gave a paper, "Roman Coins and Christian Rites," to the Berkeley Colloquium Orientologicum in April 1948, and gave the same paper in March 1951 at Dumbarton Oaks while he was there for the winter term.[1] No copy of this talk survives. What we have is a copy of a spoken version of March 1960, as well as a partial copy of a formal version meant for publication. A heading in the extant spoken version specifies "Baltimore, March 23, 1960," and we learn from a letter that the specific locus of the talk was Johns Hopkins University.[2] Evidence that Kantorowicz was working on it a few months earlier comes from gibes in letters of November 1959 and February 1960 to his student Robert Benson: he writes that Benson needed an "ani calcatio" (kick in the pants) for not getting on with his dissertation, thereby playing on "calcatio colli," the governing term of the second half of the "Roman Coins" paper.[3]

Although the author divided "Roman Coins and Christian Rites" into two parts, "Concordia" and "Calcatio colli," the first part inexplicably is

---

1. Office memo in the Kantorowicz papers, Dumbarton Oaks Archives.

2. To Vera Peters, March 1, 1960, Lerner Archive.

3. Robert E. Lerner, *Ernst Kantorowicz: A Life* (Princeton, 2017), 271. (The date and location of the paper given there are mistaken.)

absent from the formal version. (Perhaps Kantorowicz used large parts of it for another paper that he did publish in 1960.)[4] Yet it is possible to present a text of the entire paper by compensating for the absence with the text of the spoken version. (Where both versions exist, they display only minor variants.) No footnotes have been found. Since numbers for notes do appear in the surviving sections of the formal version, the author surely meant to provide them, but one must guess that he put the paper aside before he did. Where we at least have the numbers, these have been retained in parentheses to permit knowledge of what he intended to annotate.

If no footnotes survive to display Kantorowicz's erudition, the equivalent of such may be found galore in the paper itself. The first half in effect is a history of Roman marriage rites and their evolution into Christian ones. The main sources adduced are coin types spanning centuries, but Kantorowicz also adduces sarcophagi, papyri, medallions, marriage belts, and "gold-glasses." He also takes evidence from writings of such as Severinus of Gabala and Paulinus of Nola, as well as the *Book of Common Prayer*. The second half of the paper is no less erudite. Coins again provide the main evidentiary basis, but for the fullest description of the Christian (Byzantine) ceremony of "Calcatio colli" we are brought to the Book of Ceremonies of Constantine Porphyrogenitus.

Kantorowicz is on record as having been very pleased with this paper. He wrote to the director of Dumbarton Oaks in January 1951: "I think it is quite good as a method because it shows how much farther one can carry even well-known problems if one integrates liturgical aspects." At Berkeley "even Harold Cherniss [a noted classicist] who never attends lectures, heard [it] without showing that he disliked it."[5]

Cherniss might possibly even have liked it, for it is one of Kantorowicz's most accomplished pieces. According to its argument, Roman marriages were blessed first by a succession of deities from Juno through Cupid and Hercules; then reigning emperors took the place of the deities; and this led with the triumph of Christianity to Christ replacing the emperor. The underlying concept governing Roman marriages was "concord," which implied not only the concord of the bride and groom but also the greater

---

4. "On the Golden Marriage Belt and the Marriage Rings of the Dumbarton Oaks Collection," *Dumbarton Oaks Papers* 14 (1960): 2–16. The interested reader will find there much specific bibliography relating to the "Concordia" section of the present paper.

5. To Albert M. Friend, January 5, 1951, Kantorowicz papers, Dumbarton Oaks Archives. In the same letter Kantorowicz describes the ending, which might to many seem grisly, as "an amusing finale."

"harmony of the universe." Subsequently such an ideology lent itself effortlessly to the Christian view of the holiness of marriage and the treatment of the rite as a sacrament.

With panache Kantorowicz moves in his second part from harmony to violent hostility. Here too he lets the evidence underpin striking reflections. An Athenian tomb of the fourth century BC shows a horseman about to trample an enemy under the horse's hoofs, and we see "not only the glory of the victor but also the human tragedy of the defeated." Early Roman evidence as well shows victors overcoming enemies but not humiliating them. Roman coins, however, from the time of Hadrian onward, portray the defeated literally getting it in the neck. They are much smaller than the victors, and as enemies of Rome represent evil for which there is no mercy. In Christian times, these enemies, customarily barbarians, become *the* enemy and represent all that is inimical, warranting ceremonies before condemned captives that draw on Christian liturgy.

Harold Mattingly, the eminent English numismatist, once dropped an incidental remark which, I believe, will fairly describe the subject of this study. When discussing a Merovingian coin on which a Roman winged Victoria had assumed the meaning of a Christian angel, Mattingly mused:

> Victory no longer flew over the battlefield but God still sent his angel to bear triumph to the side which HE pleased to accord it; and the winged victory-angel with palm and cross still appeared on the coinage. There must be other such survivals by transference that would repay investigation.[1]

Other such "survivals by transference" indeed there are, and they are not at all rare. One might even venture to say that most of the events which ancient Rome customarily commemorated by issuing a special coin or medallion were echoed in the early Church by some ritual act—a mass, an oration, a benediction, or a lesson. And very often the Christian prayers would reproduce, in one way or another, the very keyword or technical term which the legends on Roman coins traditionally displayed.

Coins of Constantine the Great and Licinius display the legend: VOTA ORBIS ET URBIS.[2] Moreover, poets would address the emperor *Lux* [or *Spes*] *urbis et orbis*.[3] The words later appeared in the Coronation Order of the pope, for at the rite of immantling the pope with the imperial *cappa rubea*, the Prior of the Cardinal Deacons speaks the following formula: "Investi te de papatu romano, ut presis urbi et orbi."[4] And

**FIGURE 2.1**  Merovingian "Victoria" coin, 491–507 CE, with angel holding cross; the letters "CONOB" indicate imitation of Byzantine usage. CONOB stands for "Constantinopoli obryzum" (refined gold of Constantinople), 491–507. Wikimedia Commons, CC BY-SA 3.0.

who would not think of the solemn moment when the pope, from the Loggia of St. Peter's, gives his blessings *Urbi et Orbi*, he himself the successor of the Caesars, the "Light and Hope of the City and the World."

We should recall also the numerous coin issues commemorating the emperor's comings and goings to or from Rome. The emperor's departure for war, his *Profectio*, began with a lustration on the Capitol before he left the City with his army. The coins show the emperor on horseback, sometimes alone and sometimes within a procession, a *Victoria* marching in front of him while standard-bearers and soldiers representing the army formed the cortège.[5]

The echo was a highly elaborate *Ordo quando Rex cum Exercitu ad Prelium egreditur* such as is found in the Visigothic *Liber Ordinum*, reflecting the conditions of the seventh century.[6] In the ancient *Basilica Praetoriensis*, the church of the Visigothic praetorians or royal guards, a real rite of lustration was performed in the course of which the bishop

**FIGURE 2.2**    Emperor Trajan on the march—gold coin (aureus), 114–117 CE. Source: gallica.bnf. fr/Bibliothèque nationale de France.

handed to the king a golden processional cross which was to be carried during the campaign permanently before the emperor mounted on horseback, so that at the Christian *Profectio* the victorious Cross took the place of the Roman Victory.[7]

In the Visigothic Breviary there is also a *Hymnus in profectione exercitus*,[8] and there is a *Missa in profectione hostium euntibus in praelium* in the early Carolingian Sacramentary of Gellone,[9] which with slight changes remained valid for many centuries.[10] These liturgical sources have preserved also the technical term *Profectio*. Moreover, in the Carolingian mass *In profectione hostium* God was entrusted to send his angel that he may walk before the Frankish hosts now marching to war.[11] The prayer, to be sure, refers to the angel walking before Israel after the exodus from Egypt (Exod. 23:20–23). Nevertheless, the Angel walking before the Frankish army appears also like a faithful "survival by transference" of the coin images where the winged goddess of Victory walks before the Roman emperor and his army.

The Roman coins celebrating the FELIX ADVENTUS AUG[USTI]—the happy arrival of the emperor in his city—displayed a pattern almost equal with that of the *Profectio* coins: a *Victoria* leading the emperor's horse by the bridle and standard-bearers marching behind the horse.[12] To this image the Church, in its likewise rather elaborate *Ordo ad imperatorem (regem) suscipiendum,* responded with the antiphone: *Ecce mitto angelum meum*—"Behold, I send my angel who shall prepare the way before thee."[13] This too appears as though it were a faithful translation into words of the ancient Roman coin image.

All that, of course, does not imply that the rite of the early Church simply descended from the Roman medallions, or that the early liturgist who composed a blessing or a prayer or a mass, first rummaged his pockets to find a suitable Roman coin to be transposed into biblical terms. All that is to be indicated here is that both coin images and ecclesiastical rites were reflections of a language of symbols which for centuries Empire and Church had in common, which were current within the Roman world, and which were generally understood without a commentary by pagans and Christians alike. In other words, there existed a great number of immutable religious symbols or "values" which were subject to a very mutable religious "interpretation."[14] What this study is concerned with is to demonstrate, by means of a few examples, how close the interrelations were between Roman coins and Christian rites, and how some of the accepted values abiding in Roman coins survived in the rites of the Church "by transference," that is by changing their original meaning more or less completely, yet not out of recognition.

[The draft of the formal article breaks off here, but the tenor can be supplied by the copy of the spoken presentation; the text of the formal article returns later.]

From a score of possible examples, I have chosen for the present discussion only two items: CONCORDIA, here restricted to her function in marriage rites; and the CALCATIO COLLI, the treading on the neck of the enemy. Each of these subjects has its own interesting history which stands out in full relief only if the details are taken into consideration.

## 1. Concordia

I may start with the suggestive *catena iconographica* of marriage coins. Some links of that chain are well known, whereas the most interesting ones have passed unnoticed.

The ancient Roman rites were taken over by the Christian Church with very few changes. The auspices of the augurs, of course, were abolished and the *sacrificium nuptiale*, the nuptial sacrifice of wine or incense, was eventually "converted" and became a nuptial mass. But the legal and ceremonial aspects: the reading of the marriage consent from the *tabulae nuptiales*, the signing of the tablets, the handing over of the dowry, the *dextrarum iunctio* or clasping of the right hands, and the cooperation of the deity confirming the legal action and protecting the marriage, the *Pronuba* or *Pronubus*—all that underwent few changes, or changes only with regard to the tutelary deity.

In pre-imperial and early imperial times, the goddess uniting and protecting the young couple was Juno. In that capacity, *Juno pronuba* was shown standing between the young couple and putting her hands on the shoulders of groom and bride who clasped hands. This scene was often represented on the sarcophagi, as on the one in the Uffizi, or on that of the Belvedere where we also notice the altar for the *sacrificium nuptiale*.

**FIGURE 2.3**   Gold coin depicting the wedding of Caracalla and Plautilla, with the couple clasping hands, 202–205 CE. The British Museum, 1864,1128.110.

The imperial wedding coins, however, reflect with few exceptions the idea of *Concordia*, the concord of the bridal couple. They display the *dextrarum iunctio* while the inscription explains CONCORDIA or (as on a coin of Caracalla and Plautilla) CONCORDIA DIÆ AETERNÆ.

"Concord," to be sure, was not the original meaning of the ceremony. Originally the Roman bridegroom did not clasp hands with his bride, but (reminiscent, as it were, of the "Rape of the Sabine Women") took the bride by the wrist to indicate that she was given in his possession and power and was obliged to "obey and serve him." Concordia certainly was a very ancient Roman goddess, but only gradually did she grow into the role of a marriage deity, apparently at a time when the notion of concord had been assimilated to and influenced by the Stoic idea of *Homonoia*, implying not only the concord of those concerned, but also the greater "harmony of the universe." And it was that broader cosmos harmony of which eventually the bridal couple was supposed to be an exponent. Thus the "Rape of the Sabine Women" had been philosophized and philanthropized. It was replaced, under the influence of Greek philosophy by a completely different state of mind and of mood.

In the course of this development, imperial marriage coins began to display Concordia acting as a *pronuba*. As a *Concordia felix* she solemnizes the marriage of Caracalla and Plautilla or puts her hands on the shoulders of Marcus Aurelius and the younger Faustina as they clasp hands and receive the *vota publica* occasioned by their marriage.

**FIGURE 2.4**  Concordia blessing the marriage of Caracalla and Plautilla, gold coin (aureus), 202–205 CE. Berlin, Münzkabinett der Staatlichen Museen, 18277266. Photo: Benjamin Seifert.

**FIGURE 2.5**  Concordia joining Marcus Aurelius and Faustina, gold coin (aureus), 145 CE. Berlin, Münzkabinett der Staatlichen Museen, 18200264. Photo: Lutz-Jürgen Lübke.

Concordia established, as it were, both the union of the august couple and its unisonance with the eternal harmony of the universe.

Whereas Concordia prevailed as a marriage goddess, her place could yet be taken by another patron deity. The emperor Aurelian made the cult of *sol invictus* an official cult of the state. Fittingly, we find the Sun god, the new *dominus imperii*, who by his rise conquers the demons of darkness and brings peace to man, as the *pronubus*, the unifier and solemnizer of the marriage of Aurelian and Severina.

The gods began to shift. It is not surprising, of course, that in a late glass the picture of Cupid is found acting playfully as an *Amor pronubus*, his hands resting on the heads of the couple. It strikes us, however, as more curious to find, in the time of late paganism, a gold-glass displaying a *Hercules pronubus*: ORFITUS ET CONSTANTIA IN NOMINE HERCULIS reads the inscription. Hercules, it is true, offers the golden fruits of the Hesperides which form a very old nuptial symbol; and since the pomegranates contained many seeds in one skin, they were also a symbol of Concordia. But the presence of Hercules is not justified by the three fruits alone. In the political theology of the late empire, Hercules was above all the heroic savior of man who liberated the world from all sorts of monsters, and who therefore appeared as the great *pacator mundi*, the pacifier and concord-bringer of the world, whose statue, in the act of crowning himself, had its place in front of the temple of Concord on the Capitoline Hill. And in this capacity *Hercules pronubus* may well have taken the place of *Concordia pronuba*.

The more numerous the representatives of Concord, the greater of course the discord in the Roman world and the graver the political situation. According to Hellenistic political theories, it was the supreme task of the Prince to establish within his empire the *Homonoia*, the Concord, of his subjects and to attune them to the harmony of the universe. The emperor now was honored as the *pacator mundi*, the pacifier of the world, and he was recognized as the living "Concord of the human race" with regard to both the political and the private spheres. Is it surprising, then, to find the emperor himself in Concordia's place as the *imperator pronubus*?

Perhaps we should recall the fact that in the later empire contracts—including marriage contracts—were frequently signed before the emperor's image; also, that the solemn oath, if such was taken, was delivered by the *genius*, the *Tyche*, "of our unconquered lord and august emperor." That is to say, the emperor in his capacity of guardian of contracts and solemn oaths could be recognized even in the legal sphere as an incarnation of CONCORDIA. And represented in this role we find, in an *aureus* of 437, the emperor Theodosius II. The haloed emperor gives his blessings to the marriage of Valentinian III and Licinia Eudoxia, while the legend surrounding the imperial *pronubus* and the likewise haloed couple reads FELICITER NUPTIIS.

We know from the evidence of the papyri that in the later years of Theodosius II the official oath formula was Christianized. The imperial *Tyche* was still invoked, but this invocation was henceforth preceded by the invocation of Christ or the Holy Trinity. At the next issue of imperial wedding medallions, in 450, we find that *Juno pronuba* and *Concordia, Sol invictus* and Cupid, Hercules and the *imperator pronubus*, have ceded their place to *Christus pronubus*. The bridal couple, the empress Pulcheria and her consort Marcian, the first at whose coronation the Patriarch extended the blessings of the Church, are haloed and diademed like their predecessors, and the central figure appears in quasi-imperial attire. Only the cross-halo of the *pronubus* indicates the change and allows us to understand that in the Christian empire Christ was the new *pacator mundi*, who incidentally, in a verse inscription of ca. 450 in Ravenna, was praised as *cuncti concordia mundi*, "the concord of the whole world."

The *aureus* of 450, however, was not the first representation of Christ in the role of *Concordia pronuba*. In the sarcophagus reliefs of the fourth century Christ is sometimes shown in that role, and iconographic continuity here is no less striking than in the case of the coin images. The sarcophagus of the Villa Albani is badly mutilated, but enough is left

**FIGURE 2.6** Theodosius II as haloed emperor giving his blessings to the marriage of haloed Valentinian III and Licinia Eudoxia, gold coin (aureus), 437 CE. Berlin, Münzkabinett der Staatlichen Museen, 18202348. Photo: Lutz-Jürgen Lübke.

to recognize not only Christ in the place of the Roman goddess, but also the altar for the *sacrificium nuptiale* which now has been turned appropriately into a lectern carrying a Gospel Book.

Moreover, the continuity in transference disclosed by the monuments, including the gold-glasses, is strikingly confirmed by the texts of the fifth century. Around 400 A.D. Severianus of Gabala wrote a sermon which is also transmitted under the name of the bishop of Ravenna, Petrus Chrysologus, in which he says:

> When the images of the persons . . . are painted, we often notice that the painter, so as to emphasize the unanimity of the couple, places back of them a *Concordia* in female garb . . . So does now the Peace of the Lord stand in the center to teach us how separate bodies may become one in spirit.

This is the most accurate description of the change which, by 400 A.D. had taken place: the substitution of the goddess Concordia by Christ. Moreover, Paulinus of Nola, who died in 431, actually uses the Roman technical term *pronubus* for Christ when in the Epithalamium for his son he writes:

> By those of his faithful who marry in this Christian law, Jesus stands as *pronubus* . . . (Tali lege suis nubentibus adstat IESUS PRONUBUS . . .)

For all the available evidence, however, is it correct to say that *Christus pronubus* simply replaced *Concordia pronuba*? Is the change merely an iconographical problem? A masterpiece of goldsmith's work in the Dumbarton Oaks collection, a Syrian marriage belt of the fifth century, may give the answer. The central medallions show Christ as the unifier and solemnizer who unites the hands of the bridal couple. What matters is the inscription. It reads: EK ΘBOY HOMONOIA—"Harmony, Concord deriving from God" with the words XAPIC and YΓIEIA, "Grace" and "Health," in the exergue. That is to say *Homonoia* or Concord no longer ruled, or even had existence in her own right as an independent goddess, having her own temple and altar, but had become subservient. She now proceeds from God, or is an effluence of Christ.

This change reflected also on the bridal couple. No longer were groom and bride embraced by the natural harmony of the universe in which they participated and of which they became an exponent, a likeness by their own *Homonoia*. Their hands are now joined together by a sacrament, by a spiritual principle bestowing upon them concord as a special gift like Grace and Health. Although marriage rings would continue to display the word *Homonoia*, and the marriage rites mentioned the concord by which bride and groom were united, something essential had changed: the couple no longer appeared as the manifest likeness, the visible *mimesis* of the purely natural order of the world symbolized by Concordia.

And yet, the idea of *mimesis*, of reflecting an authoritative model, was not lost nor was it absent from the Christian ritual. In the Epistle to the Ephesians (5:25) St. Paul enlarged upon the image of the marriage of Christ to the Church, a chapter which appears in almost all Christian services of Solemnization of Matrimony. It serves as a Lesson and pervades the prayers; and it still is included in the *Book of Common Prayer* where, in the introductory prayer, the estate of matrimony is praised as "an honorable estate, instituted of God, signifying unto us the mystical union that is betwixt Christ and his Church." And once more, towards the end, a prayer invokes God,

> who hast consecrated the state of Matrimony to such an excellent mystery, that in it is signified and represented the spiritual marriage and unity betwixt Christ and his Church.

Thus the loving—and spiritual—unity, the *homonoia* or *concordia* between Christ and his Church, as represented by the Virgin Mary, became the model of the bridal couple.

This formula must be far older than our late liturgical texts would suggest. On the bezel of a wedding ring of the sixth century we recognize the celestial couple, Christ and Mary, the King and Queen of Heaven, as they dispense their blessings to the bridal pair. The word HOMONOIA, which appears also on a similar if more elegant ring of the Dumbarton Oaks collection, refers to both couples, to XP and Mary, or XP and his Church, as the model, and to the human couple as the antitype and *mimesis* of the exemplary harmony of king and queen of heaven. And therewith the idea of *homonoia* or harmony has required, once more, a special depth and unexpected perspective.

This then, we may assume, this doubling of the couples—celestial and terrestrial—should be considered the original contribution to the idea of *concordia* on the part of the Church. Or does this concept, too, have its antecedents on Roman coins?

In 176 A.D. the Roman Senate passed a decree that, on their wedding day, the bridal couples should offer a sacrifice on an altar placed in front of the colossal silver statues of the emperor Marcus Aurelius and his empress, the younger Faustina, in the temple of Venus and Roma. Similar decrees are known from Egypt. Most explicit, however, is an earlier inscription from Ostia. That city consecrated an altar for the imperial couple Antoninus Pius and the elder Faustina to the purpose that

> *ob insignem eorum concordiam*—for the outstanding harmony, concord, of the imperial couple, the maidens that marry at Ostia, and their grooms, shall offer on that altar on the day of their wedding.

Those were not merely words. A superb coin, a sestertius of Antoninus Pius, shows us not only the colossal statues facing each other, it shows a scene strikingly symbolizing the unison, harmony, and consonant rhythm of macrocosmos and microcosmos. In the center we recognize the altar and before it, the *dextrarum iunctio* of bride and groom. The two smaller human figures are framed, not overshadowed, by the statues (we recognize the pedestals) of the *Divi*, of emperor and empress, who clasp hands exactly as the newly wedded pair at their feet.

Moreover, the emperor carries on his left hand the statue of CONCORDIA whose name we also read in the inscription and who creates, as it were, the harmony of all three spheres: the human, the imperial, and the universal. *Concordia pronuba* is effective by her own cosmic

**FIGURE 2.7**  Bronze coin, 144–145 CE, depicting the statues of Antoninus Pius, holding a Concordia statuette, and Faustina the Elder, with a scepter, clasping hands; below are the smaller figures of Marcus Aurelius and Faustina the Younger clasping hands over an altar. Berlin, Münzkabinett der Staatlichen Museen, 18200260. Photo: Lutz-Jürgen Lübke.

power of rendering harmony; but she wields her power also through the relationship of the protypes, the *Divi*, who are the *mimetai* of the heavenly order, whereas man becomes a *mimesis* of the ruler.

All that opens some wider perspectives. We may think not only of the "holy wedlock" of Oriental rulers in imitation of the gods, but may think also of the CONCORDIA coins of emperors of the third century, of the imperial couple Septimius Severus and Julia Domna, showing the emperor radiate as Sun and the empress on the crescent as Moon. And we may recall the marriage of the *Sol Iustitiae*, Christ, to the Woman Having the Moon under Feet (Rev. 12:11), that is, according to customary exegesis, the Church.

And we may add, for what it is worth, that the Byzantine and Russian marriage rituals remember in the Dismissal not only Christ and Mary, but also Saint Constantine the Great and Saint Helen, the emperor's mother. In this concentricity of human, saintly-imperial, and divine couples there is, it is true, some resemblance with the former concentricity of human, imperial, and universal spheres. But the Christian imperial saints no longer were the exponents, or models, of that natural Concord of the World which the Roman sestertius suggested. Saints Constantine and Helen have become exponents of that spiritual world order which the inscription of the Dumbarton Oaks wedding belt proclaims: EK ΘBOY OMONOIA—Concord A GIFT COMING FROM God.

From Harmony and Concord we may now fittingly turn to the opposite, to Hostility as expressed by the CALCATIO COLLI, the stepping on, or kicking the neck of the enemy.

[Here the draft of the formal article can be resumed for what follows.]

## 2. Calcatio colli

In 695, the emperor Justinian II was swept away by a revolution. The usurper Leontius, soon followed by another usurper, Apsimar, forced Justinian to go into exile. The ex-basileus—after an adventurous life of ten years in the course of which he married a Chazar princess—recovered his throne in 705. He had sworn not to spare the head of a single one of his adversaries, and he made his promise true. But before their execution, the two usurper emperors were dragged in chains to the Hippodrome and were cast prostrate beneath the throne of Justinian II. And the emperor, comfortably planting a foot on the neck of each, cheerfully watched for an hour or so the races of the chariots.[82]

A coin of Valens and Valentinian I fairly illustrates a similar scene. It is the day of the *Vota*, January 3, which customarily was celebrated by games. Valens has lifted his right hand to cast the cloth into the arena, the sign for starting the show, while his feet, and those of his co-emperor, are resting on the backs of prisoners.[83] The two emperors might have staged the first versicle of Psalm 109: "Sit thou at my right hand, until I make thine enemies thy footstool."[84] This, however, was the way the people of Constantinople interpreted the scenario in 705. To be sure, Justinian II with the defeated and chained usurper emperors beneath his feet posed, as it were, likewise a biblical *tableau vivant* which the people translated into the Christ-centered iconographic language then current in Byzantium. They grasped the image which the imperial *christomimetes*, the imperial actor of Christ, was staging and accordingly they shouted incessantly the triumphant 90th Psalm (verse 13): "Thou shalt trample on the asp and basilisk; on the lion and dragon shalt thou set thy foot."[85] The people, by transposing a scene of life into

**FIGURE 2.8**  Mosaic of Christ trampling lion and snake. Archbishop's Chapel, Ravenna, sixth century CE. Wikimedia Commons, CC BY-SA 4.0. Photo: © José Luiz Bernardes Ribeiro / CC BY-SA 4.0.

biblical words, did what the artists had done before. For the Christian artists had translated biblical verses into the language of imperial court imagery after the court iconography had been liberally applied to the imagery of Christ: in the mosaics of Ravenna Christ appears even in the emperor's uniform when trampling on lion and snake.[86]

The problem involved is perhaps not quite as simple as that, although it is certainly true that "paradoxically . . . this pagan brutal fashion of triumph was furthered by the Christianization of the empire."[87]

To be defeated in war or battle is always a bitter fate. But it need not always imply disgrace, diffamation [*sic*], or dishonor of a moral kind for the defeated. When we look[88] at a Greek representation of victory, the tomb of Dexileos in the Athenian cemetery of the Kerameikos, a work of the early fourth century BC, we visualize not only the glory of the victor but also the human tragedy of the defeated.

Life will be blown out of the succumbing warrior at the last moment, and dying he has the terrifying sight of the charger rearing above his

**FIGURE 2.9**    Tomb of Dexileos, Athens, fourth century BCE. Wikimedia Commons, CC BY-SA 4.0. Photo: Andrzej Barabasz.

head. The horse's hooves will go down on him as the horseman's lance will pierce through him. The scene touches us directly because it touches us humanly. There is no moral element involved in this combat, no hatred for either victor or vanquished, nor love. Yet we hold our breath for a moment, for we feel that there is something dialectical in that relief which equals the dialectic of life and death itself. Dexileos, who has been slain in battle himself, appears now as the victorious horseman of the tombstone but seems to know that Fate might just as well have turned against him and reversed the roles, and that it might have been he that was defeated and was to lie under the horse's hooves. Victor and vanquished are humanly equals; they are like brothers, and therefore their roles might as well have been exchanged, perhaps even in the last minute.

All that is indeed very different when we turn to a late Roman representation of an imperial victory, to the Paris Cameo showing probably the triumph of the emperor Licinius or a later ruler.[89] A quadriga arrives, not the proverbial "prancing proconsul," but a self-righteous

**FIGURE 2.10**    The Triumph of Licinius, sardonyx cameo (308–324 CE), depicting the emperor Licinius on a quadriga (chariot) trampling his enemies. Wikimedia Commons, CC BY-SA 4.0. Photo: CRIX.

prancing emperor. Victories lead his horses, Genies (of East and West?) hand him a globe each. He is the victor, the executor of the *Providentia deorum* which on the coins of the third century is sometimes represented by a Gorgonian head.[90] His chariot wheels above his foes, barbarians perhaps or rebellious subjects. Those unfortunate devils are not a match for the emperor, and they are certainly not his equals as the difference in size indicates. They are deprived of human dignity as well as of individuality. Nor are they simply defeated; they are, so as to use our present unattractive parlance with regard to human lives, "liquidated." They are liquidated like nauseous vermin and unfortunately remind us of practices experienced in our time.

At any rate, there is not even a potentiality of dialectics, of a merciful Fate that might just as well have reversed the outcome of the struggle. The outcome is final and inevitable because it is providential, and it is politically moral to liquidate the enemies of the government of the empire. Here the roles could not have been reversed, for a new element, utterly hostile to agonal thinking, has been introduced: that of Good and Evil. The emperor, ever victorious and almost the gods' equal, is always good and just and righteous; and his adversaries are not simply defeated men, but are always bad and wicked and morally inferior: they are simply evil. The qualifications of good and evil in a purely political sense, now connected even with the security of the empire, have to justify the scene of that mass judgment or mass liquidation. And with those political qualifications the former human equilibrium of victor and vanquished has gone. The scene may reflect political morals, but it no longer touches us directly, because it does not touch us humanly, or only in the sense that it is plainly revolting.

The posture of putting the foot on the neck of the defeated or of kicking him in the neck or, as in the Cameo, the rolling of the chariot over the dwarfed vanquished enemies is of Eastern origin.[91] We find it not rarely in Egypt,[92] though it seems to have been a novelty to the Israelites when Joshua (10:24) ordered his reluctant army-chiefs to go and set their foot on the necks of the five defeated Amorite kings, and said to his officers: "Fear not, nor be dismayed. For so will the Lord do to all your enemies, against whom you fight."[93] And in the Psalms there is more than one versicle alluding to that custom. It would be difficult to tell exactly when this Eastern expression of total victory penetrated Roman art and thought,[94] although the kicking of the vanquished is found on coins of Trajan.[95]

**FIGURE 2.11** Bronze medallion, 104–107 CE, depicting Trajan treading on a personification of conquered Dacia (roughly modern Romania). Source: gallica.bnf.fr/Bibliothèque nationale de France.

There is a plaque from Niederbieber showing Caligula standing on the bodies of the defeated enemies.[96] Side by side with these representations there are others which, during the first and second centuries, display the emperor's victory still after the pattern of the Dexileos slab: the enemy is equal in size with the emperor on horseback, is brought to his knees and will probably succumb, but his defeat lacks the element of humiliation although he may have little chance to defend himself.[97]

Under Hadrian, the new posture of victor was fully developed. His colossal statue from Hierapytna on Crete, now in Constantinople, shows the emperor, his face menacing, as he puts his foot on the head of the conquered foe whose size of body now is far smaller than that of the emperor and who is defeated apparently without a preceding struggle.[98]

What Hadrian represents has been indicated by several scholars before. For his statue is apparently modeled after that of the goddess

**FIGURE 2.12**   A statue of the victorious Roman emperor Hadrian, originally from Hierapytna in Crete, 20–125 CE. Istanbul Archaeological Museum, via Wikimedia Commons, CC BY-SA 4.0. Photo: Dosseman.

Nemesis.[99] Although a very ancient Greek goddess, her representation with one foot firmly set on a human head is not Greek at all.[100] The numerous replicas of the type of Nemesis standing on *Hybris* defeated are mostly of Egyptian origin and are worked perhaps after an *ex voto* image in the Nemeseion of Alexandria.[101]

The Hadrian colossus at any rate suggests that the emperor here appears as the impersonator of Nemesis, a role which would justify his treading on the enemy. This enemy, however, was not simply an enemy, but it was, and became more so in the course of time, synonymous with the "Fiend of Mankind."

We have to remember that the emperor was identified with the *genus humanum*.[102] The legend of coins proclaim him the *salus generis humani* or the *restitutor generis humani*.[103] That is to say, resistance against the emperor was not only simply resistance against him individually but against him as the incarnation of the whole human race. And thus it

**FIGURE 2.13**   Marble statuette of Nemesis with portrait resembling the empress Faustina I (wife of Antoninus Pius), about 150 CE. The J. Paul Getty Museum, Villa Collection, Los Angeles, California, 96.AA.43. Open Content Program.

happened that the barbarians, or the rebellious subjects, were the enemy of mankind in general, and of the savior-emperor in particular. Moreover, by the third century the Sun-god, especially as *Imperator* or as ORIENS, was shown on coins time and again as he treads on, or kicks, his enemies, the spirits of darkness or demons of evil which he scares away and conquers by his rise in the morning.[(104)]

If we now consider the close relationship between the Sun-god and the emperor in the third century it can hardly surprise us to find the emperor acting in conformity with and after the fashion of his divine *comes*, as seen, for an early example, on an *aureus* of Probus to demonstrate the VIRTUS PROBI AVG.[(105)] The emperor's enemies, too, were demons of darkness without restriction and fiends of mankind.

The later Roman Empire, so we notice, was also in this respect well prepared for the great change to come under Constantine the Great. Eusebius, when referring to Constantine's victory over Licinius, says in so

**FIGURE 2.14**   Roman emperor Probus with foot placed on a kneeling captive, gold coin (aureus), reverse, 276–282 CE. © The Trustees of the British Museum.

many words that his hero "triumphed at once over the enemies and the demons."[(106)] The equation of political enemies and religious demons was more than a metaphor. For in the vestibule of his palace in Constantinople, Constantine, according to Eusebius,[(107)] had an image painted showing him as he pierces his lance through Licinius, who was represented in the shape of a serpent, the fiend of mankind and the *antiquus serpens*.[(108)] We think at once of Constantine's famous SPES PUBLICA coins: the *vexillum*, displaying the images of the three emperors (Constantine and his sons), is crowned by the christogram while the ferrule pierces the snake—a victory of Christ through the emperor over the dragon and fiend of man.[(109)]

Even more telling is perhaps a later series of coins which was started apparently by the emperor Valentinian III (425–455). The emperor holds the cross-staff in his right hand, the globe with a Victory in his left, while his foot treads on the head of a serpent, a serpent having a human head.[(110)]

This is not simply the victory over any, or just another, enemy who has been defeated. It is the victory over *the* enemy, the snake, and as such comparable to the victory of Christ over lion and dragon. Ancient tradition has it that the human head of the serpent bore the features of Attila.[(111)] This is interesting, because according to Suidas, Attila, when he conquered Milan in 452, took offense of a wall painting in the imperial

**FIGURE 2.15** Constantine the Great coin (reverse) depicting a serpent pierced by a spear topped by a christogram, 327–328 CE. Münzkabinett, Kunsthistorisches Museum, ID193289. Photographs by Münzkabinett.

**FIGURE 2.16** Gold solidus of Valentinian III (reverse), Ravenna, 426 CE. Stamped VICTORI-A AVGGG and depicting the emperor holding a cross scepter in one hand and a small image of Victory in the other, with his right foot on a human-headed serpent. American Numismatic Society, 1947.2.533.

**FIGURES 2.17**   Constantius II bronze coin, 347–348 CE. Obverse: bust of Constantius II. Reverse: two prisoners seated (bending over) on either side of a military standard (vexillum) with the inscription VOT / XX / MVLT XXX. National Museums of Berlin. Photo: Dr. Karsten Dahmen.

palace showing the two emperors sitting upon their golden thrones and, in prostration at their feet, some captured Huns. Thereupon, Attila, so we are told, ordered a painter to overpaint the wall and paint a picture of Attila sitting upon the throne and showing the Roman emperors pouring a sack of gold coins to the conqueror's feet.[(112)]

All that has yet nothing to do with the liturgy or with Christian rites. Into the liturgical sphere, however, we are led by a series of medallions of Constantine's successors. The emperors, Constans I as well as Constantius II, are shown holding the labarum with the christogram in their right hand, and through this sign the emperor becomes victor over the barbarians: TRIUMFATOR GENTIUM BARBARUM reads the inscription.[(113)] [Kantorowicz apparently indicates a mistaken inscription.]

Here is a case of an almost verbatim congruency of coins and prayers. For the great Ektene, the litany of the Eastern liturgies, contains a suffrage for the emperor imploring god that he may "subdue to him all the barbarous nations."[(114)] This suffrage has survived in the West, too, where it is found in the *Orationes solemnes* on Good Friday:

> Oremus et pro Christianissimo imperatore vel rege nostro, ut Deus omnipotens subditas illis faciat omnes barbaras nationes ad nostrum perpetuam pacem.[(115)]

Although Christian prayers for the emperor, and magistracies in general, go back to apostolic times (I Tim. 2:2),[116] there can be no doubt but that the special petition for the subjection of the barbarous nations belongs to the century after Constantine when the peace with the Church had become a fact.[117] For only after the enemies of the Empire had changed into enemies of the Church did it make sense to pray for the subjection of those beyond the frontiers of the Empire, who were pagans or infidels, at any rate barbarians. We may recall the fact that for St. Jerome the "barbarians" did not belong to the human beings, to the human species at all;[118] and Prudentius explained in so many words that the difference between a Roman and a barbarian equaled that between man and quadrupeds,[119] opinions which have stubbornly survived *mutatis mutandis* until the twentieth century.[120]

This attitude of Christian authors allows us to understand how readily there would have been accepted on the part of the Church that brutal extinction of human "vermin," that is barbarians and infidels, such as it was displayed by the Paris Cameo. At any rate, the coin inscriptions such as TRIUMFATOR or DEBALLATOR GENTIUM BARBARUM belong to the same period as the liturgical suffrage for the emperor's "subjection of all the barbarous nations," which was introduced as an addition to an older form of prayer for the ruler.[121] In fact, as a result of the equation of the emperor's enemies with enemies of the Christian Church, and further with the fiend of mankind, and also as a result of the imperial *christomimesis* on the basis of which the emperor emulated Christ setting his foot on dragon and lion, the idea of the *calcatio colli* and its equivalents had an amazingly long life. The *toga picta* of Justinian, so well described by Corippus[122] had embroideries showing not only *subiectas gentes*, but also the *emperor Vandalici calcantem colla tyranni*. An ivory plate of the Bargello in Florence displays a Carolingian ruler, probably Charlemagne himself, treading on enemy.[123] Nor was that scene absent from papal iconography.[124]

How actually the suffrage of the Litany could be combined with the performance of a *calcatio colli* may be gleaned from the *Book of Ceremonies* of Constantine Porphyrogenitus and the description of the ceremonial and ritual observed after a victory over the Arabs.[125] The emperor arrives in great procession at the Forum, and so does the patriarch. Then the captured Arabs are led before the emperor whose throne is placed on the steps of the great column bearing the cross. The task fell to the logothetes of leading the Saracen emir to the throne in order to bend the emir's head under the foot of the basileus. At the same time another officer, the protostrator, imposes a lance on the neck of the prostrate emir. The emperor now touches the lance or holds it for a little while in his right hand, this posing exactly the coin image of earlier times.[126] At that moment the precentor intones appropriate Psalms, which were followed by the Ektanie or Litany of the Liturgy of St. John Chrysostome. When the Litany arrived at the suffrage: "And subdue under their [the emperors'] feet all that is hostile and inimical" (that is the equivalent of "all the barbarous nations")[127] the crowd responded with forty *Kyrie eleison*, whereupon the patriarch said the prayer.

CHAPTER 3

# Coronation Scenarios Eastern and Western

Kantorowicz sometimes used an alternative title for this article, namely, "Epiphany and Coronation." He read it at the Dumbarton Oaks research center in April 1951. Ultimately, he intended to publish it as part of a series: *Studies Eastern and Western in the History of Late Classical and Medieval Ideas*. That volume was to include as well "Synthronos," "Roman Coins and Christian Rites," "Charles the Bald and the *Natales* of the King," and "Roma and the Coal." Although that project never came to fruition, the text given here is based on corrected proofs that Kantorowicz oversaw before his death.

The problem of the Byzantine coronation and the parts played at this performance by the Byzantine emperor and the Patriarch of Constantinople is still a subject given to controversy. More than forty years ago, W. Sickel established the authoritative interpretation which was generally accepted.[1] Sickel could not fail to realize that the patriarch from his function as coronator did not derive constitutional or legal rights of supremacy over the imperial power similar to those claimed by the

Greek translations in parentheses in this article have been supplied by Jeremy Thompson.

1. Wilhelm Sickel, "Das byzantinische Krönungsrecht bis zum 10 Jahrhundert," *Byzantinische Zeitschrift* 7 (1898), 511–57, esp. 518.

pope and the western clergy, and he therefore maintained that the patriarch in crowning the emperor performed a function of the state and not of the church. Recently, however, the tide of scholarly opinion began to change. Professor Georg Ostrogorsky, of the University of Belgrade, defines his position emphatically, if only in a footnote to his brilliant *History of the Byzantine State*. "Quite untenable—writes he[2]—is the opinion offered by Sickel and despite its strangeness generally repeated ever since saying that the patriarch did not perform the act of crowning in his capacity as representative of the church but that he always acted as a representative of the State." Incidentally at the same time, Mr. Peter Charanis, being attacked by German scholars in a rather unpleasant way, devoted an article to the coronation in the Later Roman Empire in which he has demonstrated—successfully, as I believe—that the coronation of the Byzantine emperor as introduced probably in 450 was a definitely ecclesiastical act.[3]

The controversy, it seems to me, is to some extent a controversy of distinctions and terms resulting from the practice or malpractice of applying modern legal thought to the conditions of the past, and like a too short blanket these modern distinctions finally turn out to be inappropriate to cover the whole body of the historical problem. It is strange indeed to maintain that the high priest and chief of the Byzantine Church, at the important ceremony of crowning the emperor, should have acted "not as a priest" or on behalf of the church but as an officer of the state and a civil deputy of electors—army, senate, and people. Even a Prussian *Oberhofprediger*, truly an official of the state, acts when giving his slightly colorless and uncompromising blessings to the king, on behalf of the Prussian State-Church or at least (!) of God; and even the coronation at Königsberg, though adding no element of power to the king, had the function to make the Prussian monarch visible within the state as the incarnation of divine right, a visibility not achieved but increased by the blessing of the church. So far as it goes, this, too, was an ecclesiastical act. However, with regard to the Byzantine ceremony of crownings the terms of "civil" or "ecclesiastical," the hair-splitting distinction between "first priest" and "first Roman citizen" with reference to the patriarch, or the qualifications of "dispensable ceremony" and

---

2. Georg Ostrogorsky, *Geschichte des byzantinischen Staates* (Munich, 1940), 35, n. 1.

3. Peter Charanis, "Coronation and Its Constitutional Significance in the Later Roman Empire," *Byzantion* 15 (1940–41), 49–66. For his controversy with Franz Dölger, in *Byzantinische Zeitschrift* 38 (1938), 240, see also the strange intermediation of Otto Treitinger in *Byzantinische Zeitschrift* 39 (1939), 194–202.

"essential act" with reference to the coronation, all seem to miss the vital center because they have been borrowed from a sphere significant of neither Byzantine nor general mediaeval vitality. Their application distorts the otherwise clear contours and instead of clarifying obscures a problem which is still in need of being settled even though the ecclesiastical content of the Byzantine coronation may be admitted.[4]

It is the intention of the present brief discussion to approach the involved problem from an altogether different point of view and to raise the question of the function of the Byzantine coronation with regard to what may be called the emperor's "visibility" within church and state. What were the parts played by both emperor and patriarch in the liturgical scenario of the coronation play? What was the model of the *tableau vivant* which the head of the Eastern Empire and the head of the Byzantine clergy staged on that occasion? This question is more likely to yield an answer than the previous approaches because it derives from then customary concepts; and as the controversy arose implicitly from a comparison of Eastern with Western conditions, it may be appropriate to compare and to contrast the liturgical setting of the Byzantine coronation with the one established by the Western Church.

# I

The prototype and model of the Western coronations was the anointment of David at the hands of Samuel. There are scores of possibilities available to bear out this statement. Here, however, it may meet all our needs to restrict the discussion to the central part of the liturgical action, the formula of the anointment itself. A Benedictional of Freising of the early ninth century has preserved in its Gelasian additions an apparently old formula for the consecration of kings and for the anointment of the king's hands:[5]

> Unguantur manus istae de oleo sanctificante, *unde uncti fuerunt reges et prophetae, sicut unxit Samuhel David in regem*, ut sic benedictus et constitutus rex in regno isto.

---

4. Not all the conclusions of P. Charanis, op. cit., appear to me to be acceptable; see e.g. *infra*, n. 91.

5. *Cod. lat. Monac. 6430*, fol. 30ᵛ, first published by G. Morin, "Un Receuil Gallican inédit," *Revue bénédictine* 29 (1912), 168–94. Against Morin's attribution of these benedictions to the Merovingian kings, who to our knowledge were not anointed, see Eduard Eichmann, "Die sog. römische Königskrönungsformel," *Historisches Jahrbuch* 45 (1925), 545, and the same author's "Königs- und Bischofsweihe," *Sitzungsberichte der bayerischen Akademie* 1928, 6. Abhandlung,

It has been held that this benediction was related to the anointment of King Pepin in 751 or 754 because the image "befitted the situation at that time": Pepin, the new David, taking the place of the repudiated Saul (the last Merovingian king) and being consecrated by a new Samuel, St. Boniface or Pope Stephen II.[6] Historians have been warned by a great scholar "to fix the dates of prayers by means of allusions supposed to be contained in them to current events," and the warner was right in this case.[7] Whether or not the Freising benedictions were spoken at the sacring of King Pepin is a question to which there is probably no answer. If, however, this was the case the Samuel-David benediction was spoken certainly not because it befitted this particular political situation but because it befitted any similar occasion. For regardless of current political events, the David-Samuel benediction was the, or a, liturgical formula for any consecration with oil and of oil.[8]

The Samuel-David form is first found in the *Ordo baptismi* of the sacramentary of Bobbio, which falls in the seventh century.[9] It here belongs to the exorcism of the person to be baptized. The priest touches nose, ears, and breast of the candidate, saying: "Ungo te de oleo sanctificato, *sicut unxit Samuhel David in regem et prophetam*."

Nothing can be less surprising than to find that through the liturgical formula the king's consecration here appears closely related to the rite of baptism. The French kings, until the nineteenth century, were anointed with the holy balm which an angel was alleged to have brought from heaven for the baptism of Clovis at the hands of St. Rémy. Contrariwise, the baptismal unction has often been interpreted as man's coronation to kingship. "Through the signing of the forehead

---

30 (here to be quoted as Eichmann, "Königsweihe"). See also Percy Ernst Schramm, "Die Ordines der Kaiserkrönung," *Archiv für Urkundenforschung* 11 (1930), 362, n. 2 (here quoted as Schramm, "Ordines").

6. This is the thesis of Eichmann, "Königsweihe," 32, which has been repeated by Erich Caspar, "Das Papsttum unter frankischer Herrschaft," *Zeitschrift für Kirchengeschichte* 54 (1935), 136, n. 8.

7. See Edmund Bishop, *Liturgica historica* (Oxford, 1918), 13.

8. Theodor Klauser, in *Jahrbuch für Liturgiewissenschaft* 13 (1936), 351. Most of the places adduced in the following pages are well known. They have been adduced by Eichmann, "Königsweihe," 30ff., and more broadly by Gerald Ellard, *Ordination Anointings in the Western Church before 1000 A.D.* (Cambridge, Mass., 1933), 30ff., who unfortunately omitted to discuss the development of the royal unction with the same thoroughness which he devoted to the sacerdotal and episcopal anointings; many features would have stood out more clearly. For some additions, see *infra*, n. 11.

9. PL 72, col. 502B. Ellard, *Ordination*, 21, by some mischief, has mistaken this prayer for a part of an Order for the Anointing of the Dying and therefore comes to conclusions as to the original use of the form which are not correct; see Klauser, op. cit., 351.

with oil a royal ointment and perennial chrism has been granted," says Prudentius, and Isidore of Seville explains the "royal" character of the anointed by emphasizing that the latter had become a member of the eternal king and priest and that those baptized represented a *genus regale et sacerdotale* in general.[10] As man's coronation with the diadem of glory and honor, baptism occasionally was even accompanied by acclamations.[11] Hence the inner relationship of the two rites—baptism and royal unction—is hardly in need of any further explanation, all the less so as the baptism of Christ in the Jordan was at the same time recognized as his unction with the oil of gladness.

The interrelationship between the two rites is evinced by the benedictions. The words which in the Freising Benedictional precede the Samuel-David form (*unde uncti fuerunt reges et prophetae*) are likewise to be linked to the baptismal rite. We find that phrase—in the fuller form of "*unde unxisti sacerdotes, reges et prophetas, et martyres*"[12] in the Gelasian Sacramentary at the *Benedictio olei* on Thursday in Holy Week.[13] Here it appears twice. It

---

10. Prudentius, *Psychomachia*, verse 360f, ed. Maurice Lavarenne (Paris, 1933), 161-62: "Post inscripta oleo frontis signacula, per quae / Unguentum regale datum est et chrisma perenne." Isidore of Seville, *De ecclesiasticis officiis*, 2, c. 26, PL 83, col. 823f: "Eratque … tantum in regibus et sacerdotibus mystica unctio, qua Christus figurabatur, unde et ipsum nomen a chrismate dicitur. Sed postquam Christus dominus noster verus rex et sacerdos aeternus a deo caelesti et mystico unguento est delibutus, unguento non solum pontifices et reges, sed omnis ecclesia unctione chrismatis consecratur pro eo quod membrum est aeterni regis et sacerdotis. Ergo quia genus regale et sacerdotale sumus, ideo post lavacrum ungimur, ut Christi nomine consecremur." This place, together with Johannes Diaconus, in PL 59, col. 403 ("intelligat baptizatus regnum in se sacerdole convenisa"), has been quoted by Odilbert of Milan, *Liber de baptismo*, c. 17, ed. Friedrich Wiegand, *Erzbischof Odilbert von Mailand über die Taufe* (Leipzig, 1899), pp. 34-35, 54ff., a work submitted to Charlemagne in response to his inquiry of 812; cf. Jean Michel Hanssens, "Deux documents carolingiens sur le baptême," *Ephemerides Liturgicae* 41 (1927), 69-82, who adds to the nine hitherto known answers a tenth found in Orléans (MS 116).

11. Thomas Michels, "Die Akklamationen in der Taufliturgie," *Jahrbuch für Liturgiewissenschaft* 8 (1928), 78f.

12. The formula first occurs, in relation with the consecration of oil, in the early third century; cf. *Traditio apostolica*, ed. Johannes Quastern, *Monumena eucharistica et liturgica vetustissima* (Bonn, 1935), 30, with n. 6; Louis Duchesne, *Christian Worship* (5th ed., 1931), 528. Isidore of Sevilla (cf. *supra*, n. 10) almost paraphrases the formula. It is actually found in Germanus of Constantinople's *Mystica contemplatio*, PG 98, col. 385, where it appears in connection with the baptism. The passage belongs to the later interpolations (probably of the 11th or 12th century; cf. [F. E.] Brightman, *Liturgies Eastern and Western*, Oxford, 1896, xciii), as it is not found in the Latin version of this work by Anastasius Bibliothecarius; see S. Pétridès, "Traités liturgiques de Saint Maxime et de Saint Germain traduit par Anastase le Bibliothécaire," *Revue de l'orient chrétien* 10 (1905), 290ff. On the other [hand], the Germanus formula shows not yet the additional "et martyres," an interpolation according to Duchesne, op. cit., 576, note to p. 306, which is found already in the *Gelasianum* and elsewhere and which was generally used in the 11th/12th century. Hence the Germanus interpolations might be of an earlier date.

13. The *Gelasian Sacramentary*, ed. Henry Austin Wilson (Oxford, 1894), 70-71.

first occurs in the blessing of the oil for the unction of the sick, and consequently the healing forces of the oil as a "tutamentum corporis, animae et spiritus" (a remarkable residuum of trichotomistic [three-part division] concepts within the liturgy!)[14] are emphasized. In the second place, the formula appears in the eucharistic prayer. Here the chrism is put into closest relationship to the baptism on Holy Saturday for which it was being prepared. In the prayer mention is made of King David, the prophet who foreseeingly had sung the sacramental power of the oil; of the dove which with the olive branch in its beak had found home to the ark; of baptism in general; of Moyses who by the order of God had anointed his brother Aaron priest; and of Christ who in the Jordan received the unction with the oil of gladness. Finally God is besought to sanctify the oil by his blessings and to add to the liquid the power of the Holy Ghost

> per potentiam Christi tui[15] a cuius sancto nomine chrisma nomen accepit, unde unxisti sacerdotes, reges, prophetas, et martyres tuos . . .

We now realize that the Freising Benedictional in the prayer for anointing the king's hands has combined the two formulas, the Samuel-David and the *unde unxisti* forms, which both were derived from the baptismal rite.

These formulae were used not only at the consecration of kings. Between 700 and 900, it rightly has been said, the Samuel-David as well as the more general *unde unxisti* form may be found in any rite providing for an unction with oil.[16] Consequently, when the application of oil was added to the ritual of sacerdotal and episcopal ordinations (to our

---

14. The Pauline trichotomy (1 Thess. 5:23) is found time and again in the Egyptian liturgies (Serapion, St. Mark), but also in the Syrian liturgy of St. James; cf. F. E. Brightman, "Soul, Body, Spirit," *Journal of Theological Studies* 2 (1901), 273-74. Trichonomistic concepts are quite frequent also in the works of Augustine, e.g. *De fide et symbolo*, c. 23, and passim; cf. Erich Dinkler, *Die Anthropologie Augustins* (Stuttgart, 1934), 255ff. For a few notes on later mediaeval trichonomistic concepts, see E. Kantorowicz, *Die Wiederkehr gelehrter Anachorese im Mittelalter* (Stuttgart, 1937), 4, n. 13. In the Gregorianum the trichonomistic version has been replaced [by] a dualistic ("tutamentum mentis et corporis"); cf. PL 78, col. 93. The same is true of course in the present *pontificale Romanum*.

15. The Roman liturgy, as usual, has attenuated this strong image. See *Gregorianum* (PL 78, col. 85): "*cooperante potentia Christi tui,*" diluted by the *Pontificale Romanum* into "*cooperante Christi Filii tui potentia.*" For a similar change, see Thomas Michels, "La date du couronnement de Charles-le-Chauve (9 Sept. 869) et le culte liturgique de S. Gorgon à Metz," *Revue bénédictine* 51 (1939), 2, n. 1. For the reason of these changes see Josef A. Jungmann, *Die Stellung Christi im liturgischen Gebet* (Münster, 1925), whose attention, however, the items mentioned above—and so far as I can see, also their type—has escaped.

16. Klauser, loc. cit.

knowledge in the course of the eighth century) the Samuel-David form
would appear on this occasion too. The earliest liturgical evidence for a
sacerdotal ordination anointing is found in the *Missale Francorum*, written most likely in Visigothic Aquitaine in the first decades of the eighth
century, 700–730.[17] As in the Freising Benedictional the prayer refers to
the anointment of the hands, the hands of a priest:

> Unguantur manus istae de oleo sanctificato et crismate sanctifi-
> cationes[18] *sicut unxit samuhel david in regem et prophetam ita unguan-
> tur et consummentur.*

To this there is added the trinitarian baptismal formula *In nomine patris
et filii et spiritus sancti.* This additional baptismal formula is found with
other oil anointings as well; it became inseparable from the sacerdotal
and episcopal anointments,[19] but never, it seems, to have been added to
the royal or imperial unctions—a most remarkable fact. Once more in
the course of the eighth century does the Samuel-David form appear,
in the Sacramentary of Gellone (written probably between 770 and 780,
but representing material of a somewhat earlier period). Here it serves
the episcopal consecration and more specifically, the anointment of the
bishop's head, probably "à la mode de roi."[20]

In the age of Charlemagne and the later Carolingians the Samuel-David
form seems to disappear from the rite of the episcopal ordinations, but
it was revived after the collapse of the Carolingian power.[21] It then served,
after some oscillations, for the anointing of the hands of the bishop. For
the unction of the bishop's head a new benediction was created which was
closely connected with prayers remembering the anointment of Aaron at
the hands of Moyses.[22] Hence, at the episcopal unctions there were eventually represented both the royal and sacerdotal forms, "Samuel-David" for

---

17. Ludovico Muratori, *Liturgia Romana vetus* (1748), 2, 669. Ellard, *Ordination*, 20. I am
inclined to believe that ordination anointings, not only royal unctions, were known in the
Visigothic-Spanish Church before, or about 700 A.D.; but evidence is lacking.

18. For the various kinds of oil, cf. Eichmann, "Königsweihe," 21ff., 35; see, however,
Schramm, "Ordines," 353, n. 4, for the inconsistency of the sources.

19. The baptismal formula as attached to the Anointing of the Dying is found in the
Celtic Orders; cf. F. E. Warren, *The Liturgy and Ritual of the Celtic Church* (Oxford, 1881), 172,
223. Furthermore, see Theodulf of Orléans, in PL 105, col. 221. For the episcopal unctions,
cf. Ellard, *Ordination*, 81, 95, passim, and plates III, 1–2.

20. Ellard, *Ordination*, 30. The question of which was first, royal or episcopal unction,
cannot be decided; cf. Ellard, 31; Eichmann, "Königsweihe," 35.

21. Ellard, *Ordination*, 69, has clarified this point.

22. Cf. Ellard, *Ordination*, 93, 95, for the Samuel-David, and 81–82, 87 for the Gallican
Moyses-Aaron form; see, for the latter, also Eichmann, "Königsweihe," 35.

hands and "Moyses-Aaron" for the head, as suitable for the new "genus regale et sacerdotale" which emerged from the unction with oil.

On the other hand, the Samuel-David form lingers on in the coronation rites of the Carolingians during the ninth century;[23] it disappeared from these Orders at approximately the time when its reintegration into the rite of episcopal ordinations was achieved. Instead of "Samuel-David," kings had to accept the more general *unde unxisti* form which eventually became firmly established in the rite of royal anointings. It was embedded into a long prayer in which David, Solomon, and other figures of the Old Testament were remembered.[24]

Whatever the details of the development, we find that ordinations as well as coronations were dominated by metaphors borrowed mainly from the Old, hardly from the New Testament. It is true that both the episcopal[25] and the royal consecrations were reflected elements of the baptismal idea.[26] But that was like a faint glimmer of bygone days which remained in the background of the scene, since the tableau posed at

---

23. For example, in 856, in the Order for the coronation of Judith (PL 138, col. 642), and more precisely in 888, in the Order for the coronation of Odo, ed. Percy Ernst Schramm, "Die Krönung bei den Westfranken und Angelsachsen von 878 bis um 1000," *Zeitschrift der Savigny-Stiftung für Rechtsgeschichte*, kan. Abt. 23 (1934) (quoted as Schramm, "Westfranken"), 198: "Accipiat . . . unctionem sanctificationis tuae, qui per manus sancti prophetae tui Samuelis regem et prophetam David oleo benedictionis tuae unxisti."

24. See the Order for the coronation of Charles the Bald (Metz, 869) and the important preamble to the *unde unxisti* form in the Order of Louis II (877), PL 138, cols. 741, 783. See further Paul L. Ward, "An Early Version of the Anglo-Saxon Coronation Ceremony," *English Historical Review* 57 (1942), 353, and Schramm, "Westfranken," 203, for a Continental Order of about 1000, and Schramm, op. cit., 214ff., 225 for the Anglo-Saxon Orders. For the German Orders of the Coronation, see Schramm, "Die Krönung in Deutschland bis zum Beginn des Salischen Hauses (1028); *Zeitschrift der Savigny-Stiftung für Rechtsgeschichte*, kan. Abt. 24 (1935) (quoted as Schramm, "Salier"), 316, 328.

25. Cf., *supra*, n. 19. Unambiguously "baptismal," if not quite unique is the ordination anointing according to the Ambrosian rite: "Et fundat oleum super caput eius in modum crucis dicens: 'In nomine Patris et Filii et Spiritus sancti ungeo te in sacerdotem magnum ad regendam ecclesiam Dei et plebem universam.'"Cf. Marcus Magistretti, *Pontificale in usum ecclesiae Mediolanensis* (Milan, 1897), 53; Eichmann, "Königsweihe," 38; Ellard, *Ordination*, 74. This form agrees almost verbatim with that of the later coronation anointing of the Byzantine emperors, cf. *infra*, p. XXX. For the relationship between baptismal and ordination anointings, see the most interesting discussion of Peter Damian, *Liber qui dicitur Gratissimus*, c. 3, PL 145, col. 102: "Si quis autem mihi fortassis objiciat aliud esse baptismum humanae regenerationis, aliud consecrationis ecclesiasticae dignitatem, nos quidquid in hac parte de baptismo credimus, totum nihilominus et de consecratione sentimus. Nam cum baptismus totius ecclesiastici sacramenti origo sit atque primordium . . . , ita nimirum omnis ecclesiastica consecratio illi specialiter competit, a quo omnium benedictionum plenitudo profluxit." See also PL 144, col. 529C.

26. See above all, the prayer *Deus Dei filius* of the consecration of kings in which the Lord's baptism and unction with the oil of gladness is commemorated and God is demanded that "per praesens sacri unguinis infusionem Spiritus paracliti super caput tuum infundat"; Schramm, "Salier," 316–17, and "Ordines," 380–81; Eichmann, "Königsweihe," 13, n. 7. In certain

consecrations on the liturgical stage was certainly not the baptism of Christ. This image had been definitely superseded by recollections of the Old Testament, and after the prototypes of Israel's kings, priests, and prophets all Western unctions were finally molded. "David anointed by Samuel"—sometimes replaced by Solomon anointed by Sadoc the priest and Nathan the prophet, or supplemented by other suitable images—this remained the authoritative metaphor of royal anointments in the West.[27]

"David anointed by Samuel," however, challenged inevitably theological minds to decide whether supremacy was with the anointer or the anointed. The situation was comparatively uncomplicated in the Carolingian period: supremacy then was doubtless with "David." Nor did the odds change considerably in favor of "Samuel" when the pope himself acted. Pepin, in 754, remained the protagonist; and even on that memorable Christmas morning in 800, notwithstanding the later curial interpretations, it [was] still the Frankish Charlemagne who "ab apostolico more antiquorum principum adoratus adque imperator et augustus appellatus est." There was no doubt who came first. The great change arrived during the ninth century. The Frankish Empire declined while great hierarchs resided in Rome. At the same time, however, a constitutional change took place the importance of which, to my knowledge, has hardly been recognized. During the ninth century the practice of anointing the bishops, and of anointing their heads, was increasingly carried into effect, not yet in Rome but in France. That is to say, in the moment when the episcopal unction became the general custom in the Frankish Empire, the king forfeited his hitherto unique position of solely representing the *christus Domini* in his realm. His former exclusiveness and exceptional rank now were shared by many. The one Anointed now was sided and overshadowed by scores of anointed, by scores of Frankish princes of the Church who became likewise, and literally, *christi Domini*. Their sublime rank was clearly recognized by Charles the Bald when he admitted, in 859, that it was the bishops

quorum ministerio in regem sum consecratus et qui throni Dei sunt dicti, in quibus Deus sedet, per quos sua decernit iudicia.[28]

---

English *Ordines*, the trinitarian baptismal formula is said at the unction of the queen; cf. Schramm, "Westfranken," 207, 229, 241; Ward, op. cit., 358.

27. Eichmann, "Königsweihe," 52. According to the Anglo-Saxon, so-called "Egbert" Ordo, the choir sings the antiphony "Uncaerunt Salomonem Sadoc sacerdos et Nathan propheta" during the act of anointing the king's head; cf. Schramm, "Westfranken," 214, 225; Ward (*supra*, n. 24), 353.

28. See Charles the Bald's *Libellus proclamationis*, in PL 138, col. 659C; MGH, Leges (fol. ed.), 1, 457.

The bishops, in whom God was enthroned and through whose mouth he passed his sentences, had become the king's peers. Vice versa, the anointment of the king, hitherto a unique and para-hierarchic act, was rapidly filled with hierarchic sentiment, as it was put, so to speak, on a footing with the ordinations of scores of bishops. It was caught by the hierarchic machinery and easily integrated into the inescapable hierarchic mechanism. In the earlier period we still find, heading the Orders of the Coronation, rubrics such as *Ordinatio regis* or *Benedictio ad ordinandum regem*,[29] terms which were used quite harmlessly but which promoted the assimilation of royal to episcopal sacrings. The counter-current began to set in after 900 when gradually these terms disappeared. To the Church there arose the danger that the king's "ordination" might become a sacrament like the ordination of priests, and a misinterpretation concerning the king's sacerdotal qualities was by no means desired.[30] The tendency to distinguish more clearly than hitherto between the two rites grew stronger in and after the age of Church Reform. The emperor eventually was denied the unction of the head; he was anointed only on the arm and the shoulders which symbolized, according to curial interpretation, his being instrumental to the purposes of the Church.[31] For his unction oil of catechumens was used and not the more holy chrism which was reserved for the bishops, "ut ostendatur—writes Innocent III—quanta sit differentia inter auctoritatem pontificis et principis potestatem."[32] On the ground of this general

---

29. In the Irish Collection of Canons of ca. 700, a chapter is devoted to the subject "De ordinatione regis"; cf. H. Wasserschleben, *Die irische Kanonensammlung* (2nd ed., 1885), 76; and in the *Vita sancti Columbae abbatis*, there is the narration about a dream in which the saint saw an angel "qui in manu vitreum *ordinationis regem* habebat librum"; cf. *Nova Legenda Anglie*, ed. C. Horstman (1901), 1, 202–203. To these passages my attention was called by Eichmann, "Königsweihe," 24–25. The expression is found somewhat earlier in the Visigothic-Mozarabic Liturgy in which it survived much longer than elsewhere; see G. Morin, *Liber comicus* (Anecdota Maredsolana, I): 1893, 301: "Legendum in ordinatione regis"; Marius Férotin, *Le Liber Ordinum* (Paris, 1904), col. 502, offers further examples; see also Férotin, "Deux manuscrits Wisigothiques de la bibliothèque de Ferdinand I^er, roi de Castille et de Léon," *Bibliothèque de l'école des chartes* 62 (1901), 383, an entry: "Ordinatio Domni Ferdinandi Regis" (ca. 1055). See also the Frankish Order, ed. Schramm, "Ordines," 370: "Benedictio ad ordinandum regem," and the Anglo-Continental Order of ca. 900 for the ordination of a queen; Schramm, "Westfranken," 206; Ward, op. cit.

30. Eichmann, "Königsweihe," 12–13, 57ff., 67, and Schramm, "Salier," 255ff. discuss the problem briefly.

31. See, Innocent III, *Reg.*, VII, *ep.* 3. PL 215, col. 284B/C, a decretal of 1204 (Decr. Gre. IX, I, tit.15, §5), of which a better text is found in *Corpus Juris Canonici*, ed. Emil Friedberg (Leipzig, 1879–81), 2, col. 132. Cf. Eichmann, "Königsweihe," 51; Schramm, "Salier," 256–57; see also *infra*, n. 37 for the king as instrument of the Church.

32. Innocent III, loc. cit.

tendency there is likely to be found the explanation of the fact that the baptismal trinitarian formula "In the name of the Father and of the Son and of the Holy Ghost" was constantly omitted in the rite of the royal unction. The king's consecration was not to pass for a sacrament. It was to be clearly distinguished from both the sacramental acts, baptism and ordination, even though the heptad of sacraments was not settled before the twelfth century.[33]

The king's consecration was a "quasi-ordination" without sacramental character. To ordain means to appoint. There no longer could be a doubt within canonical political theory whose appointee the ruler became at his coronation. The anointed was credited with being a son adopted by God; but the emperor was actually adopted by the pope. He was styled *a Deo coronatus*; but between God and emperor there was the pope as the most visible protagonist.[34] In short, of the Samuel-David plot was but one possible interpretation on the part of the Church, and this was definitely established as early as 881, when the synod of Frankish bishops assembled at St. Macra decided:

> So much greater is the dignity of the bishops than that of kings as the kings are consecrated to their royal sublimity by the bishops whereas bishops cannot be consecrated by kings.[35]

This argument became a standard concept of mediaeval hierarchism. The argument was based on the words of St. Paul (Hebr. 7:7), saying that "without all contradiction the less is blessed by the better" (Sine ulla autem contradictione, quod minus est, a meliore benedicitur). To this word Pope Innocent III referred when explaining:[36]

> More dignified is the one that receives the tithe than the one who pays it; and less is he that is blessed than he that blesses, as it is testified by the Apostle, who of this speaks and says "Without all contradiction the less is blessed by the better." Albeit that by divine law both kings and priests are anointed, still the kings are

---

33. Schramm, "Salier," 254ff.

34. Eduard Eichmann, "Die Adoption des deutschen Königs durch den Papst, *Zeitschrift für Rechtsgeschichte*, germ. Abt. 37 (1916), 296–99. In Rome, even the *a Deo coronatus* formula with reference to the emperor was suppressed as far as possible; cf. E. Kantorowicz, *Laudes Regiae* (Berkeley, 1946).

35. PL 125, cols. 1069–70; cf. Heinrich Lilienfein, *Die Anschauungen von Staat und Kirche im Reich der Karolinger* (Heidelberg, 1902), 145–46.

36. Innocent III, *Registrum in negotio imperii*, n. 18; PL 216, col. 1012; Eichmann, "Königsweihe," 69–70.

anointed by priests, not priests by kings. Less, however, is the one anointed than he that anoints, and more dignified the anointer than the anointed.

And as though the great pope felt that his arguments might not stand the test without being applied to the One Anointed, he exemplifies his hierarchic principles with regard to the Lord's unction and adds in a dogmatically daring way:

> Therefore he, too, Christ himself, to whom it was said by the prophet "God hath anointed thee with the oil of gladness above thy fellows" (Ps. 44:8), asserts that the Father, who anoints, is greater than the anointed. "The Father—said he—is greater than I am." For, the Father anoints according to what is God, the Son, however, is anointed inasmuch as he is man.

This was the extreme limit to which hierarchical concepts could be carried without reviving Arian and similar ideologies. However, the principle was established and sealed. "David," firmly integrated into the hierarchic functionalism of the Church through his ordination, appeared as less than "Samuel." The ruler, it is true, became visible within the Church as new David, if one whose power was considered as instrumental to the Church and the clergy;[37] but along with David there became visible the new Samuel who was to eclipse the anointed. This tendency became palpable in the times of popes such as Nicholas I and of metropolitans such as Hincmar of Reims; but it culminated in the thirteenth century. From the tombstones of the archbishops-coronators of Mainz we may gather that on the coronation stage Samuel became the prominent actor who almost smothered the visibility of little Davids whom he anointed. These stones indeed illustrate the then current conception very well, the conception according to which the "anointer is more than the anointed" and "the less is blessed by the better."[38]

Within the hierarchical rationalism of the Western Church, in which *Petrus princeps* governed through his vicegerent alone, there may have been no solution other than the one outlined. Every exception of the hierarchical order might have jeopardized the absolute sovereignty claimed

---

37. PL 125, col. 1071C: "legimus (writes the bishops in 881) in sacris historiis, quia cum sacerdotes in regimine regni reges ungebant, et diademata capitibus illorum imponebant, legem in manibus eis dabant, ut discerent et scirent qualiter se et subjectos sibi regere, et sacerdotes Domini honorare debeant." Cf. Deut. 17:8–13.

38. See Plate I, 1–2. [This note from the original unpublished version of Kantorowicz's article refers to a plate that was to have accompanied it.]

by Rome. This, however, does not imply that a different solution was not altogether impossible. The Eastern Church was under the sway of neither Peter the Prince with the tiara on his head nor by Paul the Apostle with the sword in his hand.[39] The prominent place in the East was given to John the Precursor, Prophet, and Baptist, clothed with camel's hair and bearing the lamb; and the spirit as represented by John was irrational rather than hierarchic, and mysterious rather than rational.

## II

> Miles regem baptizavit,
> Qui nos a peccatis lavit,
> Quam pradicens demonstravit
> Agnum sine macula

There seems to be nothing in particular that could rouse our interest in this unpretentious stanza which is found in a sequence to St. John the Baptist in a fifteenth-century missal of Lincoln.[40] Yet the first line deserves our attention. The image of the "knight baptizing the king" is not one of the poet's own inspiration. It has been borrowed from an antiphony which must have been quite popular in the thirteenth century at the latest when it appears in the service books of Salisbury, Worcester, and probably other cathedrals as well.[41] The antiphony then belonged to the octave-day of Epiphany and has the following text:[42]

> Baptizat miles regem, servus dominum, Johannes Salvatorem: aqua Jordanis stupuit, columba protestatur, eterna vox audita est: "Hic est filius meus."

---

39. For St. Peter, see Jeanne Vielliard, "Notes sur 'iconographie de saint Pierre,'" *Le Moyen Age* 39 (1929), 1–16, and for St. Paul, see Eugen Rosenstock-Huessy, *Out of Revolution* (New York, 1938), 529-37.

40. Clemens Blume, *Sequentiae ineditae*, n. 255, *Analecta Hymnica* 34 (1900), 208.

41. *Breviarium ad usum insignis ecclesiae Sarum*, ed. Francis Proctor and C. Wordsworth (Cambridge, 1882), 1, p. CCCL; André Mocquereau, *Le codex F 160 de la bibliothèque de la cathédrale de Worcester* (Paléographie musicale, 12: 1922), fol. 58. The chant refers in both cases to the octave-day of epiphany. To trace the history and dissemination of this canticle is beyond my intentions and my present means. However, it seems to me that it was restricted to the breviaries in which the recollection of Epiphany as the day of the Lord's baptism has survived in the West (cf. Dom Anselm Strittmatter, "Christmas and the Epiphany: Origins and Antecedents," *Thought* 17 [1942], 625–26) and that from the breviaries it has found its way into the later mediaeval rite of the Blessing of the Waters on Epiphany.

42. Cf. *infra*, p. 00 [citation missing].

Neither the canticle itself nor the office to which later it was to be attached are of Western origin. The text agrees with a Greek versicle, and the strange nocturnal ceremony in which later the antiphony was added had been imported from the East. The ceremony of the Blessing of the Waters on the eve of Epiphany now is obsolete in the West where it is observed only in one church, at Sant'Andrea della Valle in Rome.[43] The rite was a symbolico-dramatic repetition of the baptism of Christ who was credited with having consecrated the waters of the world when diving into the water of the Jordan and putting his foot on the head of the water dragon.[44] In all the Oriental Churches, Epiphany appeared as the feast devoted almost exclusively to the commemoration of the Lord's baptism, and it became one of the most important church festivals along with Christmas and Easter, a "most venerable day," as it is called in the Apostolic Constitutions.[45] Epiphany in the Western Church is of secondary importance. There is an ancient Roman tendency towards dimming the light of John the Baptist, probably in order to make all the more visible the light of St. Peter.[46] Epiphany in the Roman Church,

---

43. This I gather from Hermann Usener's fundamental article "Heilige Handlung," *Archiv für Religionswissenschaft* 7 (1904), 290–91, reprinted in his *Kleine Schriften* 4 (1913), 429.

44. In addition to Usener's article, see the most important study of Karl Holl, "Der Ursprung des Epiphanienfestes," *Sitzungsberichte der Berliner Akademie*, 1917, Abhandlung 29, 402–38. There is a broad literature on the subject; cf. Strittmatter, op. cit., 623, n. 86, and Pierre de Puniet, "Bénédiction de l'eau," *Dictionnaire d'archéologie chrétienne et de liturgie* 2 (1912), 698ff. The edition of Oriental and Latin formularies related to the Blessing of the Water by John Marquess of Bute and E. A. Wallis Budge, *The Blessing of the Waters on the Eve of Epiphany* (London, 1901), unfortunately has not been available to me. However, the most important Eastern liturgies for the Blessing of the Waters have been published by F. C. Conybeare and A. J. Maclean, *Rituale Armenorum* (Oxford, 1905), 165ff., 298ff., 415ff.

45. *Consitutiones Apostolorum*, V, c. 13, ed. F. X. Funk, *Didascalia et Constitutiones Apostolorum* (Paderborn, 1905); cf. Holl, "Epiphanienfest," 411. The importance of that day, of course, is partly due to the fact that originally January 6th was considered also the birthday of Jesus.

46. The Roman efforts of obscuring the Feast of Epiphany, which perforce was also a day of commemoration of John the Baptist according to the Eastern Rites, have been discussed rarely; the fact, however, has been clearly evidenced by Karl Holl, op. cit., 411ff., who indicates the competition between Epiphany and Christmas and Rome's championship of the latter feast. Strittmatter, "Christmas and the Epiphany," who rightly regrets that this particular phase of the problem has never been investigated, styles the issue a case "in which Rome was extraordinarily unreceptive," and suggests "dogmatically very serious" reasons to be at the back of this unreceptiveness. I am inclined to conceive of the issue as indicating but one important phase of Rome's very long struggle against the predominance of "John" in the Eastern and various "Gallican" rites, a preponderance which might have eclipsed the superiority of St. Peter in removing him to a second place. The antagonism climaxes in the well-known contest between the Roman basilicas of the Lateran and St. Peter during the 11th and 12th centuries. I have broached the problem in a study "Ivories and Litanies," *Journal of the Warburg and Courtauld Institutes* 5 (1942), 78–79, and may further substantiate it in a special study.

therefore, became mainly the day on which the Magi adored the new-born king of the Universe; the recollection of the baptism in the Jordan was blotted out as completely as possible, and the rite of the Blessing of the Waters had consequently no place in the Roman liturgy of January 6th. Not until the eleventh century does there appear in a Pontifical of Salzburg, a Latin translation of the Greek, which was vaguely accommodated to Western ecclesiastical usage.[47] This translation never gained ground within the orbit of the Roman Church whereas another Blessing of the Waters on Epiphany, a blending of Western with Oriental elements, began to spread quickly in the drama-and-symbol-loving later Middle Ages.[48]

In that later ritual the antiphony *Baptizat miles regem* had its specific function. The priest, as the holy action proceeded, had to dip a crucifix (not simply a cross) three times into the water of the font while the antiphonies sung by the choir accompanied and explained his doing:

Baptizatur Christus et sanctificatur omnia mundus . . .

and thereafter the other antiphony is chanted: "The knight baptizes the king, the serf the Lord, John the Savior . . ." The part played by the priest at this dramatic performance is obvious: he is the soldier and serf, the "John," that symbolically baptizes the king and lord, the "Savior," in dipping the crucifix into the font.[49] *Miles regem baptizat*—the less blesses the better.

---

47. The formulary has been edited by P. de Puniet, "Formulaire grec de l'Épiphanie dans une traduction latine ancienne," *Revue bénédictine* 29 (1912), 29–46. Cf. Adolf Franz, *Die kirchlichen Benediktionen im Mittelalter* (Freiburg, 1909), 1, 193ff.; for the provenience of the manuscript, which has been disputed, see Victor Leroquais, *Les pontificaux manuscrits des bibliothèques publiques de France* (Paris, 1937), 1, 292ff., n. 91.

48. This is the rite discussed by Usener, *Kleine Schriften*, 4, 429–35. Its connections with the *Benedictio maior salis et aqua*, with the breviaries, and with Eastern liturgies deserve to be studied in detail.

49. Valentin Thalhofer and L. Eisenhofer, *Handbuch der katholischen Liturgik* (Freiburg, 1912), 1, 685, connect the ritual with Exodus 15: 25, where Moyses casts the wood into the waters to make them sweet. This is certainly not the most obvious meaning of the ceremony which has been explained excellently by Usener, op. cit., 430ff. Cf. the interpretation of John of Odsun, in Conybeare and Maclean, *Rituale Armenorum*, 182: "per id commemorare (oportet) Salvatoris nostri pro nobis in Jordane baptismum," and he compares the realistic symbolism with that of Palm Sunday, "quemadmodum in die adventus ramos tollere et flabella movere (oportet) imitantes quodammodo Hebraeorum pueros." *Dies adventus* refers to the entry (*adventus*) into Jerusalem; cf. E. H. Kantorowicz, "The 'King's Advent' and the Enigmatic Panels in the Doors of Santa Sabina," *Art Bulletin* 26 (1944), pp. [left incomplete]. The male-female symbolism of the prayers at the Blessing of the Waters on Saturday in Holy Week, stressed by Usener, op. cit., 433, finds some support in Theodore of Studion, *Oratio in baptismi pervigilium*,

The image of the less that blesses the better, or at least the emphasis laid upon this mysteriously reverted order, is Oriental. "Today the lord is baptized by the serf" is a versicle of that exuberant "Today" Litany which in the Oriental liturgies is chanted on that occasion.[50] The same idea we find echoed, time and again, in the Eastern Epiphany homilies, often amplified by new elaborations: fire purified by hay, a fountain rinsed by mud, the judge baptized by the defendant, the sun illuminated by a wick, the physician healed by the sick, and similar metaphors.[51] In the Byzantine ritual, the prayer of consecration—the famous "Great art thou, O Lord, and marvelous are thy works"—is followed by a fairly long supplication for emperor, or rather a plurality of emperors, as was the custom in Byzantium:[52]

> Save your servants, our faithful emperors, and protect them in peace beneath thy shelter; subdue under them all those that are hostile

---

in Angelo Mai, *Patrum nova bibliotheca* 5 (Rome, 1849), 22, c. 7, while ibid., c. 8, a short but impressive description of the Eastern Epiphany celebration may be found.

50. For the versicle adduced, see *Rituale Armenorum*, 426, 428, 429, 433, cf. 424, 186ff. For the great hymn the clauses of which all begin with the word "Today," cf. Anton Baumstark, "Die *Hodie*-Antiphonen des römischen Breviers und der Kreis ihrer griechischen Parallelen," *Die Kirchenmusik* 10 (Paderborn, 1909), 153–60. For an early example of these "Today" clauses, see N. Borgia, "Frammenti liturgici antichissimi inediti," *Byzantinische Zeitschrift* 30 (1930), 347, which according to the editor may fall in the fourth century.

51. See, e.g., Proclus of Constantinople (434–447), *Oratio in sancta Theophania*, PG 65, col. 761; Gregory the Thaumaturge, Patriarch of Antioch (570–593), in PG 10, cols. 1179–80, with an early Latin version published by Angelo Mai, *Nova patrum bibliotheca*, 2 (Rome, 1844), 553ff. The same metaphors are found with various writers. Not only images such as "soldier-king" or "serf-lord" are repeated time and again but also the one of "judge and defendant" (Proclus and Gregory the Thaumaturge) or "potter and clay" (Gregory the Thaumaturge and Antipatros of Bostra in PG 85, col. 1763) as well as others are found frequently. In Western literature metaphors for the reverted world order are rarer; see, however, the sequence on the virginal birth by Aegidius Zamorensis [space left blank], ed. G. M. Dreves, in *Analecta Hymnica* 32 (1899), 233–35. The homiletic literature is of course enormously rich owing to the importance of that day. See, e.g., Gregory of Nyssa, PG 46, cols. 577ff., Gregory Nazianzene, PG 36, cols. 360ff.; Eusebe of Alexandria, PG 86, cols. 372ff.; see also the spurious homily ascribed to John Chrysostome, PG 64, cols 43ff. For early Western sermons which on Epiphany still refer to the Baptism, see Holl, "Epiphanienfest," 417 (Maximus of Turin, Chrysologus of Ravenna), and add the most interesting Pseudo-Augustinian sermons CXXXIV to CXXXIX in PL 39, cols. 2010–18, which often give the impression of being mere paraphrases of Greek homilies. Many of the Eastern homilies are dislogized and distinctly dramatized, e.g. the one of Gregory the Thaumaturge [citation missing], and George La Piana, *Le rappresentazioni sacre nella letteratura bizantina dalle origini al secolo IX con rapporti al Teatro sacro d'Occidente* (Grottaferrata, 1912), 72ff., points out the important role played by these "dramatic homilies" with regard to the development of the liturgical drama. See also the Epiphany *Kontakion* of Romanos, ed. J. B. Pitra, *Analecta sacra* 1 (Paris, 1876), 16–23. On the Epiphany celebration in Byzantium, see Petrus Hendrix, "La fête de l'Épiphanie," *Congrès d'histoire du christianisme: Jubilé Alfred Loisy* 2 (Paris, 1928).

52. *Rituale Armenorum*, 419; it is found also in the Latin version, see P. de Puniet, in *Revue bénédictine* 29 (1912), 34.

and harmful; grant unto them all that is needed unto salvation and eternal life, that with the elements, and men, and angels, and with all things visible and invisible they may glorify thy holy name . . .

Supplicatory prayers for the emperor along with intentions for the Church, the patriarch, the clergy, and other groups of society are anything but rare in the Byzantine service. However, long supplications for the emperor alone and at the most prominent place of the service are not found frequently. Whatever the reason may have been of commemorating the emperor so conspicuously on the day of Epiphany, it reminds us that the part played by the emperor in the Epiphany drama at Constantinople was not simply that of a spectator or passive member of the congregation. For to him there fell an important role at the staging of the feast.

The Byzantine emperor, as is well known, was considered in a most realistic fashion the living image of Christ. Accordingly, he represented the Lord in a true-to-nature manner especially on the great church festivals. On Palm Sunday, at the ceremony of the *peripatos*, he performed the Entry into Jerusalem; on Maundy he visited the infirmaries and, later, washed the feet of twelve poor men; on Easter he staged, the Cross symbolizing the Anastasis in his right hand and the sack of dust in his left, the resurrection;[53] and in a similar way it was the emperor's duty to represent the Lord on Epiphany. In conformity with the significance of this feast in the Eastern rites, the service on Epiphany rolled off with all the elaborate pomp which the Byzantine Church would display on these occasions. The emperor attended the service in Santa Sophia, and while he was moving in grand procession to the church the acclamations in their carefully studied order accompanied every important section of his way. These acclamations, as natural, stressed the elements which allowed a comparison between emperor and Savior or established through other means the "stage identity" of image and prototype. Thus the acclamations on Epiphany would allude to the events in the Jordan river; they would illustrate the part that the emperor was expected to play and at the same time prepare the minds for visualizing the emperor's appearance within the timeless space of a transcendental reality.[54]

---

53. See August Heisenberg, "Aus der Geschichte und Literatur der Palaiologenzeit," *Sitzungsberichte der Bayerischen Akademie* 1920, Abhandlung 10, 82ff., and especially the valuable study of Otto Treitinger, *Die oströmische Kaiser- und Reichsidee nach ihrer Gestaltung im höfischen Zeremoniell* (Jena, 1938), 125ff. and passim.

54. Constantinus Porphyrogenitus, *De cerimoniis aulae Byzantinae*, ed. Johann Jakob Reiske (Bonn, 1929–30; here quoted as *De cerim.*), 1, c. 3, 41ff.; cf. Treitinger, *Zeremoniell*, 35. The acclamations, to a great extent, repeat the ideas of the liturgy of the day.

Today the Logos, coeternal with God the Father, proceeds to be baptized in the Jordan; and the Lord, whom even the powers of heaven watch only with trembling, inclines his head like a slave to the Precursor; but the one that has illumined the world by his appearance, exalts the power of majesty and increases it to the happiness and glory of the Romans . . .

CHANTERS: Baptized in Jordan's water.
PEOPLE: Long live the emperors.
CHANTERS: And inclining his head like a slave to the Precursor.
PEOPLE: Long live the emperors.

The one baptized today at the hands of the Precursor, at his trembling hands, heralds you, the benefactors crowned by God, as emperors, and to the whole inhabited world he makes you manifest as his christoi. And in hallowing his bath, he baptizes the majesty with the oil of immortality and bestows on the Romans salvation and sublime support and the glory of the empire . . .

CHANTERS: Adoring the glory of the manifest Christ.
PEOPLE: May God make longlasting your holy kingship.

The acclamations, in the parts here adduced, bring the two main themes of Epiphany into relief: the baptism of the Lord in the Jordan at the hands of St. John, and the Lord's manifestation as the Son of God through the descent of the Holy Ghost.

These two themes are reflected in the court liturgy of that day. On the eve of Epiphany the emperor attended the great ἁγιασμός, the Blessing of the Waters, which was conducted by the patriarch in the palace church. The patriarch, standing beside the baptismal font, said the long series of stichoi [lines of a fixed length] which all began with "Today" and the beautiful prayer of consecration ending in the petitions for the majesties. The emperor, a burning taper in his hand, took his stand behind the font while the eunuch *protospatharioi* [court dignitaries], likewise with burning tapers in their hands, were lined up behind him. Having finished the prayers, the patriarch approached his sovereign and poured blessed water in the hands of the emperor who with it washed his head, face, and hands and who, if he so pleased, drank a few drops.[55] To miss the symbolic contents of this scene is almost impossible once

---

55. *De cerim.*, 1, c. 25, 139ff. The "Today" clauses are not recited by the patriarch, but he begins their recital with loud voice; cf. *Rituale Armenorum*, 431.

we recall the pictorial representations of the Baptism in Eastern art: John, standing on the left bank of the Jordan, pours the water; the Lord has his place in the river, while on the right bank, ready to attend the Lord, there are lined up the angels which in the imperial liturgy apparently were represented by the eunuchs.[56] In later times, the great *hagiasmos* [consecration] underwent some changes in that the patriarch "anointed" the emperor's forehead and eyes with the holy water, a rite thereafter repeated in a less ceremonious fashion at the beginning of every month.[57]

More impressive than the "baptism," which had taken place in the palace church, was the "epiphany" of the emperor which was a more public performance. The acclamations had emphasized that the Lord, who by his baptism had been "Made manifest to Israel" (John 1:31), in turn makes manifest and visible his anointed, the emperor. Yet the Lord himself heralds the *christoi* to the whole world, as the heavens open and the Holy Ghost descends from above. That is to say, from the Lord's visibility there arises as a logical and mysterious consequence the visibility of the emperor, the former's epiphany being the premise of the imperial epiphany.

The acclamations, which to some extent simply repeated the phrases of the liturgy of that day, were reflected and paraphrased by the poems and orations with which the emperors were greeted when, in the dark of the winter night, they presented themselves in the brilliant light of the *prokypsis*.[58] The *prokypsis* was a wooden tribune, erected in the open,

---

56. The basis for this, I suppose, is Matth. 19:12. Cf. Walter Bauer, "Matth. 19:12 und die alten Christen," *Neutestamentliche Studien George Heinrici zu seinem 70. Geburtstag* (Leipzig, 1914), 235–44. I am not aware that the problem of eunuchs in Byzantine civilization has been investigated. For the Greco-Roman Antique, see Arthur Darby Nock, "Eunuchs in Ancient Religion," *Archiv für Religionswissenschaft* 23 (1925), 25–33, who emphasizes that the eunuch put himself on a footing with the virgin and the pure child. For the Christian attitude toward eunuchs, see in addition to the study of Bauer also *Dictionnaire d'archéologie chrétienne et de liturgie*, 2 (1912), s.v. "Castration"; 5, col. 744, s.v. "Eunuques," where the interesting statement of St. Jerome is discussed who held that the Three Youths in the Furnace (Daniel 3) were eunuchs. Their Phrygian attire, probably meant to be "Babylonian," may have suggested the costume of Atthis actually displayed by the "Eunuchus" Chereas in the Vatican Terence. That *castus* and *castrare* (ἁγνός) derived from the same root was known to Isidore, *Origines* 10, c. 33: "castus primum a castratione dicitur"; cf. Nock, op. cit., 28.

57. Codinus, *De officialibus* rec. I. Becker (Bonn, 1839), c. 14, p. 78; cf. Reiske's notes in *De cerim.*, vol. 2, 227, who indicates that the monthly aspersions were consummated in the name of St. Mary while the Epiphany aspersion was performed in the name of Christ. With liturgical celebrations I shall deal in another connection.

58. The fundamental study on the *prokypsis* is Heisenberg, op. cit., 85ff.; cf. M. A. Andreeva, "De la cérémonie *prokypsis*," *Seminarium Kondakovianum* 1 (1927), 157–72 (in Russian); Treitinger, *Zeremoniell*, 112ff.

appropriately decorated, and veiled by golden or other curtains. The name of the fabric was transferred eventually to the whole ceremony which originally seems to have taken place only on Christmas and Epiphany, the feasts of light, but which later was performed also at the coronations and imperial weddings.[59] In the evening, while the emperors were attending the service in the church of the Blachernae, there assembled in front of the stage-like estrade the deputations of the garrison with their banners, the court, the high officials, and other dignitaries and people, who after the service were joined by the clergy in festival vestments. In the meantime, the emperors ascended from the back of the fabric the steps of the *prokypsis* which was still veiled. When they had arranged themselves on the platform, the curtains were flung open and the emperors in their glittering robes became "visible," or were "made manifest," the only luminous figures in the dark of the night.[60] It was in fact an "imperial epiphany," theatrical perhaps and not to Western taste, but in perfect agreement with the realism of the Eastern rites and mystery plays.[61]

The symbolism of this dramatic pageantry was disclosed by the chants and rhetorical effusions offered to the majesties. Chants and

---

59. Heisenberg, op. cit., 92, n. 1, believes that the *prokypsis* did not antedate the time of the Comneni.

60. For a miniature representing the *prokypsis* (late 12th century), see Joseph Strzygowski, "Das Epithalamion des Paläologen Andronikos II," *Byzantinische Zeitschrift* 10 (1901) p. VI, 2 facing p. 554; Heisenberg, op. cit., 96.

61. See in general, Treitinger, *Zeremoniell*, 79ff. Orations for the Epiphany *prokypsis* have been prepared in not small a number. Wilhelm Regel, *Fontes rerum Byzantinarum* (St. Petersburg, 1917), has edited the following orations: pp. 24ff., No. III, an oration of Eustathius, Metropolitan of Thessalonica (1174 or 1175); it is found also in PG 135, cols. 933ff., which refers to the orator's election to the See of Myron, but contains so many allusions to Epiphany that January 6th must have been the day on which it was delivered; pp. 131ff., 165ff., Nos. VIII and X, two allocutions of Michael the Rhetor of ca. 1153 and 1150 respectively; pp. 244ff., No. XIV, an allocution of John Kamateros, ca. 1186; pp. 254ff., No. XV, one of Georgios Tornikas, ca. 1193; pp. 304ff., No. XIX, one of John Diogenis. Several of these together with the newly edited Epiphany oration of John Syropulos have been discussed by Max Bachmann, *Die Rede des Johannes Syropulos an den Kaiser Isaak II. Angelos* (Munich Dissertation, 1935). Several poems for the Epiphany *prokypsis* (probably falling within the years 1172 and 1173) have been composed by Manuel Holobolos, ed. J. F. Boissonade, *Anecdota Graeca*, 5 (Paris, 1833), 164ff. (Nos. V, VI), 170ff. (Nos. X-XIII), and 176ff. (Nos. XV-XVII); they have been discussed by Heisenberg, op. cit., 112ff., according to whom (p. 129) poem XV may belong to a Christmas *prokypsis*. An additional Epiphany poem of Holobolos has been published by M. Treu, "Manuel Holobolos," *Byzantinische Zeitschrift* 5 (1896), 546ff. Three poems by Theodorus Prodromus and addressing John II Comnenus (1118-1143) have been edited by Angelo Mai, *Nova patrum bibliotheca* 6 (Rome, 1853), 412-13, Nos. XVI-XVIII; on the poet, see Carl Neumann, *Griechische Geschichtsschreiber und Geschichtsquellen im zwölften Jahrhundert* (Leipzig, 1888), 37ff. See also the general remark of Dölger, in *Gnomon* 14 (1938), 205-6, on the court rhetoric.

addresses, all saluted with few variations the *Helios basileus* and emphasized the parallelism of the Lord and the Lord-staging emperor.[62]

Resplend, Rhomaen city, once more I say: Resplend,
Radiate, in the double splendor of two suns.
You harbor, here, the Sun of Justice,
The Father's likeness naked in the Jordan;
And, there, you see the sun that rules alone,
The Father's heir that shineth in the palace . . .[63]
I view a double assembly and double joy of the Romans;
The bath of Christ and the emperor's shining trophies.
Christ has bathed for us in the bath of waters,
The man has rinsed himself for us in the bath of sweat,
The former grinds the heads of dragons in the water,
The latter bends heads of Barbarians to the ground . . .
The former is made manifest by the Spirit as a dove,
The latter is announced by victory's white dove.
The former is heralded by the Father's voice as son,
The latter, Persian-killer, is heralded by his deeds.
I hear, it seems, a second time a voice from heaven,
Crying again to peoples "This is my basileus,
This is in whom I am well pleased, and him obey."
Both purify the royal city
By baths of rebirth and of new birth . . .[64]

---

62. An evaluation of these texts has been promised by Mr. A. Kerscher, a pupil of Professor
F. Dölger (cf. *Gnomon* 14 [1938], 206), but the war may have made publication impossible.

63. Prodromus, No. XVIII, ed. Mai, op. cit., 413. The image of the "two suns" is reminiscent of Dante, *Purg.*, XVI, 106ff.:

> Soleva Roma, che il buon mondo feo,
> > Dei Soli aver, che l'una e l'altra strada
> Facean vedere, e del mondo e di Deo.

[In 1951 Kantorowicz was to publish an article on "Dante's 'Two Suns,'" wherein he includes Prodromus.]

The antithesis, *Sol Jusititiae—Sol invictus* goes back to Constantinian times; for the problem,
Franz J. Dölger, *Sol Salutis* (Münster, 1925).

64. Prodromus, No. XVI, Mai 412. The antithetical composition is found in a very similar
way, though applied to Christ and Frederick II, in a poem of ca. 1229 by Marquard of Ried,
probably a crusader cleric of Passau:

> Jerusalem gaude nomen Domini venerare
> Magnifica laude: vis ut dicam tibi quare?
> Rex quia magnificus Jesus olim, nunc Fridericus,
> Promptus uterque pati, sunt in te magnificati.

You have, my emperors, baptized me, your slave New Rome,
With all the seas of the good . . .
You have baptized me with gladness . . .[65]

It is apparent that the emperor, the *Helios basileus*, becomes the double and antitype of Christ whom Eastern art traditionally represents with the open book, saying: "I am the light of the world."[66] The emperor becomes [δεύτερος θεός] the "second God" that is the second member of the Trinity.[67] He is "the king formed after Christ" [ὁ πρὸς ἐκεῖνον τυπούμενος βασιλεὺς] he acts [χριστομιμήτως] and is quite generally spoken the "actor of Christ" [Χριστοῦ . . . μιμητήν],[68] while on the other hand "the Saviour in the Jordan has shown himself as Basileus."[69] Over and over we find these ideas repeated in poems and orations, and there is no need of adding more examples to illustrate the part played by the "imperial actor" on the Feast of Lights as on other occasions as well.

What matters here is the fact that in connection with the general preeminence of John the Baptist and the Epiphany in all Eastern rites[70]

---

Obtulit ille prior semet pro posteriore
Et pro posterior sua seque prioris honore,
Hic Deus, ille Dei pius ac prudens imitator . . .
(MGH Scriptores IX, 625)
The images in the poem of Prodromus are obviously traditional; e.g. the "Bath in the Jordan" has been rehashed by Holobolus (Nos. XVI and XX), Boissonade, op. cit., 177, and Treu, op. cit., 546, line 4.

65. Prodromus, No. XVII, Mai, 412.

66. See, for these representation, André Grabar, *L'empereur dans l'art byzantin* (Paris, 1936), 102ff. Epiphany was the Feast of Light, and all the prayers of the day refer to Christ as the φῶς τό ἐκ τοῦ φωτός or use similar terms; cf. *Rituale Armenorum*, 416ff. All this made it easy to compare the emperor with Christ as "sun"; cf. *infra*, n. 67.

67. Cf. Bachmann, *Syropulos*, 26.

68. Eustathius of Thessalonica, in Regel, *Fontes*, 61, 7; Michael the Rhetor, ibid., 131, 14; John Diogenis, ibid., 305, 2; Theodorus Prodromus, in Neumann, *Griechische Geschichtsschreiber*, 61 and 67, lines 70f.

οὐ γὰρ τολμῶ σε, τὸν Χριστόν, καὶ Φοῖβον ὀνομάσαι
σὺ γὰρ ὡς χριστομίμητος χριστώνυμος ὑπάρχεις.

The examples are no end; cf. Dölger, in *Gnomon* 14 (1938), 209. The emperor as "Helios" appears also in the official documents; see e.g. Dölger, "Der Kodikellos des Christodulos in Palermo," *Archiv für Urkundenforschung* 11 (1930), 2, and 24, n. 1. See also Heisenberg, op. cit., 93ff.; Treitinger, *Zeremoniell*, 112ff., and passim; Bachmann, *Syropulos*, 22-23.

69. Eustathius, ed. Regel, *Fontes*, 25, 10.

70. To investigate the historical development of the increasing volume of the cult of John in the East would be a promising study. In Egypt, even the *Trisagion* on Epiphany was "farced" with commemorations of the Baptist; cf. Theodor Schermann, *Ägyptische Abendmahlsliturgien des ersten Jahrhunderts* (Paderborn, 1912), 222-23. The East celebrated also the feast of St. John's Conception; cf. Anton Baumstark, "Orientalisches in altspanischer Liturgie," *Oriens*

the baptismal symbolism presented itself incomparably more often as a metaphor to Byzantine than to Western mind. In word and image alike, the baptismal metaphors were favored in the Eastern stock and trade of symbolic formulae, and they were ever ready to be applied to the emperor whenever he was to be made manifest to the world. Rhetoric and imagery, both competed in expounding and depicting the scene of how the heavens opened above the emperor to release a crown held by the deity or hovering over the emperor's head to testify him as the anointed of God. Victory, triumph, marriage, feast day—by any one of the highlights in the life of the emperor the epiphany metaphor might be evoked.[71] Above all, however, it was applied to the emperor's coronation, his true "epiphany," when first he became manifest to the universe and visible to the Romans.

The idea of baptism formed, if only dimly perceptible, the background of the crowning ritual in the West. In the East, the *eidos* [essence] of Baptism and Epiphany was in the bright foreground of the coronation scene. There has never been an episcopal ordination anointing in the Eastern Church so that an assimilation of ordination and coronation on the basis of an unction common to both could never take place. The coronation always remained a "para-hierarchic" act, and even when at a very late date, the imperial unction was introduced this act, too, remained something extraordinary and unmatched by episcopal ordinations. The emperor remained the sole *christus domini* in his empire and never had to acknowledge the bishops as his peers. Although the image of David was conjured up time and again in Byzantium as a metaphor for the emperor, for a Samuel-David ideology of Western pattern there was no thrifty ground. In the East, the baptismal and epiphanean idea maintained its position while in the West this was superseded by the idea of ordination. When Michael Paleologue crowned his son Andronikos junior emperor in 1273, at a time when the rite of imperial unctions was about to be introduced in Byzantium, it still was quite natural to a *prokypsis* poet to compare the senior emperor with God the Father at the baptism of Jesus, saying: "This is my splendid and beloved son, in whom wisely I have pleasure, with whom by divine dispensation I share the power of crown and throne." The younger caesar, accordingly, appeared at this moment as Christ, as the one "who has the words of life

---

*Christianus* 32 (1935), 18ff. St. John was represented in later times with wings (cf. Kantorowicz, "Ivories and Litanies," 71–72, and liturgical encomia were offered, in addition to Christ and Mary, only to John; cf. La Piana, *Le rappresentazioni sacre*, 49.

71. This has been excellently discussed by Grabar, *L'empereur*, 112ff.

(John 6:68) like the Anointed of the Lord" (ἔχει γὰρ ῥήματα ζωῆς, ὥσπερ Χριστὸς Κυρίου).[72] The patriarch is not mentioned, here as little as in the other *prokypsis* poems and orations. But as it was his function to take the crown from the altar, kiss it, and pass it on to the senior emperor, who then placed it on the head of the caesar, the general stage-setting suggests that the service of the patriarch compared with that of the Baptist whose cooperation was indispensable in this scene.[73]

It is here necessary to emphasize once more that the Epiphany is composed of two distinctly different, though coinciding, acts: the baptism in the Jordan and the bursting open of the heaven with the descent of the Spirit. "We again see—it said in an Epiphany sermon[74]—John baptizing the Lord who taketh away the sin of the world. And also we see the Father testifying from above his Son's stupendous descent, and we see the Pneuma equal with him descending as a dove and hovering over the one who has been made manifest." We have to keep in mind this partition in two in order to visualize the scenario of the imperial epiphany such as it was staged not only on the Feast of Lights but also at the emperor's coronation.

The first Byzantine coronation to take place in a church, the coronation of Phocas in 602, was celebrated in the church of St. John the Baptist in the Hebdomon.[75] The visit to this church had been customary at previous crownings as well. Leo I, in 457, after having been crowned in the military camp, rode on a white horse into the city and made his first halt at St. John's. At the entrance he took off his crown and handed it to the *praepositus*. He then walked to the altar, had the crown returned to him, deposed it on the altar-table, prayed, took the crown up again, handed it back to the same official, and put it on his head when leaving St. John's to continue his circuit on horseback.[76]

---

72. Holobolus, No. V, Boissonade, *Anecdota*, V, 164–65; Heisenberg, 117. See also Bachmann, *Syropulos*, 11.

73. For the cooperation of the patriarch, see *De cerim.*, 1, c. 43, 220, 15ff., and 224, 20ff.; slightly different (the patriarch says only a prayer), ibid., 1, 94, 432, 5ff., cf. *infra*, n. 90. The presentation of the ceremony by Charanis, in *Byzantion* 15 (1941), 55 (including n. 36) evokes a quite wrong impression because he combines the coronation of the emperor and that of the co-opted caesar as though it were one act: the emperor being crowned by the patriarch passes the crown on the head of the caesar. This is, to say the least, misleading.

74. PG 64, cols. 43ff., a spurious sermon ascribed to John Chrysostome.

75. See the numerous sources adduced by Treitinger, *Zeremoniell*, 13, n. 16.

76. *De cerim.*, 1, c. 91, 410ff., esp. 413, 10ff. The study of Charanis, "The Imperial Crown Modiolus and Its Constitutional Significance," *Byzantion* 12 (1937), 189ff., has not convinced me regarding the "constitutional significance."

There should probably not be attached too great weight to the choice of the church. It may be that local conditions suggested the visits to, and Phocas's coronation in, the church of St. John the Baptist.[77] The coronations were staged, for some time, in the palace church dedicated to St. Stephen, and after 641 the church of Holy Wisdom became the favored place for carrying through the imperial crownings.[78] From the *Book of Ceremonies* there may be gathered innumerable details related to the crowning punctilio; but the first description of the prayers said on that occasion is found in the *Euchologion* which may fall in the twelfth century.[79] The central act of the ceremony took place on the ambo where the imperial chlamys and crown had been deposed beforehand. While the emperor stood on the ambo, his head inclined, the patriarch spoke a benediction over the chlamys. The emperor donned the mantle, and the patriarch said a blessing over the crown. He then took the crown from the table and holding it in his two hands he crowned the emperor, saying: "In the name of the Father and of the Son and of the Holy Ghost." Thereupon the people acclaimed, chanting thrice the two angelic praises "Holy, Holy, Holy" and "Glory to God in the highest and peace on earth."[80]

What we are interested in is the crowning formula proper which was spoken by the patriarch, for it is the trinitarian baptismal formula. Its application to the imperial crownings is older than the text of the Euchologion. It can be traced back at least to the coronations of the eighth century when the senior emperor in crowning his junior colleague likewise said: "In the name of the Father and of the Son and of the Holy

---

77. See for the topography Jean Paul Richter, *Quellen der byzantinischen Kunstgeschichte* (Vienna, 1897), 146, No. 602.

78. Treitinger, 13–14.

79. Cf. [F. E.] Brightman, "Byzantine Imperial Coronations," *Journal of Theological Studies* 2 (1901), 380–81, who translates passages from the *Euchologion sive Rituale Graecorum*, ed. Jacques Goar (Paris, 1730), 726–27, a book at present inaccessible to me.

80. The prayer over the chlamys resembles the customary supplications for the emperor (cf., e.g., Brightman, *Liturgies Eastern and Western*, 1, 333, 4–25), though with some elaborations. The parallel between the angelic acclamations before God and that of the people before the emperor has been stressed already by Louis Bréhier and Pierre Batiffol, *Les survivances du culte imperial romain* (Paris, 1920), 46; Treitinger, *Zeremoniell*, 79, n. 168. Narsai, *Homily XXI*, ed. R. Hugh Connolly, *The Liturgical Homilies of Narsai* (Cambridge, 1909), 57, mentions that the priest imitates the spiritual beings, when "holily he teaches the people to cry 'Holy.' The utterance of sanctification of the heavenly beings he recites to men, that they may be crying 'Holy, Holy, Holy, Lord.'" The angelic acclamation is adduced in connection with the Baptism in the Jordan by Michael the Rhetor, in Regel, *Fontes*, 131, 17: . . .οἷον ἐξ Ἰορδάνου τὸν βαπτισθέντα Χριστὸν ἀναβαίνειν ἡ προφητεία φησὶν ἀγγελικαῖς δυνάμεσιν εὐφημούμενον.

Ghost." Probably the formula has served already at the coronation of Marcian in 450 A.D.[81]

In the thirteenth century the unction was added to the coronation rite of Byzantium. The patriarch then anointed the emperor's head in form of a cross before placing the crown on his head.[82] This may, but need not, depend on the rite of baptism. The underlying baptismal idea, however, becomes quite evident if we turn to the sacring of the Russian Czars the ceremonial of which was derived from the rite of Byzantium. In Moscow the patriarch or acting metropolitan anointed the emperor's forehead, his eyes, nostrils, mouth, ears, breast, and hands, saying: "Seal of the gift of the Holy Ghost." In this case there can be no doubt about the model, since the rubrics as well as the benediction agree verbatim with those of the oil anointing of the orthodox baptism.[83]

The crowning of the emperor, or later his unction, at the hands of the patriarch refers only to the first act of the imperial "epiphany." The mis en scène of the second act, the manifestation of the emperor by the powers of heaven, was of course bound to be symbolical and allusive rather than realistic. However, the Byzantines, inventive in theatrical matters, contrived a means of giving a somewhat realistic shape even to things transcendental. For it seems almost certain that the *prokypsis*, which at the coronations was staged not in the open but in Santa Sophia itself, symbolized the "manifestation" of the new emperor through the powers above. The golden veils of the *prokypsis* were still closed when the chanters invited the new Helios to rise, singing "Rise, rise, rise, Emperors of the Romans" (ἀνάτειλον ὁ δεῖνα καὶ ὁ δεῖνα αὐγοῦσται τῶν Ῥωμαίων), and the people likewise shouted "rise, rise, rise, may there rise the divine majesty." Finally the curtains opened right and left. The majesties appeared and received the acclamations. Then the veils closed again and deprived the people of the sight of the emperors.[84] If one

---

81. *De cerim.*, 1, c. 43, p. 225, 2. Cf. *supra*, n. 25, for the corresponding formula in the Milanese rite.

82. John Cantacuzenus, *Historiae*, 1, c. 41, ed. L. Schopen (Bonn, 1828–32), 1, 198; Codinus, c. 17, p. 90.

83. *Euchologion der orthodox-katholischen Kirche*, translated by Micahel Rajewski (Vienna, 1861–62), 3, 21; cf. 2, 36, for the baptismal unction. For the "Seal" formula cf. Franz J. Dölger, *Sphragus. Eine altchristliche Taufbezeichnung in ihren Beziehungen zur profanen und religösen Kultur des Altertums* (Paderborn, 1911), esp. pp. 184ff.

84. Heisenberg, "Aus der Geschichte und Literatur der Palaiologenzeit," 89ff., has discussed the coronation *prokypsis* very thoroughly and has reprinted also the three related texts, namely Cantacuzenus, 3, c. 95, vol. 2, 587; Codinus, c. 17, 96–97; and an anonymous fragment first published by Ch. Loparev, in *Festschrift zu Ehren von D. T. Kobeko* (St. Petersburg, 1913), 1–13 (inaccessible to me). The acclamation ἀνάτειλον, ἀνάτειλον, alluding to the rising of the

bears in mind the liturgical functions of the καταπέτασμα, the curtains, in all Eastern liturgies, there can be little, if any, doubt that the opening and closing of the veils of the *prokypsis* paralleled the exposing and concealing of the holy of holies by means of veils at the divine service.[85] The scene on the *prokypsis*, therefore, may have symbolized the "opening of heaven" and the "making manifest" the emperors crowned by God. The blessing on earth at the hands of the patriarch would have been incomplete without the second act in which the God testifies the new emperor.

However this may be, the interpretation of the transcendental part of the imperial epiphany fell mainly to the commentaries of the acclamations, poems, addresses, and images. It was, as usual, the function of words and arts to "translate" the events visible on earth into the language of the invisible and to guide the minds of the spectators in such a way that they visualized, almost unthinkingly, the bursting open of heaven and the Divine Hand reaching down to crown the emperor at the moment when the patriarch placed the material crown on the emperor's head. Therefore, the people could shout instantly the other acclamation:[86]

God has had mercy on his people.
This the great day of the Lord.
This is the day of the life of the Romans . . .
The Master and Lord of all things, who crowned you with his own hand, multiplies your years . . .

The people wanted to see, and already viewed, nothing but an "emperor crowned by God" or "crowned by Christ." The service rendered by the patriarch—important though it was, as it effected the "opening of heaven"—could never divert from the light breaking down from above. The imperial epiphany was the "great day of the Lord" because the Lord in making his emperor visible became visible himself. But there

---

"Helios" emperor (cf. Dölger, in *Gnomon*, 14, 1938, 209), is found in very much earlier times (cf. *De cerim.*, 1, c. 43, 216; 1, c. 69, 316) and might as well suggest an earlier date of the *prokypsis* than disclosed by the sources; cf. Heisenberg, 111, and also the *prokypsis* poem of Nicholas Eirenikos, verse 104, ibid., 104.

85. Carl Schneider, "Studien zum Ursprung liturgischer Einzelheiten östlicher Liturgien, I," *Kyrios* 1 (1936), 57–73.

86. Brightman, in *Journal of Theological Studies* 2 (1902), 381.

**FIGURE 3.1**   Gold Nomisma Histamenon (gold coin, reverse) of the Byzantine emperor John I Tzimiskes, Constantinople, 969–976. American Numismatic Society, 1977.158.1167.

was no question of making the patriarch visible, not at least in this connection.[87]

Even more telling are the images. In imagery the claim became true that "the crown was fitted on the emperor, not by man or through man, but from above."[88] Unless Christ himself is shown as the coronator crowning the emperor directly, there would be found angels or (indeed quite often) St. Mary performing the act of crowning. Most instructive in this respect is a coin of John Tzimisces (crowned in 969) demonstrating clearly the two coinciding actions of the imperial epiphany: the crowning proper and the manifestation from above (see figure 3.1).

The Theotokos, standing at the side of the emperor, puts the diadem on his head while at the same time the Divine Hand is released from heaven to put its blessing fingers on the diadem.[89] Most convincingly the expert on Byzantine imperial art says about this coin: "Il suffit de se rappeler certaines scènes du Baptême du Christ (où la Main Divine apparaît parfois dans un segment du ciel), pour apprécier à sa juste

---

87. The words of the Epiphany liturgy τὰ ἄνω τοῖς κάτω συνεορτάζει καὶ τὰ κάτω τοῖς ἄνω συνομιλεῖ (cf. Petrus Hendrix, "Der Mysteriencharakter der byzantinischen Liturgie," *Byzantinische Zeitschrift* 30, 338, n. 1) illustrate also the coronation.

88. A quotation from Michael Psellus, cited by Charanis, "Coronation," in *Byzantion* 15 (1941), 61, n. 58, and others. However, I cannot follow Mr. Charanis in his conclusions; see below, n. 91.

89. Grabar, *L'empereur*, pl. XXVIII, 6.

valeur la signification de ce geste: de même que saint Jean-Baptiste au-
près du Christ, la Vierge elle-même agit ici chargée d'une mission par
Dieu."[90] Mary here has taken over the part of John the Baptist which on
the liturgical stage in Santa Sophia was presented by the patriarch, the
"baptist" to the emperor.

# III

The patriarch of Constantinople in crowning the Byzantine emperor
acted on behalf of the Church. This, I believe, can no longer be the subject of scholarly dissension, and the theory according to which he acted
as the "first Roman citizen" on behalf of the state and of the constitutional electors can be safely dismissed. The part played by the patriarch
can be clearly defined once we have recognized the characters of the
liturgical play performed on the Byzantine coronation stage. The idea
of an ordination after the Roman pattern must be completely eliminated. To the earliest Roman customs, the proclamation of the annual
general as the human counterpart of *Iuppiter Imperator*, the Byzantine
coronation was more closely related than to a Jewish-Christian ordination after the model of "Moyses anointing Aaron" or "Samuel anointing David." In fact, the Byzantine coronation was the direct descendant
of the Hellenistic theophanies, as might have been expected by anyone
familiar with the cultural development of the Later Roman Empire. It
was not Iuppiter Ammon's voice that was heard above the Jordan, but
through the Epiphany of the Lord the essence of Hellenistic theophanies was passed on to the Christian era. The West has discarded this
idea and made the adoration of the three Magi kings the main content
of the feast of the Epiphany. The East clung to the earlier contents,
and after the pattern of the Lord's Epiphany, of his humble and glorious manifestation, such as it was (and still is) celebrated in the East
on Twelfth Night, the Byzantine coronation was consummated. It was
Christianized, but essentially Hellenistic, theophany that was staged at
Byzantium.

All this clarifies the action of the patriarch at the coronation. Whatever the role played by him may have been like on other occasions,[91]

---

90. Grabar, 117.

91. The patriarch as every priest represented at a given moment Christ the Highpriest;
cf. the discussion of Jungmann (*supra*, n. 15), pp. 211ff. and passim. At other times, however,
the celebrant compared with an angelic being, or with an apostle, or with John the Baptist
(see next note), and all these various relations could and would intermingle at any moment

when crowning the emperor he presented, above all, the character of
John the Baptist while the emperor represented Christ. There is more
than one evidence available to prove both that John was credited with
having acted as a priest as he baptized the Lord,[92] and vice versa that
the Lord while standing in the waters of Jordan, was anointed *Basileus*
by the descent of the Holy Ghost.[93] The cooperation of the patriarch
at the imperial epiphany was by no means negligible; it was absolutely
essential. It was essential to the same extent as John's cooperation on
the bank of the Jordan: John's obedient act of baptizing the Lord with
water effected the heaven to open, the Ghost to descend, and the voice
to testify and make visible the "beloved Son." The visibility of Christ
may not have depended on it, but is inseparable from the doing of the
Baptist.[94]

An altogether different question it is to ask whether the emperor
"needed" the coronation, whether really it was indispensable and irre-
missible in view of the image which during his reign he was supposed to

---

and thus give every action its complexity. I quite agree with Treitinger, *Zeremoniell*, 79, n. 168,
who indicates the way of how the Byzantine "hier jeden Gedanken mehrmals umschreibt und
so viel Gründe und Beziehungen für ihn aufbietet, dass der einlinige 'Kausalzusammenhang'
uner solcher Vielfalt fast zusammenbricht und eine mystische Gesamterhöhung mit vielen
Einzelbeziehungen an seine Stelle tritt." I therefore cannot accept Mr. Charanis' merciless syl-
logism when he says: "The patriarch, in crowning the emperor, represented Christ *for* Christ
alone had the power to invest an emperor with the regalia of his office," a statement he
supports by Psellos' remark (cf. *supra*, n. 87) that the emperor was crowned "not by man or
through man but from above." To my mind, Mr. Charanis drives towards overestimating the
functions of the patriarch at the coronation, though indeed he is very correct in emphasizing that the patriarchal cooperation at this ceremony was indispensable. The reason for this
"indispensable," however, should be sought in another direction.

92. Cf. Pseudo-Augustine, *Sermo* CXXXVIII, PL 39, col. 2017: "Joannes ergo implebat habi-
tum sacerdotis"; Michael the Rhetor, in Regel, *Fontes*, pp. 131–32: διεδήσω τὴν ἱερὰν κεφαλὴν
καὶ τῇ εὐλογίᾳ τῷ ἐρημικῷ κατὰ πνεῦμα καὶ ἀτρόφῳ κατ᾽ Ἰωάννην χριστομιμήτως ὑπέκλινας
ταύτην ἀρχιερεῖ. See further Theodorus Andidensis, *Commentatio liturgica*, c. 11, ed. Mai, *Patrum nova bibliotheca*, 6, 557: ὁ δέ γε ἱερεὺς ὁ τὴν ἔναρξιν τῆς θείας ἱερουργίας ποιούμενος, εἰκόνα
φέρει τοῦ προδρόμου Ἰωάννου καὶ Βαπτιστοῦ. Most interesting in this connection is a miniature of the fourteenth century, reproduced by Grabar, *L'empereur*, pl. XXIII, 2. It is a more
or less traditional "coronation" scene. The heaven is open and releases an angel putting the
crown on the head of Ivan Alexandre, Czar of the Bulgars. To his right is Christ, "Czar of czars
and czar eternal"; to his left we find the chronicler Constantine Manasses whose chronicle in
a slave [*sic*] translation is adorned by this frontispiece miniature. A later hand, however, re-
named this figure and wrote beside his head "S. Johannes Baptista" so that the Czar appears
between Christ and the Precursor and with a crown-bearing angel hovering above his head.

93. Eustathius of Thessalonica, in Regel *Fontes*, 25, 10ff.: σωτὴρ βασιλεὺς διεδείκνυτο.

94. This at least is the version found in Matth. 3:16, and Mark 1:10. According to Luke
3:21, it was the prayer of Jesus that made heaven open; cf. G. O. Williams, " The Baptism in
Luke's Gospel," *Journal of Theological Studies* 45 (1944), 31–38; see also Richard Reitzenstein,
*Die Vorgeschichte der christlichen Taufe* (Leipzig, 1929), 270.

represent. Mediaeval theology, of course, has often discussed the problem whether Jesus had needed the baptism; and the answer (at least
the orthodox answer) would always have been that he stepped in the
water of Jordan "non ad necessitatem peccati" and that the baptism
at the hands of St. John "non fuit regeneratio Christi," but that it was
indispensable in view of the economy of salvation.[95] By analogy it may
be held that the imperial *Christomimetes* likewise was "not in need" of
the patriarchal consecration in order to be emperor or to exercise imperial rights and power; the coronation added nothing to his legal com-
petences nor did it "change the man" as did the ordination. Yet, for the
economy of salvation of the empire, for the sake of the transcendental
foundation of imperial power, and the sake of his visibility as the *christos*
and human antitype of Christ, the emperor needed the coronation-
epiphany just as much as the Lord had needed the Jordan with regard
to his visibility. Hence all the Byzantine emperors, with one possible
exception,[96] had themselves crowned (or later anointed) at the hands of
the patriarch, no matter as to whether we consider this act essential or
not. To them, evidently, it was essential.

It is, to my opinion, an altogether doubtful undertaking to try to figure out whether or not the politico-liturgical ceremonies in the Middle
Ages, especially in the early Middle Ages, had a character of constitutional stringency and were *staatsrechtlich bindend* [legally binding]. The
weight of these liturgical actions is usually imponderable. Impondera-
bles, however, are often more stringent than legal clauses, and often it
may prove easier to elude the latter than to neglect the former.

The casting of the parts at Byzantine coronations makes it clear that
the Byzantine emperor never became an appointee of the Church, of his
coronator or anointer.[97] The difference between Eastern and Western
coronations stands out distinctly. In the West, the emperor was sub-
jected to a hierarchic, subordinating discipline. His anointment was
imagined into the hierarchic system as a quasi-ordination in conformity with a canonical political theory which was easily developed from
the biblical prototype of royal and other unctions, "Samuel anointing

---

95. These ideas are repeated time and again, alike in East and West; see e.g. the Epiphany
mass of the *Missale mixtum*, PL 85, col. 236, which I have quoted together with a letter of Alcuin
to Felix of Urghel, in MGH, Epistolae, 4, 270, 26, No. 166. To trace the heterodox opinions
here is not the intention.

96. Nicephorus Bryennius (1077) crowned himself but was not recognized; cf. Charanis,
"Coronation," 54, n. 31, who discusses also the case of Constantine XI.

97. This, I gather, is also the opinion of Charanis, op. cit., 59, n. 2.

David." Baptismal ideas and baptismal symbolism of language, it is true were still at the back of the Western coronations. But these elements were overruled by concepts of ordination and hierarchic discipline, and for any mysteriously reversed order on earth by which the pope would be demoted to a secondary place there was no possibility within the authoritarian hierarchic rationalism of the West. Unimpeachable and rigid was the validity of the Pauline motto *Quod minus est, a meliore benedicitur* ("The less is blessed by the better").

In the East, the baptismal idea was inseparably one with that of the epiphany. With regard to the coronation rite, this whole complex has never been replaced by other contents or any other model; nor had this current been diverted into the rite of ordinations which derived from other sources. To the model of baptism and epiphany, however, rules of hierarchical subordination could not apply. On the contrary the mystery of the Epiphany rested in the reversed order, in the device ὁ δεσπότης ὑπὸ τοῦ δούλου βαπτίζεται, "The lord is baptized by the serf, the king by the knight," and Eastern religiosity thrived in the ground of the mystery.

In fact, the two devices grow out of the very deepest layers of Western and Eastern religious sentiment. They do not only express a divergence of trends and a differing choice of metaphors and models. They hit almost directly at the life-nerves of Eastern and Western Christianity and disclose quite bluntly the differing centers of vitality. For it makes all the difference in the world whether the subject, as in the West, or the object as in the East should be placed in the center. There is no use in expatiating on generalities about East and West. Such have been poured forth often enough. But it affects our problem in a very direct way that the Eastern Church felt most strongly about the subject-centeredness of Western hierarchs. In a discussion of the rite of baptism, Symeon, Metropolitan of Thessalonica, objects vehemently to the Western baptismal formula by which the baptizing hierarch becomes the central, primarily visible figure at the baptismal scene. "Ego te baptizo in nomine Patris et Filii et Spiritus sancti" says the Western hierarchic, a formula overemphasizing the subject and obscuring the object. The formula, says the Metropolitan, does not emphasize that the one to be illuminated is baptized of his own free will. *Ego te baptizo* may imply, and sounds like, a forceful action of the hierarch, an action along the lines of power (δύναμις) rather than of grace and perhaps even against the will of the object; the formula, at any rate, brings the baptist, originally a model of humbleness, unduly and arrogantly to the fore, whereas in truth the importance is not with the baptist but with the baptized. In contradistinction to this attitude, the Eastern rite avoids even the semblance of force and applies an impersonal, object-centered formula, saying "Baptized is the servant of God NN [viz. "Nomen nescio," a filler for the name of someone unknown] in the name of the Father, and of the Son and of the Holy Ghost" (Βαπτίζεται ὁ δοῦλος τοῦ Θεοῦ. . .εἰς τό ὄνομα τοῦ Πατρός καί τοῦ Υἱοῦ καί τοῦ Ἁγίου Πνεύματος). This formula, explains the metropolitan, includes the hierarch without mentioning him, and it includes many another thing as well: it establishes an unbroken and direct relationship between the baptized and the triune deity, a relationship not overshadowed or interfered with by the acting hierarch; and it opens, as it were, the space of the cosmos. While the Roman formula, in stressing the activity of the hierarch remains "linear," the Eastern formula makes you visualize, or guess at, the cooperation of all: of the hierarch, the triune God, and the whole cosmos.[98]

The "semantics" of the metropolitan, which here have been freely rendered, are absolutely sound and irreproachable. Whoever knows something about poetry, knows the secret of activating the object so as to achieve the fullness of an image whereas the super-activity of the subject smothers the delicacy of relations.[99] Mysteries, by their very nature, are object-centered. Western subject-centerdness may lead to personal mysticism, but it necessarily encroaches upon the nature of the impersonal mysteries. This attitude was offensive to Eastern sentiment. The Eastern Church has always preserved its character of Mystery Cult,[100] a feature which did not, or only spasmodically, conform with Roman religious sentiment or Western mysticism. Of the Eastern mysteries, John the Baptist, was so to speak, the exponent and guardian; and *Petrus princeps* ruled the Church in the West.

There has survived a homily on the Baptism of Christ by Gregory the Thaumaturge, Patriarch of Antioch (570–593). It is one of the early dramatized Epiphany sermons of which mention has been made previously.[101] It here may be paraphrased briefly.

The homily begins with a praise of the humility of the Lord. The King of Heavens, so we are told, has renounced the company of angelic

---

98. Cf. the article of Hendrix, quoted above, n. 87.

99. [The manuscript contains some confusion in footnote assignments, resulting in two absences.]

100. [Missing footnote.]

101. PG 10, cols. 1178ff.; see also the old Latin translation published by Mai, *Nova patrum bibliotheca*, 2, 553ff., and the discussion of La Piana, *Le rappresentazioni sacre*, 72ff.

hosts and incorporeal precursors when making his Adventus on the banks of the Jordan: in simple military, not royal, attire, he has come to see his knight. John is frightened. "I ought to be baptized by thee, and comest thou to me? What doest thou, o Lord? Why doest thou reverse the order of things? Why doest thou demand that which thou needst not? The lamp is obscured by the sun, not the sun illuminated by the wick? The clay is formed by the potter, but not the potter molded by the clay. Thou comest to me, so great a one to one so small, the king to the forerunner, the lord to the serf? What blessing shall I speak over thee? It is up to thee to baptize the baptist. Reach out thy hand and crown my head with thy hands that I may fore-run thy kingdom and as a precursor cry to the sinners: 'Behold the lamb of God that taketh away the sins of the world.'"

To this the Lord answered: "Grant, o baptist, silence to the great moment of my dispensation. The mystery that today shall be accomplished in Jordan's waters is my secret and a mystery to those that are with me. A mystery it is which the diluvial floods of heaven have predepicted in these Jordan waters and it concerns the rebirth of man. Give to me the baptism as the Virgin gave me milk. Baptize me who in future shall baptize the faithful with water and with the Spirit and with fire."

Thereupon St. John obeys. With trembling hands he baptizes the Lord. And as so he did, a group of Jews, who had witnessed what had come to pass in the river, began to discuss what their eyes were seeing; and as though they were resuming the functions of the choir in an antique tragedy they talked to one another saying "Did we not always believe that John was more powerful and better than Jesus? Have we not been right in crediting John to be the more excellent? Does not this baptism prove the baptist as the greater? For is not he that baptizes, the better; and the baptized the least?"

Such was the buzzing talk among those blinded to view the mystery of dispensation, when out of a sudden the Father opened the gates of heaven, released the Holy Ghost as a dove, and thundered from above while pointing with his finger to Jesus: "*This* is my beloved son! This one, not that! Jesus, not John! The one baptized, not the baptist."[102]

---

102. Especially in the orbit of the Mandaean doctrines which placed St. John above Christ, it was necessary to stress the right proportions; see, e.g., the homily of the Armenian catholicos of the ninth century, Zachariah, who says: "And the Holy Spirit for this cause came down in the form of a dove, that none of the foolish might suppose that the voice from heaven referred to John." Conybeare and Maclean, *Rituale Armenorum*, 183.

Was it "Jewish perfidy" and "Hebrew superstition," branded by Rome until the present day,[103] that made the Jews incapable to understand the truth of what came to pass in the Jordan? If we consider the words which they spoke to each other, it appears to have been their fault and main error, eventually corrected by the voice from heaven, to have studied all too well St. Paul and his Epistle directed to the Hebrews (Hebr. 7:7). But their rational interpretation and false application of the Pauline words, their endeavor to exploit these words for their own purposes, for their own internal struggles and political ambitions, had made them blind to recognize the genuine mystery when they witnessed it, that "the better is blessed by the less."

---

103. The formula of invitation for abrogating Judaism at the baptism, as found in the *Rituale Romanum*, is "horresce Iudaicam perfidiam, respue Hebraicam superstitionem." That *perfidia* had originally the connotation, not of "perfidy" as at present, but of "infidelity" has been proved by Erik Peterson, "Perfidia Iudaica," *Ephemerides Liturgicae* 50 (1936), 296–311.

# CHAPTER 4

# Charles the Bald and the *Natales* of the King

This is a problematic piece, and Kantorowicz seems to have realized that himself because he put it aside well before it was finished. Of the articles recovered here it was the earliest, dating from the spring or summer of 1944. (The author "recently" read a work of 1943 [n. 1], and the latest item cited [n. 12] is an article that appeared in the first number of *Speculum* for 1944.) The English is often wobbly: "was in the rising," "resented to giving up," "authentical," "repercussed." The author also misuses English tenses. But this did not inhibit deft phrase-making: "The myth has wandered from the Empire . . . to the City, from the *orbis* to the *urbs*"; "it will be difficult to maintain that Rome actively re-Romanized France; the main current was inverted, and France above all re-Romanized Rome." Kantorowicz terms Archbishop Hincmar of Reims Charles the Bald's "Richelieu." It seems clear that he undertook this piece shortly after his engagement as an instructor in a US Army program was terminated (March 1943) and his prospects for future employment were uncertain. Whereas two subsequent pieces, "Epiphany and Coronation" and "Synthronos," were meant for the Berkeley Colloquium Orientologicum (respectively given in October 1944 and December 1945) this one was not fashioned for that purpose, obviously because its subject matter was not "Oriental," and Kantorowicz may have been distracted from the Carolingians for that reason.

The work with the title "Charles the Bald and the *Natales* of the King" is a torso. (The manuscript from the Kantorowicz papers drawn on here appears to be the original.) It consists of a highly stimulating essay, presumably designed to lead into the main subject, but toward the end the footnotes are not supplied. An extensive inventory of documents follows, and then the work stops. The opening essay, which neither announces the subject in the title nor begins to broach it until its last paragraph, is a gem. Rather than treating Charles the Bald, it is nothing less than an original estimation of the nature of the Carolingian Renaissance. It begins with a startling paradox: the "brutal fact that life dies from life." To understand the law of the "killing revival" is to understand "the essence of history." Applied, then, to the nature of the Carolingian Renaissance, the truth that had never been recognized was that developments associated with Charlemagne "abolished to a considerable extent other antique substances which then were still alive."

Had Kantorowicz published this piece exclusive of the last paragraph he would have contributed a memorable small classic: "A New Approach to the Nature of the Carolingian Renaissance." But from the author's point of view what he had written was meant to introduce the late-Carolingian ruler Charles the Bald. Thus he broaches effectively a new proposition in the last paragraph of the present manuscript: Charles "established a new center of royal and dynastical devotion, or rather a great number of such centers which dotted his empire. And the monastery being a world by itself lent itself to forms of a personal attachment to the king and the royal house far greater than the cathedral." Then Kantorowicz introduces summaries of excerpts from thirty-three charters, which offer a substantial hint of what his main purpose was to be. But the purpose is not developed, and the word "natales" located in the title never appears before the work abruptly ends.

One can easily see where the truncated article was heading from the register of documents. Kantorowicz evidently was planning to show how first Charles the Bald and then some of his successors followed a policy of binding monasteries throughout his realm to himself by ordering liturgical celebrations of anniversaries in return for grants of land or revenues. The celebrations were familial. Prayers were to be said on the king's birthday and that of other members of his family, as well as death dates of his predecessors and his own death date after it transpired. By these means Late-Carolingian monasteries became intimately tied to the person of the king and inevitably represented his interests. Charles the Bald nurtured a system of alliances that hitherto had been unprecedented.

Although the thesis concerning a governmental strategy of Charles the Bald was original, Kantorowicz put the piece aside after completing the heroic task of identifying and summarizing the contents of thirty-three documents lodged in unwieldy folio-size volumes. The question inevitably arises as to whether this article should be published, but two reasons argue in favor. First, Kantorowicz liked it well enough for years after to plan on returning to it: in 1963 Ralph Giesey reported that it was meant to be finished and included in a volume called *Studies Eastern and Western in the History of Late Classical and Medieval Ideas*.[1] Second, what we have by itself is in no way inferior.

## 1. Revival and Survival of Antiquity

There is the well-known charge against the humanists of the Italian Renaissance indicting them to have murdered Latin as a living language when they started to revive the classical Latinity. Correct or not, the oxymoron of a "killing revival" remains true because it contains a general truth. There is not a page in the ledger of History which does not reveal the brutal fact that life dies from life. Any single one of the manifestations of life—creation, revival, progress, stagnation, or chaos—has its "murderous" potentialities the simultaneity and inextricable interplay of which are the essence of History. There is no reason for restricting the concept of a "killing revival" to the Italian Renaissance. It is applicable to many another movement as well, and here it shall be applied to the epoch which, for about two generations, we are used to call the "Carolingian Renaissance." Whatever the antique forms may have been which that artistic, intellectual, religious, and political movement wished to revive, or actually had revived, there no longer can be the slightest doubt that this "renaissance" has abolished to a considerable extent other antique substances which then were still alive. Antiquity and Antiquity were not always the same thing, and in the Carolingian period neither the Antiquity proposed revived nor the one still alive were all-embracing or synonymous with that of the Classical Age.

The objectives of the Carolingian revival of Antiquity have recently been studied in a most efficient and sober manner so that the limitations of the movement now are greatly clarified.[2] The revival was re-

---

1. *Dumbarton Oaks Papers* 17 (1963): 118.

2. For what follows, the excellent study of Richard Krautheimer, "The Carolingian Revival of Early Christian Architecture," *Art Bulletin* 24 (1942), 1–38, from which here I have drawn

stricted, by and large, to a small segment of Antiquity which in space was bound by the city of Rome—not to the World Empire of Roman origin—and which in time confined itself to the age following after Constantine and the "Victory of Christianity," that is the fourth and early fifth centuries. For the last five thousand years of history, every "renaissance" has been backed by the mirage of an *aurea aetas*, a daydream of innumerable facets.[3] The Golden Age of the Carolingian epoch was, if a simplifying formula may be used, the vision of a Christian, and at the same time pre-Byzantine, Rome, an imaginary and idealized Christian Rome of Constantine and Theodosius which, as it were, was stripped of its pagan past as well as of its Byzantine bondage. Both the Roman See and the Frankish King could meet on the anti-Byzantine ground, if each for different reasons. The overlordship of an iconoclastic Byzantium, which proved ineffective, became intolerable to the Frankish King. Both strove toward eliminating Byzantium from Rome and loosing the ties by which great parts of Italy were bound to the East. The device, "back to a pre-Byzantine Rome" conveniently sums up the essence of a program in which the Western spiritual and secular powers could line up. The "Donation of Constantine," the great forgery of the eighth century, and the *Libri Carolini*, Charlemagne's great settling of accounts with Byzantium, finally the re-establishment of the imperial dignity in the West, whatever its contents may have been, are the landmarks of the anti-Byzantine movement and at the same time the stepping-stones toward a new Rome-orientation; and the myth of all that focused equally in Constantine and St. Peter.

However, Rome and Italy at their low in the fourth and fifth centuries, were by no means representative of the world. Italy's often very fine Classicism of the Fourth Century clung to an ideal estranged from the rest of the world and the still living, highly emotional Antiquity which, in a Christian garb, continued to flourish without a visible break of tradition everywhere on the shores of the Mediterranean, from the Pillars

---

freely, should be consulted. Ludwig Traube's remark that in poetry the Carolingian was an *aetas Vergiliana*, which recently has been called back to memory in the delightful pages of E. K. Rand, *The Building of Eternal Rome* (Cambridge, Mass., 1943), 243ff., remains true despite the "Christian" restrictions of the Carolingian Renaissance. Krautheimer, 31, puts the things in the right place by stressing the *reinterpretatio christiana* of the classical authors which holds good also for the image of Augustus as far as this was of any importance in the Carolingian era; cf. Erik Peterson, "Kaiser Augustus im Urteil des antiken Christentums. Ein Beitrag zur Geschichte der politischen Theologie," *Hochland* 30 (1932-33), 289-99.

3. Cf. Samuel Noah Kramer, "Man's Golden Age: A Sumerian Parallel to Genesis, XI, 1," *Journal of the American Oriental Society* 63 (1943), 191-94.

of Hercules to the Delta of the Nile, from the sacred cities of Syria to the banks of the Bosphorus and to the lands skirting the Black Sea. *Divus Constantinus* was a god of the threshold and hence two-faced. He is not sufficiently described by recalling the Battle of the Milvian Bridge and the triumphal arch in Rome, nor by things Roman and Latin in general. His other face, shining forth from Byzantium, is Hellenistic; and the Near Eastern Constantine, who represents the unbroken antique continuity, has proved to be of much greater momentum than the one reflecting true, imaginary, or faked Roman reminiscences in the chaotic West. "Roman" Antiquity, in fact was dead or dying with Constantine, and the full vigor of antique life had been shifted to Near Eastern Hellenistic Christianity. This imperial Christian Antiquity, Near Eastern or Hellenistic, was alive not only in the Balkans, in Asia Minor, Syria, and Egypt, in North Africa, South Italy, and Spain, but it had equally penetrated by various channels, Lombardy, Gaul, and the British Isles. Rome herself formed no exception to the rule. Rome, with her fifteen "Orientals" among twenty-three popes in 130 years (619–771), Rome with her Greek monasteries and churches, her Greek saints and Greek diaconates, Rome with her Eastern iconostases [screens bearing icons], her Byzantine mosaics, and Alexandrian wall paintings, was at times almost as Hellenistic as she was Roman.[4]

Of the late antique elements which at the beginning and during the Carolingian period still were alive in Gaul, only a relatively small portion was truly "Roman." The probably greater part was "Imperial," that is Hellenistic, Near Eastern, or Mediterranean; it belonged, not to Rome in particular, but to the civilization of the late antique Mediterranean Empire in general. In this compound, there were substances of Roman origin, to be sure, but they were embedded in Hellenistic, or blended with Oriental elements and then appeared as Byzantine, Syrian, or Coptic. They had reached Gaul either directly or through the agencies of others, or Visigothic Spain and of what eventually became Lombard North Italy. They had been transmitted by Irish monks and Oriental clerics. They survived, which is often forgotten, with the bishops who had adopted almost the complete court ceremonial of Hellenistic and

---

4. Cf. Jules Gay, "Quelques remarques sur les papes Grecs et Syriens avant la querelle des Iconoclastes," *Mélanges Gustave Schlumberger* 1 (Paris, 1924), 40–54, and his "Notes sur la crise du monde chrétien après les conquêtes arabes," *Mélanges d'archéologie et d'histoire* 45 (1928), 1–7; H.-I. Marrou, "L'origine orientale des diaconies romaines," *Mélanges d'archéologie et d'histoire* 57 (1940), 95–142; Myrtilla Avery, "The Alexandrian Style at Santa Maria Antiqua," *Art Bulletin* 7 (1925), 131–49.

Roman ruler cults. Nor should we forget that the Jewish-Oriental Antiquity gained momentum in Gaul when the Franks began to consider
themselves the new "chosen people," to favor the Old Testament, and to
revive, along with the tribal-universal ideology of Israel's *regnum Davidi-
cum*, the rite of royal, and probably also sacramental, anointments. For
a long time, these Near Eastern substances have determined the designs
of church buildings, the illuminations of manuscripts, the decorations
of works of applied art, and the liturgical functions in the churches of
Gaul, Spain, and Milan. These late antique forms dwelled and throve
in the climate of the Mediterranean World Empire which had given
birth to Christianity. Rome herself, in this respect, was comparatively
unimportant.

Hence, when talking about a "Carolingian Renaissance" we should
immediately recall the fact that there was also a vigorous "Carolingian
Late Antique." Revival and currents—the one Near Eastern and the
other "Roman," or one imperial and the other Urban—it has been said
very correctly that "one terminated in, the other is introduced during,
the Carolingian period."[5] This has generally not been recognized. We
are inclined to forget how deeply the Carolingian era still was steeped
into late antique customs and problems or how often "Rome Renaissance" clashed with, or even excluded, the still living "Late Antiquity."
The christological struggles had been the symptom of the religious fe-
ver shaking the late antique world. We should not forget, however, that
one of the very last christological heterodoxies, the Adoptionism, was
vigorous more in Spain when it was broken by Charlemagne. We should
remember that the Gallican rite, which in form, sentiment, and splendor betrays the Hellenistic and Near Eastern influx,[6] was abolished in
the Carolingian period and was replaced, in theory and largely in practice, by the rite of the city of Rome. Or else, we may recall that the late
antique coinage of Justinian—displaying a winged Victory on the
victorious cross-staff with the legend *Victoria* (fig. 4.1)—which until the
eighth century had served as a model to the coins of the continental
Germanic states and even to those of Pope Hadrian I (771–785) has
been discarded by the Carolingians and replaced by Charlemagne's

---

5. Krautheimer, op. cit., 29.
6. To what extent this is true, now may be gathered conveniently from the study of Johannes Quasten, "Oriental Influence in the Gallican Liturgy," *Traditio* 1 (1943), 55–78; see
also Anton Baumstark, "Orientalisches in der altspanischen Liturgie," *Oriens Christianus* 32
(1935), 3–37.

**FIGURE 4.1**   Gold tremissis (coin, reverse) of Justinian I, Constantinople, 527–565 CE. American Numismatic Society, 1977.158.1033.

*denarius* with the legend *Christiana religio* surrounding the *templum Romae* which was topped by a cross.[7]

In short, the still living late Antiquity, Hellenistic and Near Eastern, which Justinian once more had called into consciousness and had made "universal," definitely lost ground in the Carolingian period. It lost, which means more, its myth and therewith its attraction. Western myth was then shifting to the city of Rome, to a Rome of imaginary Christian Caesars and of a very substantial St. Peter. This change in fact signifies the transition from "Carolingian Late Antiquity" to "Carolingian Renaissance." The myth has wandered from the Empire, whose one half was Saracene-occupied, to the City, from the *orbis* to the *urbs*. And to the *urbs* the myth clung during the Middle Ages. Ottonians and

---

7. J. de Morgan, "Évolutions et révolutions numismatiques," *Mélanges offerts à M. Gustave Schlumberger* (Paris, 1924), 285–95 (pl. IX, 14–24, facing p. 288); Camillo Serafini, *Le monete e le bolle plumbee pontifice del medagliere vaticano* (Milan, 1910), I, 4–5, pl. I, 3–4; the Lombard duchies in South Italy preserved that type even longer; cf. [space left blank].

Hohenstaufen, Gregories and Innocents, Arnalds and Rienzos: their renaissances and their *aureae aetates* were inseparable from Aurea Roma.

The Carolingian centuries thus represent the period in which "Imperial" survival and "Urban" revival had to come to an arrangement. The forms of this arrangement are too manyfold [*sic*] as to be easily summed up on a common denominator. Sometimes the Carolingians acted quite consciously when breaking with a Justinianean or Hellenistic tradition. In other cases, the old "Imperial" tradition petered out when a new stress was laid upon those survivals which appeared as genuine "Roman" or complied with the new vision of Rome. Even the word "Roman" often seems to have changed its meaning; it has become narrower, more urban, more city-bound, and the Frankish liturgy in its prayers readily changed *Romanus* into *Christianus* whenever a universal connotation was desired.[8] On some occasions the elements of late antique survival were, so to speak, laid dry because the main stress had been deviated. Finally, the two currents of survival and revival would sometimes merge to form something new.

It would be an idle effort to seek for system and consistency in the attitude of the Carolingian rulers toward those two currents. It is *we*, not they, that have distinguished between "Renaissance" and "Late Antiquity." Charlemagne was certainly anti-Byzantine in his feelings. This, however, did not prevent him from ordering transposed the Frankish antiphonies of Epiphany into Byzantine music after having listened, with enchantment, to some Greek clerics as they performed the service on that day; and yet he was keen to introduce the Roman chant into the Frankish cathedrals.[9] Charlemagne was certainly pro-Roman, and from Pope Hadrian I he had demanded a Gregorian Sacramentary which was to become the *Liber authenticus*, the authentical service book for the whole Frankish Empire. This, however, again did not prevent him from ordering Alcuin to make certain additions to the Roman sacramentary, and among these additions we find all the Gallic-Frankish "political prayers," the masses and benedictions which referred to the king and the Frankish State. That is to say he had all the elements added which were related to the "liturgical ruler worship," as for convenience we

---

8. See in general Gerd Tellenbach, "Römischer und christlicher Reichsgedanke in der Liturgie des frühen Mittelalters," *Sitzungsberichte der Heidelberger Akademie, Jahrgang 1934/35,* 1. Abhandlung; in the *Laudes* the form *Romanus* has a definitely urban constitution. Cf. E. H. Kantorowicz, *Laudes Regiae* [no publication date offered; the book appeared in 1946].

9. Monachus Sangallensis, MGH Scriptores, II, 7, ed. P. Jaffé, *Bibliotheca rerum Germanicaum*; Suitbert Bäumer, *Geschichte des Breviers* (Freiburg, 1895), 233, with note 2.

may call the Christian equivalent of the Hellenistic and Roman ruler cults.[10] Charlemagne, it is true, had thrown in his lot with Rome. But this did not make him a "jingo" in the Roman sense, nor did he intend to bind his empire to Rome, to make himself the horse and Rome the rider. He wished to bind Rome to his Frankish Empire, to his *Imperium christianum*. This is true also with regard to the imperial diadem which Charlemagne did not consider "Rome-bound" but immediately tried to bind to Aachen where later he crowned his son Louis emperor and Louis Lothar.[11]

In Aachen, in the *bibliotheca cubiculi*, Charlemagne kept the standard sacramentary of the empire as well as the authoritative copy of the *Regula Sancti Benedicti* which was to become the norm for the Frankish monasteries. In Aachen, too, he built a palace which he called the "Lateran," a replica, as it were, of the Constantinian palace in Rome which served as the papal residence while the Lateran Basilica figured as the "Mother of all churches."[12] In other words, Aachen, and not Rome, was to be the new center of the Carolingian Empire. Rome was to be transferred to Aachen, or Aachen was to become another Rome aside of, or even eclipsing, Ancient Rome on the Tiber as well as New Rome on the Bosphorus. This, we may gather, was the true meaning of Charlemagne's "Renaissance," of his favoring the Urban-Roman Christian Antiquity.

These trends of Roman revival overlapped in Aachen, or France in general, with the survivals of Late Antiquity, and quite often this overlapping produced something new. Against Charlemagne's liturgical Romanization there was also opposition, more latent under this great man himself, more and more open under his less powerful heirs.[13] Many a Frankish bishop resented to giving up radically the old Gallo-Frankish ritual customs. They thwarted, to some extent, Charlemagne's efforts to "Romanize" uniformly the old rites. They smuggled "Gallican" benedictions, prayers, and customs once more into the Frankish sacramentaries so that formerly discarded late antique survivals resurrected once more. And in the end, many of these Gallican rites and

---

10. See, for the general development, Edmund Bishop, "The Liturgical Reforms of Charlemagne," *Downside Review* 38 (1919), 1–16.

11. Cf. Eugen Rosenstock-Huessy, "Die Furt der Franken," in E. Rosenstock-Huessy and Joseph Wittig, *Das Alter der Kirche* (Berlin, 1927), II.

12. Krautheimer, op. cit., 35; see also William Hammer, "The Concept of the New or Second Rome in the Middle Ages," *Speculum* 19 (1944), 50–62, at 56, who however does not exhaust the interesting subject.

13. Bishop, op. cit.

forms became valid again and eventually penetrated even the liturgy of the city of Rome, conquering the Roman rite through the agency of the Ottonian empire.[14] Thus indeed something "new" had been created as the late antique Gallo-Frankish rivulets merged with those of the Roman current.

These late antique and generally Near Eastern elements, as far as they found their way to Rome through Gaul, have never been summed up efficiently, and to do so would probably be premature. However, it was through Gaul that Rome received innumerable Near Eastern elements of the Christian Late Antiquity. To stage on Palm Sunday the Entry of Christ in a most realistic fashion was an Oriental, Palestinian custom which Rome adopted from Gaul.[15] The old Oriental title of Hellenistic kings and Roman emperors, "Savior of the world" (*Salvator mundi*), which the Near East had transferred on Christ at an early date, was introduced into the Roman liturgy through the mediatorship of Gaul.[16] From Gaul came the doxology *qui vivit et regnat* invoking Christ, not as the mediator but as the glorified king, the throne-sharer (ΣΥΝΘΡΟΝΟΣ) and co-regent of God in Heaven.[17] The Syrian *Improperia* with the generally Oriental *Triangion* of the service on Good Friday reached Rome through Gaul.[18] The Jewish-Oriental rite of sacerdotal anointings, completely strange to Rome as late as the ninth century, came to the city from France.[19] And even the feasts of most of the apostles were taken over by the City of Apostles from Gaul where they were celebrated in the order of the Egyptian calendar.[20]

---

14. Theodor Klauser, "Die liturgischen Austauschbeziehungen zwischen der römischen und der frankisch-deutschen Kirche vom 8. bis 11. Jahrhundert," *Historisches Jahrbuch* 53 (1933), 169–89.

15. Cf. Anton Baumstark, "Orientalisches in den Texten der abendländischen Palmfeier," *Jahrbuch für Liturgiewissenschaft* 7 (1927), 148–53, and the same author's "La solemnité des palmes dans l'ancienne et la nouvelle Rome," *Irénikon* 13 (1936), 1–24; see also Adolf Franz, *Die kirchlichen Benediktionen im Mittelalter* (Freiburg, 1909), 1, 470ff., 477–78.

16. Heinrich Linssen, *ΘΕΟΣ ΣΩΤΡ. Die Entwicklung und Verbreitung einer liturgischen Formelgruppe* (diss. Bonn, 1925; Münster, 1929), esp. 33ff., 42–43; Baumstark, *Vom geschichtlichen Werden der Liturgie* (Freiburg, 1923), 82, n. 3.

17. Josef A. Jungmann, *Die Stellung Christi im liturgischen Gebet* (Münster, 1925), 184ff., cf. 103ff.

18. Anton Baumstark, "Der Orient und die Adoratio Crucis," *Jahrbuch für Liturgiewissenschaft* 2 (1922), 16; Erik Peterson "Perfidia Iudaica," *Ephemerides Liturgicae* 50 (1936), 296–311, at 310; Quasten, op. cit., 57–61.

19. Gerald Ellard, *Ordination Anointings in the Western Church* (Cambridge, Mass., 1933).

20. Theodor Klauser, *Das römische Capitulare Evangeliorum* (Münster, 1925), 131–32; A. Dold and Anton Baumstark, *Das Palimpsestkommentar im Codex Augiensis CXII* (Beuron, 1935), XIV f. For the "Egyptian" dates of the feasts, see J. W. S. Sewell, in *Legacy of Egypt*, ed. S. R. E.

It was not only the Near Eastern survivals that flooded to Rome from France. Elements of genuinely Roman character came back to Rome from the Frankish Empire. France, literally, rendered to Peter the things that were Peter's, and to Constantine the things that were Constantine's. The feast of the *Cathedra Petri*, which by the fifth century—incredible though it is—had fallen into oblivion at Peter's See, was returned to Rome in the ninth century by Carolingian France.[21] And as far as Constantine is concerned, we may remember that the great revival of the Early Christian, "Constantinian" Basilica style, which showed up in Rome and north of the Alps after 600, was started probably not on the Tiber, but in France where this type of architecture may have existed in St. Denis before 775 A.D.[22] It will be difficult to maintain that Rome actively re-Romanized France. The main current was inverted, and France above all re-Romanized Rome. It is, to say the least, greatly exaggerated to assert that a stream of strength effused from Rome and that Rome produced actively a "Renaissance" climate. The impulse came chiefly from Gaul. The Frankish Empire revived Gaul, and mainly reverberating forces met France [and] began to influence and even transform her in the sense of the "Carolingian Renaissance," a period in which the "Carolingian Late Antiquity" was still quite alive.

We thus have to face a crisscross of intersecting, overlapping, and reverberating forces of revival and survival which is difficult to disentangle. Odds and ends of the "Imperial" Late Antiquity, as far as they had not been absorbed or abolished, lingered on throughout the ninth century. Thereafter, indeed, they faded away. The new monastic movement which then began to determine religious life, and the monastic spirit which eventually was to sway over the West, had no proper use for, or affinity to, those Caesarian Christian elements which formed the bulk of the "Imperial" late antique tradition. New concepts of society, state, and church were being prepared in the pale of the monasteries where a spirit of "enthusiasm" in the Oriental sense began to develop. And yet, it was in relation with the "monastery," as contradistinguished from the "cathedral," that we find the most surprising similarities to, and perhaps vestiges of, the late antique "Imperial" ruler cult—if only

---

Glanville (Oxford, 1942), a study to which Professor Eugen Rosenstock-Huessy kindly called my attention.

21. See the fascinating discussion of Theodor Klauser, *Die Cathedra im Totenkult der heidnischen und christlichen Antike* (Münster, 1927), esp. 157ff., 173ff., 183; see also Hans Lietzmann, *Petrus und Paulus in Rom* (Berlin, 1927), 93–102.

22. Krautheimer, op. cit., 23–24.

for a short time and mainly under the influence of one Carolingian prince, King Charles the Bald.

The statesmanship of this learned grandson of Charlemagne, son of Louis the Pious and the latter's beautiful second Empress Judith, is doubtless a problematic matter. The faint reflections of former glamour and glory, which still were hovering around the government of Charles II [= Charles the Bald], are owed primarily to Hincmar, Archbishop of Reims, the ninth century Richelieu of the West Frankish kingdom.[23] If, however, we look out for the most genuine representative of the Carolingian Renaissance, we have to turn to Charles the Bald, who appears as the true continuator of Charlemagne's cultural and intellectual endeavors. Theological problems, it is true, attracted him more than anything else; but Antiquity both revived and surviving were likewise within the range of his interests, and to that he added new, mainly Byzantine components. The revival as instituted by Charlemagne did not culminate under the initiator himself. It reached its full growth a few decades later and thus fell in the reign of Charles the Bald who personally was the only one among the later Carolingians to inherit to the full his grandfather's delight in things related to knowledge, arts, and letters. The surviving Antiquity stimulated Charles the Bald because he was an "antiquarian" who took a sometimes surprising interest in usages and customs of the past of which he knew that they were superannuated and obsolete. Moreover, he was wide open to the influences emanating from Byzantium, whose general culture was rapidly recovering as the wounds of the long, iconoclast struggles began to heal. The Eastern Empire then was on the way toward its own Byzantine Renaissance. Charles the Bald thus appears as the exponent of the various antique currents meandering though the Frankish Empire, and it was at his personal instigation that seemingly scattered elements of antique ruler worship became effective again as they reappeared where least they might be expected, in the monasteries.

The ninth century experienced the flaring up of that monastic spirit which eventually led to the portentous championship of Cluny within the Western Church. In the Carolingian age, however, the monastery was as yet far from inspiring its later independence from the state. It was still embedded in the nursery of the state and throve in the protection

---

23. For a sober approach appreciation of Hincmar, see, in addition to H. Schrörs, *Hinkmar, Erzbischof von Reims* (Freiburg, 1884), Hans von Schubert, *Geschichte der christlichen Kirche im Frühmittelalter* (Tübingen, 1921), 439ff.

of secular power.[24] In the Eastern Empire, crown and monastery had gone different ways and were at times in strongest opposition against each other. The Carolingian princes may have learned from these mistakes. They prudently avoided such antagonism and began to draw the monastery closely to the state and the dynasty. The importance of the monastery and of monastic devotion as a buttress of the empire and the crown had been clearly recognized by Charlemagne. After a visit to Monte Casino in 787, the king decided to unify Frankish monasticism on the basis of St. Benedict's rule, that is in the Roman manner as opposed to the Irish, just as he was willing to unify the Frankish Church on the basis of the Roman Gregorian rite. A leaning to a monasticism controlled, encouraged, privileged, and regulated by the state thus began to become visible already under Charlemagne. But it was up to his son Louis the Pious to take an almost revolutionary step in this direction. Suffice it here to mention the name of Benedict of Aniane, the "Goth," with whom Louis as a prince had become acquainted in Aquitania, whom then he brought to Aachen after having achieved the imperial throne, and whom he entrusted, as it were, with the "Ministry of Monastic Affairs" throughout the Frankish Empire. It became Benedict's task to unify the Frankish monasteries and to organize them uniformly, a work the idea and the execution of which emanated from and centered in the palace of Aachen, and not in Rome. There is no doubt that the authority of the monastery then was in the rising; it was the model of the organization of the regular chapters of some cathedrals, and with the increasing appreciation of monastic devotion there developed the profound respect which the laity, high and low, attached to the monastic prayer. We find more often than in any other period members of the royal clan holding the office of abbot in a Frankish monastery. Louis the Pious himself seems to have cherished the plan of becoming a monk; and Charles the Bald, Louis' son, actually took over the abbey of St. Denis (867) so that he displayed the unusual dignity of king-abbot. He was, in more than one respect, the usufructor of that state-monasticism which Charlemagne had initiated and which the unfortunate Louis the Pious has been unable to make really fruitful.

It is not here intended to discuss the general relations of Charles the Bald with Frankish monasticism. His monastic policy cannot be separated from his Church policy and from his complicated relations with

---

24. In general Karl Voigt, *Die karolingische Klosterpolitik und der Niedergang des westfränkischen Königtums* (Stuttgart, 1917).

the Frankish episcopate and the Holy See. Pope, bishop, and monastery represented a complex entity although there existed strongly divergent trends of interest. One hundred years after Charles the Bald, the Saxon King and Emperor Otto I would skillfully utilize the diverging interests of the three ecclesiastical groups and play off one party against the other. Through cooperating with the Holy See and the abbeys, Otto was in a position to outbalance the powers which he had bestowed upon the German episcopate, to check the episcopal power from above and below, and to secure the firm hold on the bishops upon whose shoulders he established the equilibrium of the empire. It would be an overestimation of Charles the Bald's statesmanship to assume that he pursued a similar political line. However, Charles the Bald anticipated the policy of Otto the Great in so far as he, too, had to move and act between those three entities which had not yet been a problem with Charlemagne.

When the Carolingian Empire broke up during the fraternal wars, the crown lost prestige within the Churches of the various realms; it lost prestige within the "cathedral." The West Frankish episcopate and its head Hincmar, the metropolitan of Reims, would resist, it is true, any papal effort of encroaching upon the prerogatives of the crown, for such encroachment would have repercussed unfavorably upon the metropolitans and the bishops themselves. On the other hand, however, Charles had to surrender to the episcopate. A man such as Hincmar despite his unimpeachable loyalty to the king, would let Charles know and feel that the king's dignity as the Anointed of God depended on the bishops who had the privilege of anointing their master. The general "clericalization" of the royal office and ceremonial may have been on the way anyhow; yet it was more or less the work of Hincmar of Reims. It was mainly through him that the consecration of the king was rapidly assimilated to the ceremonial of an episcopal ordination and that the king's sacring, hitherto a parahierarchical act, was fit into the hierarchical pattern of ordination which implied the spiritual superiority of the ordainer over the one ordained. It was to the interest of the Frankish bishops to enhance the king's authority by multiplying the "mystical" ingredients of rulership. But these elements exactly made the king all the more dependent upon the high clergy. Hincmar stressed to the utmost the king's dependency, not on the Roman pontiff, but on the Frankish episcopate, and he attributed far less weight to the idea of the king's direct investiture through God or to that of the royal accession by right of inheritance than to the king's consecration and unction at the hands of the bishops. In 859, Charles the Bald, a manageable pupil of Hincmar, acknowledged that he owed his unction to the bishops. He recognized as authoritative the judgment of the bishops who, said the king, "are called the thrones of God, in whom God resides, and through whom God pronounces his judgments."[25] Thus the general prestige of the king, despite an increase of politico-liturgical elaborations, had diminished considerably within the Frankish Church as compared with the standards prevailing under Charlemagne.

To square these losses, two ways were open to the king, one leading to Rome, the other to the monastery. No matter what considerations may have prompted Charles the Bald—policy or vanity or piety or a bit of all of them—he took both ways. He revised his policy toward Rome and began to fawn on the Holy See. In return, Pope John VIII courted the king who finally was crowned emperor in Rome, on Christmas Day in 875, a step through which the imperial diadem became definitely and irrevocably Rome-bound.

On the other hand, he found a new hold within the monasteries and therewith brought to a conclusion the development inaugurated by Charlemagne and Louis the Pious. For it was Charles II who systematically linked the monastery and the dynasty and inoculated in the important abbeys forms of worship of the ruler and the royal house such as they were almost unknown in the West during that age. It would be wrong to maintain that Charles the Bald shifted the liturgical ruler worship from the "cathedral" to the "monastery" because the liturgical position of the ruler with the secular Church had not suffered losses; but he successfully opened and exploited a new province which had not been fully utilized for the purpose of dynastic worship. In the monastery, which depended upon the ruler and the ruler's largesse to a far greater extent than the general Church, he established a new center of royal and dynastical devotion, or rather a great number of such centers which dotted his empire. And the monastery being a world by itself lent itself to forms of a personal attachment to the king and the royal house far greater than the cathedral which was part of a wider organization and lacked the organic individualism of the abbey. The personal tie and the dynastical relations between king and abbey produced forms of devotion which had been forsaken in the Western Church for a long time and which recall the ancient customs of antique ruler worship no matter whether we have to account for true survivals or mere analogies. The monks, to say it bluntly, became the *Kaiserpriester*, the new *augustales*

---

25. PL 138, col. 659C; MGH, Leges (Fol. ed.) I, 457.

and *flamines* of the Frankish monarch, a role which the secular hier-
archy could never have played. Like in the Roman Empire in and after
the times of Augustus there began to mushroom individual islands of
ruler worship throughout the realm which were independent of, and
not strictly co-ordinated with, the general cults of the state, so to speak
the "King's Owns" that were distributed all over the country. Within
these *collegia* of monastic *Kaiserpriester* there matured forms of monar-
chic worship and devotion which had faded away in the West and which
had nothing or very little to do with the cult and rite as propagated from
the city of Rome. Most of these strange forms, which hitherto have not
attracted the attention of scholars, were still alive in Byzantium; and
through the deeper layers of the late antique tradition the reminiscences
may have trickled of what in former days had been the general custom.

An inspection of the documents will immediately disclose the problems with which we shall have to deal.

## 2. The Documents

The following collection of excerpts is taken from charters of Charles the
Bald (823–877) and of some of the later Carolingian and German rulers.
All the documents are well known, but their politico-liturgical contents
have not yet been evaluated. [The abbreviated citations following each
entry correspond to the list of sources at the end of this section.]

### 1. April 3, 852

Charles the Bald makes a grant of land to the monastery of Marmoutier;
he stipulates that from the revenues the monks are to hold special services and receive special meals on the following days of commemoration: (a) on the anniversary of the king's father, the late Emperor Louis
the Pious; (b) on that of his mother, the late *augusta* Judith, which is to
be celebrated together with the late emperor's anniversary; (c) on the
king's birthday on June 13th; the birthday celebration is to be replaced
by (d) an annual obit [requiem mass] after the king's death.

(Bouquet, VIII, n. 109, p. 521)

### 2. May 21, 853

The same king makes a similar grant to the chapter of St. Vincent's at
Mâcon and stipulates that the brethren receive special meals and hold

commemorative services on the following days: (a) on the anniversary of the late Emperor Louis; (b), on that of the late *augusta* Judith; (c) on the king's birthday; (d) on the anniversary of his anointment (*in die inunctionis nostrae*) which is to be commuted into (e) an obit after the king's death.

   (Ragut, n. 56, p. 44; Bouquet, VIII, n. 113, p. 524)

### 3. December 4, 861

The same king makes another donation to the chapter of St. Vincent's at Mâcon stipulating that the brethren receive special meals and hold commemorative services on the following days: (a) on the king's birthday (*nativitatis nostrae die*); (b) on the anniversary of his anointment (*inunctio*) which shall be commuted into (c) an obit after his death; (d) on the birthday (*ortus die*) of his Queen Irmintrude, which shall likewise be commuted into (e) an annual obit after her death.

   (Ragut, n. 109, p. 84; Bouquet, VIII, n. 169, p. 570)

### 4. April 23, 862

The same king makes a grant to the monastery of St. Martin at Tours and stipulates that the monks receive special meals and hold commemorative services on the following days: (a) on the anniversary of the late Emperor Louis; (b) on that of the late Empress Judith; (c) on that of the king's consecration and ordination (*die quo . . . consecrati et ordinati sumus*); (d) on the day of a supplication for the king, the universal Church, and the universal peace (*quatenus eisdem fratribus pro nobis ac totius sanctae Dei ecclesiae statu et pro universali pace devotius Deum exorare complaceat*).

   (Bouquet, VIII, n. 172, p. 574; cf. Tessier, p. 201 [2:32–41, no. 239])

### 5. September 19, 862

The same king grants the revenues of certain titles to the monks of St. Denis. The monks shall receive special meals on the days of St. Denis and three other saints who are buried in the abbey, and also (a) on the anniversary of King Dagobert (623–659), founder of the abbey. In addition to smaller charities from the cellar of the abbey *in anniversariis regum et abbatum*, the king stipulates for special meals and commemorative services on the following days: (b) his birthday; (c) the day of his anointment; (d) the day which he calls his "restitution in the kingdom," which shall be exchanged for (e) an annual obit on the day of his death; (f) his wedding-day; (g) the birthday of the queen which (h) is to be replaced after he death by an annual obit. Some additional provisions are found in this charter: (i) during this lifetime as well as after his death, the monks are to sing daily after Prime five psalms in front of the altar of the Holy Trinity where the king wishes to be buried; (j) for the celebration of a daily mass for the king, a special priest shall be committed; (k) into the hands of this priest, three brethren are to place the oblations to be offered at the mass for the king; (l) a portion of royal wine, grown in the royal villa which the king had granted to the abbey, was to be admixed daily to the mass wine "lest there was lacking to the most holy sacrifice a portion from the treasures of our vow"; (m) a lamp should burn ever in front of his burial altar. There follow provisions for the celebration of the feasts of St. Mary and St. Peter, for the anniversaries of Abbot Hilduin of St. Denis, of (n) Louis the Pious, (o) Charlemagne, (p) Berta, the king's aunt, and (q) Queen Hildegardis, his grandmother.

(Bouquet, VIII, n. 176; Tardif, n. 186, p. 116; Giry, p. 689, n. 1 [discussion only]; Jusselin, p. 228)

## 6. September 19, 862

The same king makes another donation to St. Denis containing the stipulations (a) to (m) as enumerated in the preceding charter.

(Bouquet, VIII, n. 177, p. 582)

## 7. January 12, 863

The same king makes a grant to the monastery of St. Quentin and orders daily prayers of commemoration for (a) Louis the Pious; (b) for the king's welfare (*pro salute nostra*); (c) for the empress Judith; (d) *pro incolumitate* of his Queen Irmintrude; (e) for the royal progeny, and for several other persons. He further arranges for a daily meal to be given to twelve poor men and orders that one of the brethren should be in charge with the distribution of the food and with the office of ritually washing the feet of the poor, that on Maundy [Thursday] twelve poor are to receive a meal and clothes, and that on St. John's Day one hundred poor are to receive food and the monks a special meal.

(Bouquet, VIII, n. 180, p. 585)

## 8. (869–870)

The same king makes a grant to the chapter of St. Stephen's at Lyon and stipulates that the brethren receive special meals and perform commemorative services on the following days: (a) on the anniversary of Louis the Pious; (b) on that of Empress Judith; (c) on that of his beloved consort Queen Irmintrude, who died in October, 869; (d) on the king's birthday; (e) on the day of his unction; (f) on the birthday of his now consort and *augusta* Richildis; and (g) on the day of his second wedding.

(Bouquet, VIII, n. 223, p. 622; Dümmler, II, p. 286, n. 1 [discussion])

## 9. May 12 (871–874)

The same king gives as a donation to the cathedral of Paris the abbey of St. Éloi and makes the customary provisions for meals and liturgical celebrations on the following days: (a) on the anniversaries of Louis the Pious and (b) the Empress Judith; (c) on the king's birthday; (d) on the day of his anointment, a celebration to be replaced (e) by an annual obit on the day of the king's death; (f) on the queen's birthday; and (g) on the wedding-day of the royal couple. Provision is made also (h) for commemorating the royal progeny in that the bishop with his clergy as well as the monks, should the queen give birth to a prince are held to celebrate this event with continuous prayers and masses; a general banquet is granted on this occasion to both clerics and monks, and (i) special services are to be held for the king, his queen, his descendants, and for the welfare of the realm.

(Bouquet, VIII, n. 240, p. 635 [dated to 871]; Tardif, n. 207, p. 133 [dated to 871], and n. 152, p. 98; Jusselin, p. 231; Tessier, p. 201 [2:312–15, no. 364])

## 10. April 20, 872

The same king agrees to the division of property between the abbot and the monks of the abbey of St. Germain-des-Prés; he stipulates that the monks receive special meals and hold special services on several ecclesiastical feasts and on the following commemorative days: (a) on the anniversary of King Childebert (511–558), founder of the abbey; (b) on the king's birthday; and (c) on the day of his anointment which shall be converted (d) into an annual obit after his death.

(Bouquet, VIII, n. 244, p. 639; Tardif, n. 208, p. 133; Jusselin, p. 231 [summary only]; Poupardin, n. 36, p. 61)

### 11. (October 9, 873)

The same king makes a donation to St. Denis. Forgery drafted after the model of no. 12.

(Giry, p. 713; Jusselin, 231)

### 12. March 27, 875

The same king makes a grant to the abbey of St. Denis. He orders that (a) seven lamps are to burn night and day before the altar of the Holy Trinity, that is one each for Louis the Pious, Empress Judith, the king himself, the late Queen Irmintrude, Queen Richildis, the king's descendants living and dead, and for several relatives of the new queen. He orders (b) a monthly banquet to be given to the monks with the understanding that these monthly refections are not to coincide with feast-days or with other special meals granted to the monks for other reasons, and he orders that these monthly general banquets are to be connected with a monthly *commemoratio generalis* for the king which, however should impair the *specialis supplicatio* for the king as established from the revenues of other titles given to the abbey; that (c) a similar general banquet should in later times unite the monks on the anniversaries of the deaths of the king and his Queen Richildis; and (d) that the special meal on the king's birthday (see no. 5) was *not* to be transferred to the date of the king's death, but that in addition to the annual obit the *nativitas* of the king was to be celebrated even after his death.

(Bouquet, VIII, n. 234, p. 630; Tardif, n. 205, p. 132 [dated to 870]; Giry, p. 710; Jusselin, p. 232 [summary only])

### 13. (875)

The same king confirms the possessions of the abbey of St. Médard at Soissons stipulating that the monks receive special meals and perform special services on the following days: (a) on the days of St. Médard; (b) on the anniversaries of Louis the Pious and (c) Empress Judith; (d) on the *anniversaria* of the king, (e) the queen, (f) the royal progeny; (g) on the birthday of Carloman, the king's beloved son, a celebration to be shifted later on (h) to the date of the latter's death; (i) on the anniversary of the king's aunt Bertha; he further orders (j) the burning of lamps in the chapel of St. Sophie on the feast-day of the Holy Trinity.

(Tardif, n. 212, p. 135; Jusselin, p. 232; Tessier, p. 201 [2:248–54, no. 338])

### 14. May 5, 877

The same ruler, emperor since 875, wishes to follow the example of his grand-father Charlemagne who founded the palace chapel at Aachen. Therefore he founds a palace chapel at Compiègne and combines it with a convent. He endows the abbey, which he wishes to be called the "Royal" (it was called also *Carlopolis*), and decrees that the abbey shall harbor one hundred monks whose occupation shall be to pray continuously for the welfare of the most holy Church, for the emperor's parents and ancestors, for the emperor himself, his consort and children, as well as for the stability of the whole realm.

   (Bouquet, VIII, n. 272, p. 659; Tessier, p. 201 [2:448–54, no. 425]; De Grandmaison, p. 116 [discussion]; Schramm, *Bildnisse*, p. 66 [discussion])

### 15. April 2, 878

King Louis the Stammerer confirms the privileges granted by his father, the late Emperor Charles the Bald (died October 6, 877), as regards the donation of the monastery of St. Éloi to the bishop of Paris (see no. 9) and stipulates that monks and clerics receive special meals on, and celebrate with prayers and masses, the anniversary of the king's anointment which, later on, is the be transferred to the date of his death, and that they pray continuously for the king, his queen, his descendants, and for the welfare of the realm.

   (Bouquet, IX, n. 5, p. 402)

### 16. June 20, 878

The same king grants a privilege to the abbey of St. Martin at Tours and stipulates that the monks receive special meals and perform special services (a) on the king's birthday; (b) on the anniversary of his unction; and that they pray with vigils and masses for (c) his father, (d) his mother, (e) his brothers, (f) for the king himself, (g) his consort, and (h) his progeny.

   (Bouquet, IX, n. 7, p. 404)

### 17. February 7, 879

The same king makes a grant to the monastery of St. Médard at Soissons and orders that the monks receive, in return for special services, special meals on the following days: (a) on the anniversaries of Louis the Pious, (b) Empress Judith, (c) the king's parents, (d) on the king's anniversary after his death, (e) on the anniversaries of his queen and descendants after their death, (f) on the anniversaries of his brother Carloman and (g) his aunt Bertha.

(Bouquet, IX, n. 21, p. 416)


## 18. (ca. 883)

Chadolt, Bishop of Novara, makes a grant to the monastery of Reichenau on the condition that annually, on the day of the consecration of Emperor Charles III (the Fat) a service *cum omni abundantia* be held for the soul of the emperor, that the priests sing a mass and the monks chant thirty psalms each, that the monks on this day should be *hilares atque gaudentes* in the refectory, and that after the death of the *augustus* this celebration be shifted to the date of his anniversary.

(Mabillon, *Analecta*, p. 427; Dümmler, III, p. 290 [280–281n57, partial transcription only]; C. B. A. Fickler, *Quellen und Forschungen zur Geschichte Schwabens und der Ostschweiz* (1859), n. 2, p. 6 [document is dated to between 878 and 887, and probably to 883])


## 19. August 28, 885

Emperor Charles III (the Fat) returns to the cathedral of Langres the abbey of Rouvray on the condition that the monks receive, in return for a special service, a special meal on the day of his consecration and that, after his death, this celebration be converted into an obit.

(BM, 1667; MGH, Dipl. Karl III, n. 129, p. 207)


## 20. September 23, 885

The same emperor makes a grant to the monastery of Fulda on the condition that the monks receive a special meal when they celebrate the anniversary of his consecration and, later on, that of his death.

(BM, n. 1670; MGH, Dipl. Karl III, n. 132, p. 211)


## 21. October 29, 886

The same emperor makes a donation to the cathedral of Langres on the same conditions as before (no. 19).

(BM, n. 1684; MGH, ibid., n. 147, p. 238)

## 22. January 15, 887

The same emperor makes a donation to the same cathedral on the same conditions as before (nos. 19, 21).
   (BM, 1694; MGH, ibid., n. 153, p. 248)

## 23. January 20, 912

King Charles the Simple donates to the cathedral of Toul the monastery of [Bonmoutier] and stipulates that canons and monks receive a special meal in return for special services on the day of his consecration which, after his death, is to be changed into an obit.
   (Bouquet, IX, n. 46, p. 515)

## 24. March 18, 917

The same king makes a grant to the monastery of St. Remy at Reims and orders that the monks receive a special meal when they celebrate the anniversary of his anointment and commemorate his late Queen Frederuna and the children of royal stock.
   (Bouquet, IX, n. 64, p. 531)

## 25. March 28, 917

The same king grants a privilege to the abbey of St. Denis and orders that the monks receive a special meal when they celebrate and commemorate (a) the king's birthday, (b) his day of anointment, (c) the anniversary of the late Queen Frederuna, and (d) his obit after his death.
   (Bouquet, IX, n. 65, p. 531; Tardif, n. 228, p. 142)

## 26. March 14, 918

The same king makes a donation to the abbey of St. Germain-des-Prés and orders that the monks receive a special meal when they celebrate (a) the anniversary of the late Queen Frederuna, (b) the day of his unction, and (c) his obit by which, after his death, the celebration of the unction shall be replaced.
   (Bouquet, IX, n. 69, p. 536; Tardif, n. 229, p. 143)

## 27. April 28, 918

The same king, having transferred the relics of St. Walburgis to the royal palace at Attigny and therein having founded a chapel dedicated to her veneration, makes the following arrangements: (a) twelve monks shall observe by day and night the offices in the chapel; (b) the chapel, under the supervision of Saints Mary, Corneille, and Cyprian of Compiègne, has to send through the treasurer of Attigny on the feast days of those saints two candles of twelve pounds each to Compiègne; (c) the day of the king's anointment is to observed annually with rites and a banquet of the monks; and (d) this celebration shall be commuted into an obit after the king's death.

    (Bouquet, IX, n. 71, p. 538; Tardif, n. 227, p. 142)

## 28. September 1, 918

The same king makes a donation to the chapel of St. Clement at Compiègne and orders that the monks (a) commemorate him and the late Queen Frederuna with daily vigils and masses, (b) that during his lifetime and in honor of the late queen the monks chant daily at tierces six psalms which he has designated, and (c) that on the feast of St. Clement the brethren sing the fifteen gradual psalms for the late queen.

    (Bouquet, IX, n. 72, p. 539)

## 29. [June 27, 919]

The same king makes a grant to St. Martin of Tours and orders that the monks commemorate (a) the day of his ordination during his lifetime, (b) after his death the anniversary of his death, and (c) the anniversary of Queen Frederuna.

    (Bouquet, IX, n. 77, p. 545)

## 30. April 22, 921

The same king gives a privilege to the abbey of St. Maur-des-Fossés providing (as in no. 29) for the celebration of (a) the day of his unction, (b) his anniversary after his death, and (c) the anniversary of the late queen, and orders that on all these occasions the king's *consanguinei* are likewise to be commemorated.

    (Bouquet, IX, n. 84, p. 552; Tardif, n. 230, p. 144)

## 31. March 26, 1013

King, later Emperor, Henry II makes a grant to the cathedral of Hildesheim and orders that the canons receive a special meal when annually they celebrate the day of his ordination which, after his death, shall be replaced by an annual obit.
  (MGH, Dipl. Henrici II, n. 263, p. 311)

## 32. February 14, 1026

King, later Emperor, Conrad II makes a grant to the chapter of Worms and orders that the canons annually celebrate the day of his unction with a *memoria* for the king, Queen Gisela, and the king's son Henry (later Emperor Henry III).
  (MGH, Dipl. Konrad II, n. 51, p. 59)

## Sources

BM: Böhmer, Johann Friedrich, and Engelbert Mühlbacher. *Die Regesten des Kaiserreichs unter den Karolingern, 751–918.* Innsbruck: Wagner, 1908. Kantorowicz cited this by item (not page) number.

Bouquet: Bouquet, Martin, ed. *Recueil des historiens des Gaules et de la France.* 24 vols. Paris, 1738–1904. Reprint, Gregg: Farnborough, 1967, vols. 8 and 9.

Dümmler:
  Dümmler III: Dümmler, Ernst. *Geschichte des ostfränkischen Reiches, III: Die letzten Karolinger: Konrad I.* Berlin, 1865.
  Dümmler II: Dümmler, Ernst. *Geschichte des ostfränkischen Reiches, II: Ludwig der Deutsche bis zum Frieden vom Konstanz 860.* Berlin, 1862.

Fickler: Fickler, Carl Borromäus Alois. *Quellen und Forschungen zur Geschichte Schwabens und der Ost-Schweiz.* Mannheim: Schneider, 1859.

Giry: Giry, Arthur. "La donation de Rueil à l'abbaye de Saint-Denis; examen critique de trois diplômes de Charles-le-Chauve." In *Mélanges Julien Havet: Recueil des travaux d'érudition dédiés à la mémoire de Julien Havet; (1853–1893),* 683–717. Paris: Ernest Leroux, 1895.

Grandmaison: Grandmaison, Charles de. "Les bulles d'or de Saint-Martin de Tours." In *Mélanges Julien Havet: Recueil des travaux d'érudition dédiés à la mémoire de Julien Havet; (1853–1893),* 111–29. Paris: Ernest Leroux, 1895.

Jusselin: Jusselin, Maurice. "Liste chronologique et lecture des mentions en notes tironiennes dans les diplômes de Charles le Chauve." *Le Moyen Âge* 39 (1929): 217–32. Jusselin provides summaries only of the documents.

Mabillon: Mabillon, Jean. *Vetera analecta, sive Collectio veterum aliquot operum & opusculorum omnis generis, carminum, epistolarum, diplomatum, epitaphiorum.* Nova editio ed. Paris: Apud Montalant, 1723.

MGH: *Monumenta Germaniae Historica.*

MGH, Dipl. Henrici II: *Die Urkunden der deutschen König und Kaiser.* MGH Diplomata 3 Die Urkunden Heinrichs II. und Arduins. Hannover, 1900–1903.

MGH, Dipl. Karl III: Paul Kehr, ed. *Die Urkunden der deutschen Karolinger, 2: Karoli III.* Diplomata. Berlin: MGH, 1937.

MGH, Dipl. Konrad II: Harry Bresslau, ed. *Die Urkunden der deutschen Könige und Kaiser,* MGH Diplomata 4. Die Urkunden Konrads II. (Conradi II. Diplomata). Hannover: MGH, 1909.

Poupardin: Poupardin, René. *Recueil des chartes de l'abbaye de Saint-Germain-des-Prés.* Paris: 1909.

Ragut: Ragut, Camille. *Cartulaire de Saint-Vincent de Mâcon—connu sous le nom de Livre enchainé.* Mâcon: Impr. d'É. Protat, 1864.

Schramm, Bildnisse: Schramm, Percy Ernst. *Die zeitgenössischen bildnisse Karls des Grossen: Mit einem Anhang über die Metallbullen der Karolinger,* Beiträge zur Kulturgeschichte des Mittelalters und der Renaissance. Leipzig etc.: B. G. Teubner, 1928.

Tardif: Tardif, Jules. *Monuments historiques [Cartons des rois, 528–1789].* Paris: J. Claye, 1866. Chartes et diplômes relatifs à l'Histoire de France, publiés par les soins de l'Académie des inscriptions et belles-lettres. Paris: Impr. Nationale, 1943–1955. Kantorowicz cited Tessier at p. 202 throughout. The document's more precise citation within the edition has been added within square brackets.

# CHAPTER 5

# Roma and the Coal

Ernst Kantorowicz worked on "Roma and the Coal" over a long period of time and invested much energy on it. He wrote a first version in Berkeley before 1945, when the title was "Roma and the Carbon." A thoroughly revised second version with the present title dates from around 1945, as can be seen from one of its footnotes. This refers to the author's article "The 'King's Advent'. . ." as having been published in the *Art Bulletin* for 1944 but omits page numbers, doubtless because Kantorowicz had not yet seen page proofs. Further confirmation comes from a letter of November 1945, which refers to an article, "Roma and the Coal," that he intended to publish in a volume to be called "Studies in Political Liturgy" that would also include articles called "Synthronos" and "Epiphany and Coronation." Since these were given as papers to the Berkeley Colloquium Orientologicum in October of 1944 and December of 1945, a date of ca. 1945 seems right for the third article.

But the author was not satisfied with his product, for he twice made extensive penciled revisions to copies of the typescript of ca. 1945. (Remarkably enough the penciled revisions adding up to version three are not carried over into version four.) Versions three and four can be dated to between ca. 1945 and 1950, for version five followed in the latter year. Now Kantorowicz effectively started all over again, producing a new typescript that conveyed major overhauling. A dating index is a reference to the "address of Pope Pius XII on December 17, 1949," offering a *terminus post quem*, and a *terminus ante* the mention of help offered to him by the interlibrary loan facilities of the Berkeley library, for Kantorowicz was fired by the Regents of the University of California at the end of August 1950. At the time in question Kantorowicz was deeply engaged in the Berkeley "Loyalty Oath" controversy. Those circumstances might explain the fact that version five breaks off at what seems to be its middle.

What happened then? The author had not put aside version five because he had abandoned intentions of finishing it. This can be seen from the fact that in 1959 he showed the article (probably version four) to Bernhard Bischoff, a scholar who then was a visitor at the Institute for Advanced Study in Princeton.[1] Kantorowicz also referred to his "forthcoming study, 'Roma and the Coal,'" in two of his last completed articles, both dating from about 1960.[2] Then he planned for it to be part of a book to be called "Studies Eastern and Western in the History of Late Classical and Medieval Ideas."[3] But the truncated fifth version is the last he wrote, for there is no reference in either four or five to a work on "Epiphany" of 1955 by his close colleague Theodore E. Mommsen that Kantorowicz did cite in his "Oriens Augusti" of ca. 1960.[4]

The overarching theme of "Roma and the Coal" is the meeting of Christianity with Rome. But within this framework the work contains many parts. It begins with an expressive introduction that portrays "efforts to bestow transparency" on "Caesarean Rome." In the Rome of the Caesars "all [was] substance and firmness"; in opposition came "the medieval tendency to dematerialize." In a characteristic digression, Kantorowicz refers to occasional tendencies that "conjured the fluorescent light of Jerusalem to make Rome less weighty and transcendental." Nevertheless, such efforts were in vain, for "Roma has refused to be identified with any Jerusalem or to give her sap to that scion." Instead, Rome became "dematerialized" by an "otherness" derived from being the city of "Apostles and Martyrs." Thus

---

1. Bischoff to Kantorowicz, written from Planegg (near Munich), January 6, 1960, and now in the Michael Cherniavsky papers, Hillmann Library, University of Pittsburgh. All the surviving drafts of "Roma and the Coal" were located originally in the Cherniavsky papers as well. (Kantorowicz often showed his works to his students.)

2. *"Puer exoriens:* On the Hypapante in the Mosaics of S. Maria Maggiore," in *Perennitas: P. Thomas Michels OSB zum 70. Geburtstag* (Münster, 1963), 118–35, at 123, n. 27 (reprinted in Kantorowicz, *Selected Studies* [Locust Valley, NY, 1965], 29, n. 27); "Oriens Augusti," *Dumbarton Oaks Papers* 17 (1963): 119–77, at 142, n. 137.

3. As noted by Ralph Giesey in *Dumbarton Oaks Papers* 17 (1963): 118.

4. "Oriens Augusti," 149, n. 182.

"when placed against this, her proper background, Rome gained indeed the touch of weightless transparency which during the Middle Ages enveloped the former city of Caesars." This statement introduces the article's proper subject matter—"the literary and poetical pattern of setting over one Rome against the other," or, in plain English, Christianity over ancient Rome.

The body of the article contains four sections: the poem; the "coal"; possible pagan survivals; and (in a brief coda) a comparison of Western and Eastern pictorial representations of the poem's culminating event. The poem is an anonymous Latin work written in "serpentine" distichs (each distich ending with the words with which it began) around the year 1000 that describes nocturnal ceremonies in Rome celebrating the feast of the Assumption of the Virgin. Kantorowicz devotes nine pages to presenting the text. He shows that it can be apprehended in terms of units and then moves to view them one by one, quoting the Latin for each set and offering his own translations. A lifelong devotee of poetry, he translates poetically. Thus "Pulvere multiplici crines fedaverat ille. Hic te mundat aquas pulvere multiplici" becomes "With dirt and dust the ploughman's hair was stained; the fisher cleanses thee with water from dirt and dust." (The author's care to polish his translation can be seen by comparing this with his initial version which reads "Now it is the fisherman that approaches thy precincts and cleanses thee from dirt and dust with water.")

The poem opens with an evocative description of a midnight procession in Rome: torches carried through the streets "mingling with the light of the moon." There follows a direct address to a woman, "Roma," who heads the procession and is understood to be a personification of the city. The address refers to Rome's magnificent past, an opportunity for her renewal, and the implicit presence of Peter and Paul, the greatest of Christian Roman martyrs. "Roma" then answers. She castigates her own prior sins and points to the *Volto santo*, the icon of Christ that the crowd is carrying through the streets to meet Christ's mother. By now the *Volto santo* has reached its destination, the sanctuary of Mary, which is the church of Santa Maria Maggiore. The poet then returns to his own voice and closes with exultant prayers to the Virgin and finally to the reigning ruler, Otto III.

Kantorowicz has not yet proposed an argument, but he develops one in the central following section. At the midpoint of both Roma's speech and the entire poem is a distich that reads: "Nec procul est opifex gemmam carbone refingens et gremium pandens, nec procul est opifex." The author's translation here is sufficiently literal: "Not far away is the artisan who with a coal refashions the gem and expands the pale; not far away is the artisan." Kantorowicz reads the verse figuratively and determines that the "artisan" is Christ and the "gem" Rome. But what is the meaning of the "coal"? He answers this by showing that it must be the Eucharist. Thus Christ refashions Rome by the power of the Eucharist and thereby extends its pale. The meaning of the article's lapidary title thus becomes clear: the subject is the transformation of Rome (the city and a larger sense the civilization) by Christianity.

Once the central line of the poem is decoded (at considerable length), the remainder of the article is more routine. Although Kantorowicz heads his final section "Lustration and Theophany," this can be called more intelligibly "Pagan Survivals." The "refashioning of the gem" is an act of purification, or "lustration," and purification rites were known in ancient times. Similarly the torchlight procession to meet the appearance of a deity ("theophany") has pagan antecedents. (Kantorowicz here is not referring to direct influences, but to antecedents that he still finds noteworthy and revels in exhibiting.) As for Western and Eastern "pictorial representations," the author limits himself to representations of the coronation of the Virgin by Christ. In the Byzantine East Christ always meets his mother on earth (as happens in the Roman Assumption Day poem), and the coronation of the Virgin is subsidiary, while Western art refrains from such depictions and after the twelfth century features the crowning of the Virgin in heaven.

Whereas there are many original observations in "Roma and the Coal," it is reasonable to ask whether the central argument that the "coal" in the poem stands for the Eucharist is original. Kantorowicz maintained in the first four versions that "the allusion has never been understood by modern interpreters," and that the coal metaphor "has received little attention." The documentation for the second remark reads: "a few notes by Joseph Brinktrine [. . .] *Ephemerides Liturgicae*, 50 (1936), p. 35, is all that came to my attention." But in the unfinished fifth version we find: "before revising my manuscript I fortunately chanced upon the study by E. A. Pezopoulos, 'CYMBOLAI KPITIKAI [. . .],' a mainly lexicographical collection of places, and upon Johann E. Eschenbach, *Die glühende Kohle* [. . .] a far more penetrating study from which I was able to supplement my patristic material in a few instances and whose observations always proved to be valuable." There follow several footnote citations of both Pezopoulos and Eschenbach, after which fourteen footnotes are left blank before the entire version comes to an abrupt end.

Given the circumstance that the footnotes were left unfinished, the conclusion forces itself that further pages of the fifth version did not go astray but that the author simply stopped his work. How can we explain this? One answer might lie in the date of the writing. Perhaps Kantorowicz's engagement with the Loyalty Oath struggle and its immediate aftermath became too great to allow him to continue directly with the writing of the fifth version and that he then never came back to it. On the other hand, perhaps he stopped because he was demoralized by the appearance of two studies that he originally had overlooked. Not only would these have made him seem less original, but they would have created a need to cite them frequently and engage in discussions with them, an unappealing task. It should also be recognized that the range and nature of the author's references are more recondite than usual even for Kantorowicz. He must have relied heavily on the services of Interlibrary Loan at Berkeley, and in his last phase at that institution he may have decided to forgo them.

My procedure here has been to publish version five as far as it extends and then attach version four, beginning roughly at the place where version five breaks off. Certainly the uncompleted fifth version shows its superiority to the prior effort in many ways. For one, Kantorowicz perfected his prose. To take a few examples, "perpetual" in version four becomes "permanent" in version five; "as he moved out of Jerusalem" becomes "as he moved proudly out of Jerusalem"; "effused the strongest perfume and the fullest tones" becomes "effused the strongest perfume and resounded the fullest tones"; "the custom is remindful" becomes "the custom recalls."

Version five is also richer in terms of meaningful content. Whereas version four alludes to a later " 'Caesarean' subcurrent which so thoroughly has imbued Roman life" without offering examples, version five documents how Frederick II and Manfred related to that subcurrent, and version five documents with secondary literature how "to the present day, papal pageantry challenges the spectator to recall customs, shows and ceremonials of the Caesars." Above all, Kantorowicz's revised account of the nocturnal ceremonies and the Assumption poem is much richer. For example, only version five reports that the pope walked with the procession until the time of the Gregorian Reform and (drawing on additional research) "later only received the procession at its destination." When "Roma" admits to having been "a nocturnal whore," Kantorowicz expatiates: "she herself is that *meretrix Augusta*, Messalina, who, according to Juvenal, despite all her treasures sneaked away at night from the imperial couch and offered herself in one of Rome's brothels to any comer, asking and taking from each his fee."

While the surviving part of the ultimate version of "Roma and the Coal" is superior to its predecessor, the earlier second half needs to be read in the lack of an alternative. Thus Kantorowicz's demonstration that the "coal" is the coal of Isaiah 6:1–7, and that this in turn was interpreted as the Eucharist in diverse eastern Christian liturgies until the identification reached

Rome (under Greek influence) in the poem of ca. 1000, appears fully only in the version he had previously completed. (Whether or not parts of it had already been known to E. A. Pezopoulos and/or J. E. Eschenbach is irrelevant because these authors lacked the flair of a Kantorowicz.) Additionally, the final two sections of the merged article are engaging.

It has been mentioned that in 1959 Kantorowicz showed a draft of the article to Bernhard Bischoff.[5] The latter, a prominent medieval Latin philologist, had been a guest at the Princeton Institute in the spring of 1959, at which time he read a version of "Roma and the Coal." It remained on Bischoff's mind for many months, as we know from the fact that he sent a letter to Kantorowicz regarding it from his home near Munich in early January 1960. His purpose was to express his objection to the symbolic reading of the line "not far away is the artisan who with a coal refashions the gem." Rather than the artisan being Christ, the coal the Eucharist, and the gem Rome, Bischoff proposed that the terms should be understood literally: "not far away an artisan refashions a literal gem with a literal coal." To support his view, he referred to a work of ca. 1100 on artisan crafts by a certain "Theophilus" which prescribed the cleansing of gold and silver with coals. Granted that gold and silver were not gems and that according to "Theophilus" gems were to be cleansed with goat milk, Bischoff elsewhere found reference to the use of coals in grinding animal horn. Thus without claiming certainty he thought that the literal interpretation was the strongest.

Kantorowicz almost certainly replied, for his copy of Bischoff's letter contains a jotting that shows he had gone to the trouble of locating Bischoff's return address. But unfortunately, the putative answer does not survive. (At least not in the Bischoff papers.) Clearly, however, he held to the symbolic interpretation of the coal because of his reiterated intention toward the end of his life to publish an article with "coal" featured in the title.

With regrets about lacking a fully revised article it still may be said that the current stitched-together piece is immensely rewarding. The close reading of the Latin poem is masterful and the thick description of the torchlight procession highly evocative. To that comes the learning concerning the "coal of Isaiah" and the Eastern liturgical instances of "coal" as Eucharist. And not least is the poetically couched, overarching argument about the meeting of Rome and Christianity whereby Kantorowicz the workman polishes a gem.

---

5. Above, with note 1.

The Romans, wrote Cardinal Guido of Santa Sabina, will fall for any man who offers them *et gestus magnificos et verba tonantia et facta terribilia.*[6] The Cardinal, who as pope Clement IV (1265–1268) was destined to end the century-old struggle of the Holy See against the Hohenstaufen Emperors, had seen many princes and princely pretenders paying court to Rome, enough to know how a man could win applause in the city.[7] His experience has general validity. Time and time again, Rome, in the course of her long history of twenty-seven centuries, had proven the essential truth of his words which indicate simply the permanent existence of a "Caesarean" subcurrent with which Roman life had been imbued so thoroughly. Rome would not be Rome lest she intoxicated herself periodically with magnificent gestures, stunned her people with resounding words, and bewildered others with stupendous feats. Her predilection for the theatrical, the rhetorical, and the prodigious must be taken into account by anyone who wishes to understand imperial, papal, or modern Rome. From that stratum there arose her monuments of ugly grandeur and great beauty. From the same source there originated her remarkable ability to excel in splendid display and colorful pageantry, or to stir emotions through various kinds of exciting *circenses.* Such was Rome in Antiquity, and her intrinsic nature was not abated when the Rome of the Caesars changed into that of the Popes. The world-ruling pontiffs took full advantage of the imperial legacy. Never have the Roman popes abandoned the Caesarian stratum on which their universal power rested and their towering claims were founded. To the present day, papal pageantry challenges the spectator to recall customs, shows, and ceremonial of the Caesars.[8] In Caesarian Rome, the Spirit has found, for good or evil, a body to live in; and where all is substance and firmness, there the Spirit, too, no longer is indefinite, hazy or floating: He becomes compact, factual, and material through that incredible reality of Caesarian Rome.

---

6. *Regesta Imperii*, ed. J. F. Böhmer, J. Ficker, and E. Winkelmann (Innsbruck, 1892–1901), 5, no. 9482.

7. See, for the princely ambitions in Rome after 1250, Paul Schmitthenner, *Die Ansprüche des Adels und Volks der Stadt Rom auf Vergebung der Kaiserkrone während des Interregnums* (Berlin, 1923). The letters of Frederick II, or the Manifesto of Manfred, to the Romans (see, for the latter, MGH, *Constitutiones et acta publica*, 2, no. 424, pp. 559ff.) alone would justify the cardinal's judgment.

8. In addition to Andreas Alföldi, "Die Ausgestaltung des monarchischen Zeremoniells am römischen Kaiserhofe," and "Insignien und Tracht der römischen Kaiser," *Römische Mitteilungen* 49 (1934), 1–118, and 50 (1935), 1–171, see Theodor Klauser, *Der Ursprung der bischöflichen Insignien* (Krefeld, 1949), with further literature, 31, n. 1.

Less manifest, though hardly less effective, than the Caesarian strand was the mediaeval tendency to dematerialize, though not dim out, ancient Rome's too great reality, to make the city, as it were, transparent by viewing it in a more spiritual fashion. Efforts to bestow transparency upon Rome have been made in various directions. Artists and men of letters have occasionally conjured the fluorescent light of Jerusalem to make Rome less weighty and more transcendental. In the mosaics of Santa Maria Maggiore, executed under Pope Sixtus III (432–440), we recognize St. Peter in the garb of Israel's holy man Simeon, who took the new-born saviour in his arms, and accordingly we find the Roman *Templum Urbis* represented as the Temple of Jerusalem.[9]

We know also that strange equation of St. Peter and Moses which lingered on through the Middle Ages and which fulfilled the task to establish also in view of the Old Testament a Roman apostolic succession.[10] We know the discussions of the very obvious questions why, after all, not Jerusalem but Rome became, according to Western theologians, the *caput omnium ecclesiarum*.[11] We are familiar with the curial endeavors to bind Jerusalem's halo to the glamour of Rome through the medium of the crusades, the leadership of which was finally claimed by the pope.[12] In a hierarchical reinterpretation of an early Christian iconographic pattern—the meeting of the *Ecclesia ex circumcisione*, Jerusalem, with the *Ecclesia ex gentibus*, Bethlehem, where the Magi adored Christ—that is, the now destroyed mosaics in the apse of the Vatican, people may have admired Pope Innocent III as he moved proudly out of Jerusalem to meet the Church, his papal Church, stepping forth from Bethlehem.[13]

---

9. André Grabar, *L'Empereur dans l'art byzantin* (Paris, 1936), 216ff., has solved the iconographic problem of the mosaic; for additional evidence, see Jean Gagé, "Le *Templum Urbis* et les origines de l'idée de *Renovatio*," *Mélanges Franz Cumont* (Brussels, 1936), 151–87, and "Saeculum novum," *Transactions of the International Numismatic Congress . . . in London: June 30–July 3, 1936* (London, 1938), 179–86.

10. C. A. Kneller, "Moses und Petrus," *Stimmen aus Maria Laach* 60 (1901), 237–57; G. A. van den Bergh van Eysinga, "Saint Pierre, Second Moïse," *Congrès d'Histoire de Christianisme: Jubilé Alfred Loisy* (Paris and Amsterdam, 1928), 2, 181–91.

11. See, e.g., Petrus Damiani, *De picturis*, c. 4, PL 145, col. 594.

12. Innocent III actually thought of becoming the general of a new crusade: see his *Epistolae*, XVI, 28, and 108, PL 216, cols. 817, 905; also Joseph Greven, "Frankreich und der fünfte Kreuzzug," *Historisches Jahrbuch* 43 (1923), 23ff., and for the earlier stage of that idea, Carl Erdmann, *Die Entstehung des Kreuzzugsgedankens* (Stuttgart, 1935). [English translation by Marshall W. Baldwin and Walter Goffart as *The Origin of the Idea of Crusade* (Princeton, 1977)].

13. Joseph Wilpert, *Die römischen Mosaiken und Malerein der kirchlichen Bauten vom IV. bis XIII. Jahrhundert* (Freiburg, 1916), 1, 361ff., 1168; cf. Wart Arsland, "Un frammento dell'antico mosaico absidale Vaticano," *Dedalo* 7 (1926–27), 754ff. The iconographic pattern of confronting Jerusalem and Bethlehem to indicate their unity was very popular in early Christian art,

There are other items indicating the vain efforts to blend the Rome-Idea with the Jerusalem Idea, to graft "Jerusalem" upon Rome, and to transcendentalize Rome by making her visible as an antitype and effigy of the Celestial City: "This city of ours—the city of God, the city in which truth and sanctity are taught," as Pope Pius XII still expressed it.[14] But in the end Roma has refused to be identified with any Jerusalem or to give her sap to that scion.

Rome's earthbound reality was not to become less material and heavy-weighing by calling in the metaphysics bound to another city and climate. Rome had an otherness of her own. She was the city of Apostles and Martyrs. When placed against this, her proper background, Rome gained indeed the touch of weightless transparency which during the Middle Ages enveloped and transfigured the former city of the Caesars. It appears that for several centuries, until the antique tradition re-emerged as an all-domineering mirage during the Renaissance, the inner tension of Roman thought and life vibrated between the two extreme poles of Caesars and Martyrs. The poems which during the Middle Ages effused the strongest perfume and resounded the fullest tones, poems which still move us directly as, for example, *O Roma nobilis*, were those inspired and vitalized by the confrontation of the factual grandeur of Caesarian Rome with the sweetness of the self-sacrifice of the martyrs. Romulus and Remus replaced by Petrus and Paulus—this was the formula which the Church liked to apply.[15]

The literary and poetical patterns of setting over one Rome against the other is old. It begins, roughly, with Prudentius's songs on Roman martyrs and with the sermons of Leo the Great on the Roman Apostles. It ends in the early twelfth century in Hildebert of Lavardin's elegy on Rome. Thereafter the Pre-Renaissance produced a new variety of

especially in Roman churches (S. Maria Maggiore, S. Pudenziana, S. Prassede, S. Clemente, and others); see Wilpert, op. cit., 1, pp. 520, 1182, also Frederic van den Meer, *Maiestas Domini: Théophanies de l'Apocalypse dans l'art chrétien* (Vatican City, 1938), 74. It is significant that the later Spiritual Franciscans and other defenders of ecclesiastical poverty worshipped Bethlehem as the prototype of the poor, and therefore true, Church whereas "royal" Jerusalem appeared to them as the symbol of the carnal papal Church: cf. Ernst Benz, *Ecclesia Spiritualis: Die Kirchenidee der franziskanischen Reformation* (Stuttgart, 1934), 39.

14. Address of Pope Pius XII, on December 17, 1949, before the start of the Holy Year 1950. The history of the Jerusalem Idea, as planned by the late Professor Hans Lewy, of the University of Jerusalem, still remains to be written—a major desideratum of medieval studies.

15. Humbert of Silva Candida, *De sancta Romana ecclesia*, Fragment B, ed. Percy Ernst Schramm, *Kaiser, Rom und renovatio* (Leipzig, 1929), II, 129–30, also I, 34, 244.

Rome-Sentiment, although even Petrarch could occasionally fall back on the old scheme:

> "Assuming that ancient Rome left me cold—how sweet, then, is it to view in a Christian spirit that city, the effigy of heaven on earth, the city fit together by the flesh and bones of the martyrs."[16]

However, the climax of that literary genre should be sought in the later part of the ninth, in the tenth, and early eleventh century, thus preceding and coinciding with that surprising bloom of the mediaeval Rome-Idea in the Ottonian period which has found already its competent interpreter.[17] In that period, during which Byzantium exercised once more her powerful influence on the West and on Rome, there originated in Italy, written in or near the year 1000 by an anonymous poet, the stirring and highly emotional song, often discussed and recently published anew in a critical edition, which may form the starting point of this study, the *Carmen in Assumptione Sanctae Mariae*.[18]

## The *Koimesis* [Assumption] Poem

The sixty-six lines, or thirty-three distichs, of which the poem is composed, refer to the celebration of the Dormition and Assumption of St. Mary such as it was observed in Rome on August 15th. Like most of the feasts of St. Mary, the Assumption was based on apocryphal sources.[19] Probably since the fifth century the *Koimesis* of the Virgin was observed in the East. The celebration of that day then wandered to the West, perhaps along the customary Gallican trails.[20] To Rome it can be traced

---

16. In general, Schramm, op. cit. For Petrarch [?].

17. Schramm, op. cit. See also Schneider and Burdach (next note).

18. The authoritative edition by Karl Strecker is found in MGH, Poetae latini, 5 (1939), 465–68. The poem has been discussed by Francesco Novati, *L'Influsso del pensiero latino sopra la civiltà italiana del medio evo* (2nd ed.; Milan, 1899), pp. 47, 169–75; Fedor Schneider, *Rom und Romgedanke im Mittelatler* (Munich, 1926), 150–52, cf. 29; Konrad Burdach, *Vom Mittelalter zur Reformation* (Berlin, 1913–28), II, 1, pp. 456ff.; Schramm, op. cit., 150ff. For manuscripts, earlier editions, and additional literature, see Strecker's edition, p. 465.

19. K. A. H. Kellner, *Heortologie* (2nd ed., Freiburg, 1911), 177ff. Ernst Lucius, *Die Anfänge des Heiligenkults in der christlichen Kirche* (Tübingen, 1904), 487–89. Karl Holl, "Die Enstehung der vier Fastenzeiten in der griechischen Kirche," in Holl, *Gesammelte Aufsätze zur Kirchengeschichte* 2 (Tübingen, 1928), 165ff. A discussion of the vast, and often amusing, literature on the subject, evoked by the dogmatization of the myth of the Virgin's Assumption of the Flesh, is beyond the scope of this study.

20. For the Gallican and Mozarabic currents, see Bernhard Capelle, "La messe gallicane de l'Assomption," *Miscellanea liturgica in honorem L. Cuniberti Mohlberg* (Rome, 1948), 2, 33–59; Also Kellner and Lucius, loc. cit.

in the seventh century when Pope Sergius I (687–701) made arrangements for a procession on the vigil of Assumption Day.[21] It became a
Roman custom to carry during the night preceding that feast the *Volto
santo* in a solemn, perhaps somewhat orgiastic, torch procession from
the oratory of San Lorenzo, near the Lateran (now known as the *Sancta
Sanctorum*) to Santa Maria Maggiore.[22] The *Volto santo*, now discolored
out of recognition and almost totally covered by a silver screen by which
Innocent III tried to protect the image, was a holy icon of Christ.[23] It
was painted in the early Christian and Byzantine manner displaying
the "Emmanuel," the God incarnate and therefore manifest, seated on
his throne. That stern image was said to be an *acheropita*, an icon not
painted by human hands. Saint Luke, allegedly, had made the design,
whereas angels had finished it by adding the colors.[24] About the origin
of the panel, which undoubtedly is old (fifth or sixth century, perhaps,
since the type can be traced even to the fourth),[25] there circulated a great
number of legends. Saint Peter himself was claimed to have brought
the icon to the city. Others, who believed in the Abgar story, held that it
was found in the booty which Titus brought from Jerusalem to Rome.
A third version maintained that the iconophile Patriarch Germanus of
Constantinople, who was deposed by the Emperor Leo III at the *Silen-
tion* of 730, had saved the icon from the fervor of the Iconoclasts and
that the panel finally swam over the seas to reach Rome, thus taking,

---

21. *Liber pontificalis*, ed. Duchesne (Paris, 1886–1892), 1, 376.

22. The procession, described also in the preamble of the poem (Strecker's edition, p. 466)
which has the full title: *Incipit Carmen in Assumptione Sanctae Mariae in nocte quando Tabula
portatur*, may go back to Pope Sergius himself; the image is mentioned under Pope Stephen II
(752–57): see *Liber pontificalis*, 1, 443. For the procession in general see A. Gui, *Rassegna Grego-
riana* 5 (1906), 381, and the works quoted in the next note.

23. For the *Volto santo*, see Wilpert, "Die Acheropita in der Kapelle Sancta Sanctorum,"
*Römische Quartalschrift*, 21 (1907), 65–92; "L'Acheropita ossia l'immagine del Salvatore nella
cappella Sancta Sanctorum," *Arte* 10 (1907), 161–77, 247–62; and Wilpert, *Die römischen Mo-
saiken*, op. cit., 2, 1101ff. Not accessible to me were Hartmann Grisar, *Die römische Kapelle
Sancta Sanctorum und ihr Schatz* (Freiburg, 1908), 39ff., 53ff.; P. Stanislao dell' Addolorata,
*La cappella pontificia del Sancta Sanctorum ed i suoi sacri tesori* (Grottaferrata, 1920), quoted by
Carlo Cecchelli in his very thorough study "Il tesoro del Laterano, III: L'Acheropita," *Dedalo* 7
(1926–27), 295–319. Most valuable, and otherwise unnoticed, material has been collected by
W. F. Volbach, "Il Cristo di Sutri e la venerazione del SS. Salvatore nel Lazio," *Rendiconti della
Pont. Accademia Romana di Archeologia* 17 (1940–41), 97–126, who adduces many other relevant
studies which are inaccessible to me.

24. See, in general, Ernst von Dobschütz, *Christusbilder: Untersuchungen zur christlichen Leg-
ende* (Leipzig, 1899).

25. Grabar, *L'Empereur*, 196ff.; Volbach, 121ff., for the models in imperial art.

by and large, the familiar and classical way of the Palladium, from the Hellespont to the Tiber.[26]

The nocturnal celebration resembled in many respects a national holiday. The Romans compared their city, the *patriae parens*, to Mary, the *Deiparens*, and hallowed, as it were, in the *Assunta* also the *Roma* and vice versa.[27] The feast had a certain political character, both in Rome and in the cities of Latium which ever since early times were proud of copying the Roman model, so that their practices now shed some light also on the Roman customs.[28] The whole population was arranged according to its civic organizations, headed by the prefect of the city and the regional magistrates as well as by the clergy. The people assembled, burning torches in their hands, in or near the old Constantinian Basilica, the Lateran, to form the procession which led through the illuminated streets.[29] A mediaeval inscription from the Capitol is preserved in the Palazzo dei Conservatori, and it renders the idea of the feast, or one aspect of it, not badly: "The triumphal procession of the pagans, which one was used to perform in honor of Caesar Augustus, has been adjusted to the devotional cult of the Christian religion on the feast of the Godbearing Virgin."[30] It was in fact a *triumphalis pompa* in honor of the celestial *Augusta*—and the *Augustus*.

---

26. The legends have been summed up by Cecchelli, op. cit., 304–5; see also Burdach, op. cit., 475–76. For the swimming images of gods, see Ernst Schmidt, *Kulturübertragungen* (Giessen, 1909), 88–89.

27. Schneider, *Romgedanke*, 151–52, exaggerates when he writes: "Wie wenig ist diese Maria, für die man ohne weiteres Roma sagen kann, christliche Gottesmutter!" However, in the poem quoted below (lines 13–14) the apostrophe of Roma as *parens patriae* certainly parallels Mary as *deiparens*.

28. Volbach, 114ff.; in general see the rich material collected by Giovanni Marangoni, *Istoria dell' antichissimo oratorio o capella di San Lorenzo nel patriarchio lateranense comunemente appellato Sancta Sanctorum* (Rome, 1747), passim. For the "political" character, see also below: the invocations for the Emperors Otto and Henry.

29. A description of the procession is found in a note preceding, in some manuscripts, the text of the poem; see MGH, Poetae latini, 5, p. 466; also Benedict of St. Peter's (*Ordo Romanus* XI) describes the procession; PL 78, col. 868 and 1052; Roberto Valentini and Giuseppe Zucchetti, *Codice topografico della Città di Roma* (Rome, 1946), 3, 221. See also the literature quoted above, n. 23, and for the later period, Marangoni, op. cit.; Volbach, 120.

30. The inscription, actually a decree of the Senate, is interesting in many respects. The text, published by Marangoni, 125–26, and mentioned by Volbach, 118, 121, is not easily accessible and this therefore may justify a reprint of the preamble:

"Triumphalis gentilium pompa Augustorum honori reddi solita, ad devotum Christianae religionis cultum redacta, Dei Genitricis Virginis festo die, dum Christi Salvatoris nostri mirabile simulacrum ex Laterano in exquilias ad Mariae Matris maiorem aedem quotannis ingenti plausu solemnique processione defertur pro Senatus Magistratuumque et totius Equestris Ordinis dignitate populique et plaebis observantia,

From the Lateran, the procession took its way first to the Forum, to S. Maria Nova, now S. Francesca Romana. This church, very suitingly, was the old *templum Veneris et Romae*. This was the first station of the procession, and on the steps of the old national shrine the image was deposed. While the feet of the image were washed, the mourning over the death of the Virgin began. The people went down on their knees. They beat their chests with their fists, and sang a hundred *Kyrie eleison*, a hundred *Christe eleison*, and another hundred *Kyrie eleison*. There followed various other stations where the ritual of washing the feet of the image with basilicum was repeated. Finally the icon was carried to Santa Maria Maggiore, where it remained for the night. The pope, who until the age of the Church Reform in the eleventh century had walked in the procession, but later only received the procession at its destination,[31] sang the Mass, which according to a later legend originally had been celebrated by St. Peter himself, and then gave his blessing to the exhausted people (*benedicit populum fatigatum*).[32] The visit of Christ to the shrine of his mother came to an end. In the early hours of the morning the *Volto santo* returned to its own temple, the present *Sancta Sanctorum*. The task of the divine epiphany had been fulfilled: the Virgin's soul was received by the Son; it was conducted by the angels to Heaven, where the Virgin finally was to share the throne of the Deity.

This spectacular pageantry, the greatest feast of medieval Rome, may have been celebrated in the year 1000 with more than the customary elaboration, since the young emperor of Saxon and Byzantine stock, Otto III, then was present in the city, which he intended to restore to her old dignity as the capital of a renewed Roman Empire.[33] However this may be, we are told that "some one"—Roman or stranger—who

---

neve ulla post hac inter plebeia collegia contentio fiat, decretum est, ut hoc statuto ordine universi cum suis faculis thalamisque et luminaribus sacram imaginem, qua iter fecerit, comitentur ea ratione, ut qui proximiores simulacro sint, digniores habeantur."

The inscription then describes in great detail in what order the guilds were to march in the procession. The inscription is late. Dr. Wolfgang Hagemann, in Rome, who was kind enough to collate the text of the inscription, believes that it is not earlier than the fifteenth century.

31. Volbach, p. 118, seems to refer to the Order of Benedict of St. Peter's (PL 78, col. 1052) where indeed the pope (Innocent II) expects the parade at Santa Maria Maggiore.

32. Benedict, in PL 78, 1052C.

33. For the date of the poem, suggested by the *supplicatio* for Otto III, see Schramm, *Renovatio*, 1, 150. However, the commemoration of the emperor does not necessarily prove his personal presence; in the poem MGH, Poetae, 5, pp. 468-69, the Emperor Henry II is commemorated in Assumption Day. Was he, too, "present"? On the other hand, it is sometimes assumed that the poem is older and that the *supplicatio* for Otto was added; Volbach, p. 118, believes the poem may go back to the seventh or eighth centuries; see also Schramm, loc. cit. To my opinion the whole poem belongs to the times of Otto III.

witnessed the midnight procession, was overwhelmed by the spectacle and, taken by rapture and admiration, broke out with the words:

> Sancta Maria, quid est? Si celi climata scandis,
>   Esto benigna tuis! Sancta Maria, quid est?
> Unde fremit populus, vel cur vexilla coruscant?
>   Quid sibi vult strepitus? Unde fremit populus?
> 5   Quare volant facule, lucent per strata corone?
>   Lumine cum lune quare volant facule?
> Astra nitent radiis rutilant et tecta laternis,

In a simple translation those four distichs may be rendered as follows:[34]

(1)  Holy Virgin, what is it? When thou ascendest to the dwellings of Heaven, be thou gracious to those that are thine! Holy Virgin, what is it?

(2)  Why is this buzzing of the crowd, and why do the banners glisten? Why this noise and the buzzing of the crowd?

(3)  Why are torch-lights floating through the streets and pitch-crowns sparkling? Why, mingling with the light of the moon, are torch-lights floating?

(4)  The beams of the stars are glittering, but also the roofs resplend with lanterns. All is reddened by flames, and the beams of the stars glitter.

With those four picturesque distichs the poem opens, and the poet skill-fully prepares the reader for the approaching torch-procession. As the poem proceeds, the procession will advance, too. It is one of the artifices of that highly artistic poet to make the reader visualize, as if by means of *teichoskopia* [viewing from above], the whole train of the faithful as it passes by conducting the holy icon of the Emmanuel. At the same time however, the poet actively interferes with the procession: he stops one of the mourners, a woman marching at the head of the parade. She is *Roma*, herself, and the poet addresses her in what he calls the *Allocutio Romae*:

> Aedita consulibus numerasti, Roma, triumphos;
> 10   Signa moves planctus aedita consulibus?
> Que tibi causa mali, felix o gloria mundi?

---

34. "Une quidam cum interesset, ita mirando prorupit: *Sancta Maria quid est . . .*" See *Poeta*, V, 466.

Cur manant oculi? Que tibi causa mali?
Plaude, parens patriae, rorantia lumina terge,
   Spem retinens venie plaude parens patriae.
15  Martyrii precio cecidit si prima propago,
   Stas renovata modo martyrii precio.
Limina primus adit silvis digressus arator,
   Nunc tua piscator limina primus adit.
Pulvere multiplici crines fedaverat ille,
20   Hic te mundat aquis pulvere multiplici.
Paulus ovile tuum pascens educit aquatum
   atque refert stabulis Paulus ovile tuum.

(5)  A scion of consuls, O Rome, thou has counted thy triumphs;
   and thou showest signs of mourning, a scion of consuls?

(6)  What causes thy grief, O happy glory of the world? Why are
   thine eyes wettened? What causes thy grief?

(7)  Be joyful, fatherland-bearer; dry thy bedewed eyes. Thou hast
   not forfeited hope of forgiveness; be joyful, fatherland-bearer.

(8)  If by the price of martyrdom thy first offspring drooped, it is
   for price of martyrdom only that thou standest renewed.

(9)  The first to leave the forests and approach thy precincts was
   the ploughman; now it's the fisherman who first approaches
   thy precincts.

(10) With dirt and dust the ploughman's hair was stained; the
   fisher cleanses thee with water from dirt and dust.

(11) Paul tending thy flock leads the sheep out of the water, and
   back to the fold Paul leads thy flock

The poet addressing Rome has chosen and composed his words with
very great care. The first three distichs (5–7) are balanced by the last
three (9–11), and the whole allocution hinges on the central distich
(8). The first three refer to Roma's great past: she had her triumphs
and there is no reason for her to mourn and weep because it is not too
late for forgiveness. The last three hail the presence of the Apostles
Peter and Paul: they are responsible for the baptism of the Roman peas-
ant who founded the city. The antithesis of pagan past and Christian
present dissolves in the central couplet: Rome's first race languished
when it rudely martyred the first heroes of Christian faith—Rome,
today, stands renewed on account of those heroes of faith which she

martyred. The central distich contains also the catchword of the Roman *Renovatio* movement of those days—*stas renovata*. But the renewal
has not the political connotations which that notion has on so many
other occasions.[35] Rome is renewed by baptism, because her second race
has received through the blood of her martyr-apostles the sacrament of
rebirth and regeneration. To these words of the poet Rome gives a long
reply, which here shall be broken up in three sections of first five, then
four, finally again five distichs.

> Respondet Roma
>     Quid memoras titulos aut cur insignia prisca
> Obicis in vultum? Quid memoras titulos?
> 25    Enitui facie toto memorabilis orbe,
>     Callida sed vulpes enitui facie.
> In mediis opibus meretrix nocturna
>     Induo prostituens, in mediis opibus.
> Nec metuens dominum proieci carmine vultum
> 30    Offendens nimium nec metuens dominum.
>     Semino nunc lacrimas ad sere gaudia messis
> Et post dilicias semino nunc lacrimas.

(12)  Why do you recall my titles or cast to my face insignia of
      by-gone days? Why do you recall my titles?

(13)  Resplendent was my face and memorable in the whole world;
      but it was the face of a sly vixen that was resplendent.

(14)  In the midst of treasures I prostituted myself, a nocturnal
      whore cloaking herself in her huds [?] in the midst of
      treasures.

(15)  Lacking fear of the Lord, I debased my face through charms,[36]
      too great an offense and lacking fear of the Lord.

(16)  Tears I sow now for the joy of a late reaping, and after
      delights, tears I sow now.

---

35. Schramm, *Renovatio*, 1, 151, says that the *renovatio* is "*ganz ins Kirchliche gewendet.*" This
is correct, but the main thing is the reference to the *renovatio* of baptism.

36. Novati (above, n. 18), p. 173, has changed *carmine* into *crimine* against all manuscripts.
There is no reason for an emendation. Rome charges herself, not with crime, but with su-
perstition, her belief in charms and incantations. Cf. Juvenal, *Sat.*, VI, 133, from whom, as
Strecker has pointed out, the author has borrowed. See next note.

Since the poet started by conjuring Rome's great past, Roma too recalls in her reply her former glories as well as her former sins. She herself is that *meretrix Augusta*, Messalina, who, according to Juvenal, despite all her treasures sneaked away at night from the imperial couch and offered herself in one of Rome's brothels to any comer, asking and taking from each his fee.[37] Therefore Roma, while identifying herself with the imperial harlot and other sinners of the past, had good reasons for being in tears. However, mediaeval Rome has learnt where to find salvation, and now indicates to the poet the God whose image was approaching the procession.

[Handwritten addendum to typed manuscript: "As Basil of Seleucia put it—Roma herself takes off her diadem and casts herself in the dust at the message of the Cross. *Oratio*, 30, 1, PG 85, 336A/337A. Hugo Rahner, "Navicula Petri," *Zeitschrift für katholische Theologie* 69 (1947), 11, n. 47."]

> Gaudia sustinui, lucrum si prima recepi,
> > Purificancte deo gaudia sustinui.
> 35   Nec procul est opifex gemmam carbone refingens,
> > Et gremium pandens nec procul est opifex.
> En ubi vultus adest querens oracula matris,
> > Pre natis hominum en ubi vultus adest?
> Vultus adest domini, cui totus sternitur orbis,
> 40   Signo iudicii vultus adest domini.

(17)   Joys I sustained, but if really I profited from being the first in the world, it is through the purifying God that joys I sustained.

(18)   Not far away is the artisan who with a coal refashions the gem and expands the pale, not far away is the artisan.

---

37. Rome as whore before her conversion is a common phrase; see e.g. Humbert of Silva Candida (Schramm, *Renovatio*, 2, 131): ". . . haec etsi meretrix magna prius . . . tamen postmodum desponsata uni viro Christo virginem castam seipsam exhibet." See also the Norman Anonymous, *De ecclesia Romana et Hierosolymtana*, ed. Heinrich Böhmer, *Kirche und Staat in England und in der Normandie im XI. und XII. Jahrhundert* (Leipzig, 1899), 460: "purpuratam meretricem, demonibus prostitutam." It all goes back lastly to the Apocalypse (17, 1ff.) with its clear allusion to Rome; cf. Harold Fuchs, *Der geistige Widerstand gegen Rom in der Antiken Welt* (Berlin, 1938). What the poet, however, alludes to, or repeats verbatim, is Juvenal's story of Messalina (*Sat.*, VI, 166ff.): "sumere nocturnos meretrix Augusta cucullos . . ."

(19) Lo, where actually does the *Volto* appear to seek the shrine of the Mother, he who is far above those born of man, where does the *Volto* appear?

(20) Here [in Rome] it is present, the *Volto* of the Lord before whom the whole world prostrates; in the sign of Judgment it is present, the *Volto* of the Lord.

Rome's supremacy of former days, which has turned into the primacy of the Roman See, has at least one advantage: within her walls Christ himself makes his appearance to visit his Mother. Here, in Rome, he dwells, and before his image the world sinks to the ground like formerly before the Caesars. This then explains the torch procession and the excitement of the people.

> Ergo fremit populus, nec cessant tundere pectus
>     Matres cum senibus, ergo fremit populus.
> Sistitur in solio domini spectabile signum,
>     Theotocosque suo sistitur in solio.
> 45  Hinc thimiama dabunt, hinc balsama prima reponunt,
>     Thus myrramque ferunt, hinc thimiama dabunt.
> Dat scola Greca melos et plebs Romana susurros,
>     Et variis modulis dat scola Greca melos.
> "Kyrie" centuplicant et pugnis pectora pulsant,
>     "Christe faveto" tonant, "Kyrie" centuplicant.

(21) Therefore the people cries, and matrons as well as old men incessantly beat their breasts, therefore the people cries.

(22) On the throne there is seated the venerable sign of the Lord, and the Theotocos is seated on his (her?) throne.[38]

(23) That is why they will offer scents, why they depose the first balm, carry incense and myrrh, why they will offer scents.

(24) The Greek school proffers its chants, and the Roman people add murmur; and in varified tunes the Greek school proffers its chants.

---

38. There is no means to tell whether *suo sistitur in solio* refers to the throne of Christ or to that of Mary, since both are of some importance on that occasion. The Coronation of the Virgin, following her Assumption, was not yet represented in art (see below), but in literature it was a common subject. On the other hand, the throne of the Virgin herself is, according to later legends, carried by angels through the air. See Cecchelli in *Dedalo* 7 [as in n. 23]. Also the representation in . . . [left incomplete].

(25)  "Kyrie'" they centuple and beat their breast with the fists. "Be merciful, Christ" it resounds, and the "Kyrie'" they centuple.

While Roma speaks, the procession has moved forward. The Emmanuel has appeared and has passed by. Now the holy icon has reached the sanctuary of St. Mary. We view, as it were, the back of the individuals who kneel on the steps of the temple, who prepare the ointments for the washing of the feet of the image, listen to the chants of the Greek school and beat their breast while singing three-hundred *Kyrie* and *Christe eleison*. By their cries they now invite also the Virgin to appear. The poet, so to speak, joins the faithful who call for the Virgin, by adding his *Invocatio ad orationem*:

> Sollicitemus ob hoc dominum prece, carmine, lingua,
>     Et matrem domini sollicitemus ob hoc.
> Virgo Maria, tuos clementius aspice natos,
>     Exaudi famulos, virgo Maria, tuos.
> 55  Supplicibus lacrimis tibi grex conspargitur urbis,
>     Alma Maria, fave supplicibus lacrimis.
> Turba gemit populi modico discrimine leti,
>     Sancta Maria, tibi turba gemit populi.

(26)  Let us solicit, therefore, the Lord with prayer, chant and word; also the Lord's mother, let us solicit therefore.
(27)  Virgin Mary, with greater clemency look at your children. Hear thy servants, Virgin Mary.
(28)  In suppliant tears for thee the flock of the City is swimming. Bounteous Mary, be gracious to those suppliant tears.
(29)  The throng groans, a people happy because thou art so little distant. It is for thee that the throng groans.

With this invocation of Christ and Mary the poem might have ended. However, the poet turned back once more to earth, and to the invocations of *Virgo Maria*, *alma Maria*, and *Sancta Maria* he adds that to the *Dei genetrix*, to the mother of the incarnate God, which introduces the supplication for the Emperor.

> Sancta dei genitrix, Romanam respice plebem,
> 60  Ottonique fave, sancta dei genitrix.
> Tercius Otto tue nixus solamine palme,
>     Presto sit venie tercius Otto tue.

Hic tibi, si quid habet, devoto pectore prestat,
  Spargere non dubitat hic tibi, si quid habet.
65   Gaudeat omnis homo, quia regnat tercius Otto
  Illius impero gaudeat omnis homo.

(30)  Holy God-bearer, heed the Roman people and be merciful to
    Otto, holy God-bearer.
(31)  The third Otto, bent on the solace of thy hand, shall be ready
    for thy forgiveness, he, the third Otto.
(32)  If anything he owns, he will give thee all from his heart's
    devotion, nor will he hesitate to distribute for thee all, if
    anything he owns.
(33)  Be there merry every man, for the third Otto rules, and of his
    empire be there merry every man.

It is certainly true that the last four distichs—that is, the *supplicatio* for
the emperor—are of a somewhat inferior quality, and the feeling thrusts
itself upon the reader that those conventional lines might be a later addition. However, they are found in all manuscripts, they are essential,
as shall be seen. Their mediocre quality may derive from the fact that
those traditional phrases of homage to the ruler would usually have
a ring of banality, a banality for which the reader of the highly emotional verses preceding the *supplicatio pro imperatore* has been in no way
prepared.[39]

The artful structure and composition of this extraordinarily finished poem deserve a few words. The poem is written in so-called
"reciprocal" or "serpentine" verses: the pentameter ends in the words
with which the hexameter begins. This playful, if most effectful, com-
positional scheme goes back to Antiquity and was often used in Carolingian circles of poetry. It is not a clue that would allow us to guess
at the home or education of the poet.[40] The inner parallelisms of the
composition at large have been indicated. The Introduction consists
of four distichs, the Conclusion of eight. Similarly, we find that the
"Allocution of Rome" is composed of seven distichs, whereas "Rome's
Answer" doubles that number to fourteen. It is evident that the axis of

39. See, in general Schramm, *Renovatio*, 1, 150, and above, n. 33. It is not likely, however,
that the poem should have ended in line 58: "Sancta Maria, tibi turba gemit populi." A prayer
for the blessing of the Roman People was the natural conclusion.

40. Schramm, loc. cit., says too assuredly: "*jedenfalls war er ein Römer*." There is nothing
to prove either this or the hypothesis of Schneider, *Romgedanke*, that he was a south Italian.

the *Allocutio* is represented by the central distich (8) in which the martyry of Roman Christians is hailed as the cause of the *renovatio* of Christian Rome. A similarly meticulous balance is observed in the *Responsio* of Rome. The fourteen distichs have been grouped in the following way: 5 (12–16), 4 (17–20), 5 (21–25). In the first group of five, Rome repents her former sinful lust. In the last group of five, Roma describes the repentance of the Christian Roman People. The central four distichs are devoted exclusively to the epiphany of the *Deus purificans*, the divine purifyer who makes his appearance as the Emmanuel of the *Volto santo*. Those distichs are actually the axis, not only of Rome's answer, but of the whole poem. It is important, therefore, to eliminate every obscurity from those lines. And an obscurity there certainly is in the 18th distich:

> Nec procul est opifex gemmam carbone refingens,
> Et gremium pandens nec procul est opifex.

## The Coal

What is the meaning of that distich? Who, in the first place, is the craftsman that refashions the "gem" through a "coal"? It is easy enough to point out who alone that craftsman could be. In the preceding distich (17) the poet mentions the Divine Purifyer—*purificancte deo gaudia sustinui*. In the following distich (19), Roma indicates the imminence of the epiphany of the *Volto santo*—*en ubi vultus adest?* In 20, finally, the God is present—*Vultus adest domini*. There can be no doubt that 18, too refers to the God, and that the *opifex* "not far away" can only be Christ Emmanuel. But why does Christ refashion a gem with a coal? Who, or what, is the gem, and what is the coal? If we think of the central distich (8) of the "Allocution" where it is said that Roma stands "renewed" for the price of martyrdom, it may be expected that the other "renewal," the "refashioning" through the Divine Purifyer, would refer likewise to Rome. In other words, the "gem" is undoubtedly Rome. Rome shall be remolded by a *carbo*, and this operation eventually shall result in an expansion of Roma's pale.

But who or what is the miraculous *carbo* which apparently owns the power to transform and expand Rome? We may think of "penitence." We may also think of "purifying fire."[41] But though in the notion "coal"

---

41. Carl-Martin Edsman, *Le baptême de feu* (Uppsala, 1940) has dealt with the fire problem in its theological aspects, but has disregarded the rich material connected with the "coal."

those meanings are certainly implied, they are not very satisfactory in view of the second image, the expansion of Rome's pale, *et gremium pandens*. To think that Rome's *gremium* be burnt out by purifying fire is not a pleasant metaphor; but if so, why should this doleful operation expand the pale? Nor has penitence, all by itself, an expanding power. Those would be not only vague, but bad images—unlikely with a poet who is quite specific and conclusive in the choice of his similes. In distichs 9–11, for example, the allusion to Rome's baptism through St. Peter is very obvious, and so is the allusion to St. Paul's missionary activity which effected the return of the baptized flock (*ovile aquatum*) to the Roman fold. Similarly, the refashioning of the "gem"—Rome— through a "coal" must have some quite specific, and not vague or abstruse, meaning. After all, the "coal" forms the center of Rome's answer just as the "baptism" formed the center of the *Allocutio*.

It is evident that the allusion contained in the 18th distich of the poem has never been given a thought by modern interpreters. In the fragmentary translations and paraphrases of the poem those central lines have been disregarded.[42] Even Karl Strecker, in his careful edition for the *Monumenta Germaniae Historica*, has apparently not realized the full meaning of that figure, since otherwise he would have indicated in his useful commentary that the Bible was referred to. The editor cannot be blamed for negligence. Even though he may have consulted the concordance of the Vulgate, he could not have found the clue, for in the decisive place the Vulgate reads *calculus*, a little stone, instead of *carbo*, the coal. And even had the editor thought of the Roman Mass in which the relevant Bible verse is quoted, it would have been of little avail because the Ordinary of the Mass, as natural, follows the authoritative text of the Vulgate. The Septuaginta, indeed, offers the correct translation and says ἄνδραξ, and this is also that of the King James version which renders the Vision of Isaiah (Is. 6:1–7) as follows:

(1)  . . . I saw also the Lord sitting upon a throne, high and lifted up, and his train filled the temple.
(2)  Above it stood the seraphim . . .
(3)  And one cried unto another, and said Holy, holy, holy, is the Lord of hosts: the whole earth is full of glory . . .

---

42. Paraphrases by Burdach, Schneider, Schramm.

(4)  Then said I, Woe is me! for I am undone; because I am a
man of unclean lips, and I dwell in the midst of a people of
unclean lips: for mine eyes have seen the King, the Lord of
hosts.

(5)  Then flew one of the seraphim unto me, having a live coal
in his hand, which he had taken with the tongs from off the
altar:

(6)  And he laid it upon my mouth, and said, Lo this has touch[ed]
thy lips; and thine iniquity is taken away, and thy sin purged.

It may have been the seventh versicle—"and he laid it [the coal] upon
my mouth"—which eventually caused that seemingly strange interpretation according to which the coal was a foreshadowing of the eucharistic bread, or even signified the eucharist itself, and therewith also
the Emmanuel, the incarnate Christ. This meaning has not passed
unnoticed by modern scholars.[43] The literary and liturgical sources
have been collected, but the dogmatic, ritual, and archeological radiations of that metaphor have never been studied, and also the historical development still needs clarification. It seems justified, therefore,
to trace the history of the coal metaphor here and to spread out the
material relevant to an image which has been generally accepted and
still is recognized by all Eastern Churches. The liturgical sources may
take the lead.

In the West-Syrian liturgy of St. James we find the following prayer
over the censer:

Master and Lord Jesus Christ, O Logos of God, who by his own
free will offered himself to the God and Father on the cross as a

---

43. A few notes by Joseph Brinktrine, "Duae denominationes quibus in liturgiis orientalibus particulae consecratae significantur," *Ephemerides Liturgicae* 50 (1936), 35, was all that
had come to my knowledge when I concluded the manuscript of this paper. Before revising
my manuscript I fortunately chanced upon the study by E. A. Pezopoulos, "CYMBOLAI KPI-
TIKAI KAI GPAMMATIKAI," *Hepetreis Hetaireias Byzantinon Spoudon* 1 (1924), 263ff., a mainly
lexicographical collection of places, and upon Johann E. Eschenbach, *Die glühende Kohle: Die
Auffassung der Stelle Isaias, Kap. 6, Vers 6 und 7, bei den Kirchenvätern und ihre Verwendung in der
Liturgie* (Würzburg, 1927), a far more penetrating study from which I was able to supplement
my patristic material in a few instances and whose observations always proved to be valuable.
I was able to use, through the kindness of the U.C. Library, the copy of this rare book of Drop-
sie College Library. Edsman (above, n. 41) strangely enough has missed that material although
the "coal" is connected also with baptism.

blameless sacrifice, <u>the coal of two natures</u>, which with the tongs touched the lips of the prophet and took away the sin.[44]

In the same liturgy the image appears once more. This time it precedes the communion, as the priest humbly speaks:

> The Lord shall bless us and make us dignified to <u>take with the pure tongs of our fingers the fiery coal</u> and to lay it on the mouths of the faithful as a purification and a renovation of their souls and bodies.[45]

"Coal" appears in that Greek liturgy of the Syrians in two different meanings: (1) it is used as an epithet of the divine and human Christ whereby the phrasing "coal of two natures" would indicate that the prayer over the censer was couched during the early phases of the struggle against the Monophysites, around the middle of the fifth century;[46] and (2) the "fiery coal" of the pre-communion prayer refers directly to the eucharist whereby the tongs of the seraphim and the hands of the priest are put into parallel.

In the Syriac liturgy of the Jacobites (that is Monophysites) a rubric prescribes that the priest, when he himself communicates, "takes the coal from the chalice in the spoon" and speaks:

> *The propitiatory coal of the body and blood of Christ* our God is given to a sinful servant for the pardon of offenses and for the remission of sins.[47]

With due alterations this became the ordinary formula for communicating the clergy at large.[48] The rubric makes it clear that "coal" in this

---

44. F. E. Brightman, *Liturgies Eastern and Western* (Oxford, 1896), 1, p. 32, 4; C. A. Swainson, *The Greek Liturgies Chiefly from Original Authorities* (London, 1884), 216. For the connection of the censer with Isaiah's Vision verse 6:4, may be responsible: "and the house was filled with smoke." Accordingly John the Faster interprets the vessel of the censer as Christ's humanity, the coal in it as his divinity, and the vapor as the sweet savor of the Spirit (J. B. Pitra, *Spicilegium Solesmense*, 4 [Paris, 1853], 442). Also in the Coptic Orders the metaphor is found frequently; see e.g. the Order for the Consecration of the Baptistry, attributed to Peter, Bishop of Benhsa in Upper Egypt (ca. 1086 A.D.): "Tu es thuribulum ex auro mundo quod portat carbonem ignitum benedictum"; H. J. D. Denzinger, *Ritus Orientalium, Coptorum, Syrorum et Armenorum* (Würzburg, 1863–1864), 1, 238; Angelo Mai, *Scriptorum veterum nova collectio* (Rome, 1827), 147.

45. Brightman, 63, 19; Swainson, 314.

46. Eschenbach, 84.

47. Brightman, 103, 2; cf. 102, 28.

48. Brightman, 103, 18, shows the same formula for the communion of priest, deacon, or "Antonian" monk.

case means the consecrated particle of the eucharistic bread placed on
the liturgical spoon with which communion is usually administered in
the Eastern Churches where also the laity, not only the clergy, is communicated in the two species together. The spoon itself appeared as a
simile of the seraphic tongs—just like the hands of the priests in the
Greek St. James—and it was actually called λαβίς, tongs, and in Arabic
*labidan*.[49] That the spoon was not generally used can be gathered from
the Greek liturgies of Syria from the fifth to the eighth century, since
the rubric advises the faithful to receive the holy bread in their crossed
hands and to touch "with the divine coal eyes, lips, and faces."[50] The
purification of the senses with the eucharist, or "coal," was a custom
of Syro-Egyptian origin;[51] it is mentioned as late as the eighth century
by John of Damascus who frequently refers also otherwise to the coal
of Isaiah.[52]

In Syria, the equation of "coal" with Christ and the eucharist must
go back to relatively early times. It is found in the liturgies of the
Eastern Syrian Churches, above all in the rite of the Nestorians; and
since the secession of the Nestorians from the orthodox Church and
from Antioch took place after 431 A.D., it follows that the expression
"coal" for the eucharistic bread or the particles must have been popular among the Eastern Syrians before that secession. A rubric in the

---

49. For the liturgical spoon in general, see Joseph Braun, *Das christliche Altargerät in seinem
Sein und in seine Entwicklung* (Munich, 1932), 265-79, with reproductions, also Eschenbach,
78ff. Those spoons are not at all rare; see Enrico Giovagnoli, "Una collezione di vasi eucaris-
tici scoperti a Canoscia," *Rivista di archeologia cristiana* 12 (1935), 323-25, figs. 6-7, who dates
the spoons fifth to sixth century; a great number of early eucharistic spoons is found in the
Dumbarton Oaks Collection, in Washington. See for the name λαβίς Brightman, 588, and for
*labidan*, Eusèbe Renaudot, *Liturgiarum orientalium collectio* (Paris, 1715-16), 1, 283. According
to Braun, 272, the spoon was made in Constantinople for the first time by the Patriarch Pho-
tius, at the Synod of 861 [followed by parenthesis remaining blank in the typescript]. However, in *De sacra Liturgia*, ascribed to John the Faster (582-95 Patriarch of Constantinople), the
spoon seems to be known: [much Greek given here]. Pitra, *Spicilegium Solesmense*. See below,
notes 63, 64 [but these notes are missing].

50. Brightman, 484, 11. Appendix D.

51. John of Damascus, *De fide orthodoxa*, IV, c. 13, PG 94, 1149, is the source of Brightman's reconstruction (p. 484, 11). The place is interesting also for the custom of touching
eyes, lips, and face with the eucharist. See also Origen, *Homily 5*, PG 13, 236. For the problem,
see Franz Joseph Dölger, "Das Segnen der Sinne mit der Eucharistie," *Antike und Christentum* 3
(1932), 231-44. The custom recalls the *taurobilium* since the neophyte took care that his senses
(ear, nose, eyes, lips) were touched by the blood of the victim; see the frequently quoted lines
of Prudentius, *Liber Peristephanon*, X, 1034-39, ed. Albert Dressel, *Aurelii Prudenti Clementi quae
extant carmina* (Leipzig, 1860); Nock, *Conversion*. . . [rest is blank in typescript].

52. See, e.g. PG 94, 1149B; PG 96, 630C-D, 677A, 689C, 848D; and below, p. [left blank
in typescript].

Nestorian liturgy—so-called of Addai and Mari, the East Syrian apostles—prescribes at the Fraction of the Bread that "the priest shall break the body and dip a coal (into the chalice) for the children," the faithful.[53] This rubric might be a later insertion. However, there is more than one fifth-century evidence for the fact that the East Syrians and the Nestorian liturgists were well acquainted with the coal metaphor. Narsai, the former professor of Edessa and, after 457, the head of the Nestorian school of Nisibis, writes in his "Homily on the Mysteries of the Church":[54]

> A coal of fire Isaiah saw coming towards him, which the Seraph of fire held in a hand of fire . . . It was not a sensible vision that the seer saw; nor did the spiritual one bring towards him a material coal. An intimation he saw in the coal of the Mystery of the Body and Blood, which, like fire, consumes the iniquity of mortal man. The power of that mystery which the prophet saw, the priest interprets; and as with a tongs he holds fire in his hand with the bread. The priest fills the place of the seraph in regard of the people . . . The seraph of the spirit did not hold in his hand the vision of spirit: and this is a marvel—that a hand of flesh holds the Spirit.

Here the coal is clearly the simile of the eucharistic bread; the seraph is the prototype of the priest, though less privileged, for whereas the angel dared touch the fiery coal with the tongs only the priest is allowed to hold it with his hands of flesh without being burnt.[55]

Narsai introduces the discussion of Isaiah's coal in connection with the *Sanctus* of the Mass. This is, of course, a most legitimate association, since the angelic cry "Holy! Holy! Holy!" belongs to the vision of Isaiah: it immediately precedes the action of the seraph who touches the prophet's lips with the coal. Accordingly, Narsai discusses the "coal" after the *Sanctus*. This agrees with the Nestorian liturgy of Addai and Mari in which immediately after the "Holy!" a prayer is said which consists practically in a paraphrase of the Vision of Isaiah: the priest entreats the Lord of Hosts that he may purge the lips of the officiating priest from uncleanliness and also those of the faithful.[56] The Nestorian liturgy likens in that respect the liturgy as represented by Theodore of Mopsuestia who likewise elaborates on Isaiah and the coal after the

53. Brightman, 293, 38.

54. R. H. Connolly and Edmund Bishop, *The Liturgical Homilies of Narsai* (Cambridge, 1909), pp. 57–58, cf. p. 67, last paragraph.

55. Above, n. 45, and below . . . [left blank].

56. Brightman, 284, 21ff.

"Holy!" of the Mass whereas the West-Syrian liturgies usually adduce the coal metaphor before the "Holy!" In the West-Syrian Anaphorae ascribed to John Chrysostom, Philoxenos of Hierapolis or Mabogh (†ca. 523), James of Serugh (†521), James of Edessa (†708), and doubtless in other liturgies as well, the coal of Isaiah leads to the "Holy" rather than from the "Holy!" away.[57] In those liturgies, however, it is the angels who are compared with coals or themselves become coals whose fiery being equals Christ or borrows its flame from the Spirit. They are mediators of the true coal which descends from the celestial altar to the terrestrial and though they are bearers of the divine coal, they themselves have a "coal-like being."[58] In other words, the mediator of the coal himself becomes a likeness of the coal. Hence, the apostles are sometimes called coals.[59] Here then enters also that ever repeated comparison of the Mass-celebrating priest with the fiery seraph. He, the priest, takes "with the tongs of his hands" the "coal of two natures" from off the altar to distribute the particles to the faithful who become a likeness of the prophet: "Ye all are Isaiahs."[60]

Although in the Alexandrian theological literature the equation of coal and host was indeed very popular, the classical Egyptian liturgy of "St. Mark" does not contain the metaphor, nor is it found in the earlier forms of Egyptian liturgies.[61] However, in the Coptic Anaphora of Cyril

---

57. Alphonse Mingana, *Commentary of Theodore of Mopsuestia on the Lord's Prayer and on the Sacraments of Baptism and the Eucharist* (Cambridge, 1933), p. 101?? [*sic*]. See Francis J. Reine, *The Eucharistic Doctrine and Liturgy of the Mystagogical Catecheses of Theodore of Mopsuestia* (Washington, 1942), p. 132, also 134, n. 35. For other places in which Theodore quotes Isaiah 6:6, see Reine, pp. 42–43, and below. Syrian Chrysostomos: Renaudot, 2, 244 ("virtutes mirandae carbonis ardentis"); Jean Michel Hanssens, *Institutiones liturgicae de ritibus orientalibus* (Rome, 1932), 3:2, 607, No. 45; Anton Baumstark, *Geschichte der syrischen Literatur mit Anschluss der christlichen Texte* (Bonn, 1922), p. 301, n. 8. Philoxenos: Renaudot, 2, 311 ("Seraphim . . . qui oribus igne textis et labiis carbonibus opertis trinam sanctificationem concinunt"); Hanssens, p. 613, No. 66; Baumstark, 143, n. 13. James of Serugh: Renaudot, 2, 358 ("[*Seraphim*] oribus igneo ardore et labiis carbonum instar inflammatis"); Hanssens, p. 605, No. 33; Baumstark, 158, n. 5. James of Edessa: Renaudot, 2, 372 ("Ordines mirabilles et timendi ex carbonibus ignis levissimi constantes, qui te laudant" and "Cherubim carbones ferentes"); Hanssens, 605, No. 32; Baumstark, 254, n. 8. See also Eschenbach, 87–88, who rightly stresses the intimate interrelations between the *Sanctus* and Isaiah's coal.

58. Pezopoulos, p. 266, adduces several places.

59. Pezopoulos, p. 266; see also *Triodion* [no more citation given], p. 273, the chant sung at the morning service on Thursday of the second week in Lent (on the same day Isaiah 6, 1ff., was the lesson; p. 277) composed by Josephus, one of the martyrs of iconoclasm (see Wilhelm von Christ and Matthaios K. Paranikas, *Anthologia graeca carminum christianorum* [Leipzig, 1871], p. XLVIII).

60. [From here through note 69 indication of notes appear in the text, but the notes themselves either were never written or are lost.]

61.

of Alexandria, which served the Jacobites (Monophysites) and which was under the influence of the Syrian liturgies, we find the coal simile. A prayer after the Fraction reads:[62]

> As thou didst cleanse the lips of thy servant Isaiah, the prophet, when one of the seraphim took a live coal in the tongs from off the altar and laid it on his mouth . . . , in like manner for us . . . , thy servants, vouchsafe to purge our souls and our lips and our hearts, and grant us this true coal, quickening soul and body and spirit,[63] which is the holy body and the precious blood of thy Christ.

Here the "true coal" indicates clearly the eucharist. The metaphor appears once more in a very late prayer over the liturgical spoon: the priest entreats God to bestow upon the spoon ready to hold the coals the power and glory of seraphic tongs.[64] That prayer is found verbatim in the liturgy of the Abyssinian Monophysites which depended on the Coptic rite of Alexandria;[65] and in the Abyssinian ritual the image appears once more when the priest, while setting the host on the paten, speaks:[66]

> Now our God, bless with thine hands and hallow and cleanse this paten *filled with live coal*, even thine own holy body, which we have presented on thine holy altar.

From the Byzantine liturgies, Basil and Chrysostom, the metaphor is plainly absent. Only in the Byzantine period a formula has been integrated into the Chrysostomos liturgy which at the communion recalls the heavenly prototype, the words of the seraph: "This touched thy lips and has taken away thine iniquity, and thy sins purged." These words are repeated by the priest when he offers the spoon, to the communicant.[67] The Armenian liturgy, finally, has in the "Apologies" when the priest first approaches the altar, a prayer in which the priest asks God to cleanse him like Isaiah by means of a coal before he, the priest, takes the "manna of life."[68]

---

62.
63.
64.
65.
66.
67.
68.

To the Byzantine liturgical orbit, however, there belongs yet another prayer to be said at the dismissal "behind the ambon" which clearly equals Isaiah's coal with the eucharist. The Greek has not always the same wording; it varies according to the occasion and the feast of the day.[69] For the dismissal on Holy Saturday there was used, at some date, a form containing the following versicles:[70]

To-day we have seen our Lord Jesus Christ on the altar.
To-day we have seized upon the *coal of fire* in the
shadow of which the cherubim have sung.

The learned editor of that prayer claims that it belongs to the fourth century or even to the third.[71] Therewith the question arises at what date the equation of Isaiah's coal with the eucharist could possibly have entered into the liturgies, and this question makes an examination of the literary texts imperative.

Origen, who died in 253, seems to have been one of the first authors to have linked the Vision of Isaiah with Christ.[72] However, his interpretation of that Vision is not connected with communion. He holds that the seraphim standing on the right and left sides of the divine throne were only two in number and that they were Christ and the Holy Spirit; and he maintains that the seraph holding the coal—and not the coal itself—was a prefiguration of Christ.[73] To be sure, Christ with the coal in his hand approached the prophet and cleansed his lips. But the spiritualist Origen does not believe in the efficacy of the action *ex opere operato*. He admits that "the fire shall cleanse my mouth" but adds that "unless my mouth has been cleansed, the fire does not touch my lips."[74] That is to say, an inner purification has to precede the purification by the seraph with the coal. That on other occasions Origen interprets the divine fire as the word of God is true, and it is true also that by this circle the coal or fire would be the Word, the incarnate Christ.[75] But Origen does not draw that conclusion, as has been noticed already by St. Jerome . . .

---

69.
70. [Supplied from penultimate version: N. Borgia, "Frammentini liturgici antichissimi inediti," *Byzantinische Zeitschrift* 30 (1930), 347.]
71.
72.
73.
74.
75.

[At this point the "final draft" of the article breaks off. Since the remainder can be supplied by the "penultimate draft," that is done here, with renumbered footnotes.]

St. Jerome discusses the verse of Isaiah on various occasions. He puts forth his arguments against Origen's "nebulous allegory," which he himself had adhered to in former days, and declared that the coal represents the purifying *sermo Dei*, that is the Logos.[76] However, he does not equate the coal with the Host although this equation then has been already, so to speak, on the tip of the pen of his contemporaries. Basil, like Jerome, compares the coal with the Logos, but he adds the words "which is placed on our mouths."[77] It may be that by the time of St. Basil (†379) the "coal" has been introduced already into the liturgy proper provided that some liturgical fragments, which are claimed to fall in the fourth century, really belong to that period. [Here Kantorowicz presents the "Today we have seen" versicle used in the "final draft" and hence omitted.]

This, indeed, seems to imply that the "coal of fire" was equal with the host. The equation at any rate is fully developed by the late fourth century as may be gathered from St. John Chrysostom (†407). On one occasion he says that the seraph took the coal from the altar where the hosts were laid out.[78] In another connection, Chrysostom offers the interpretation characteristic of Syria. The seraphim, says he in a sermon, did not dare to touch the coal with the hand, they used tongs—"you, however, take the coal with the hand."[79] We may conclude that the metaphor reached its final growth by the end of the fourth century and that it spread very quickly. The double nature of the coal—live and dead, red and black[80]—made it a symbol applicable to the dogmatic struggle, and the phrasing of the liturgy of St. James—"the coal of two natures"—indeed shows clearly that the metaphor was involved in these disputes.

---

76. Hieronymus, *In Esaiam*, VI, 1–7, ed. G. Morin, *Anecdota Maredsolana*, III, 3 (*Maredsou* [*sic*], 1903), p. 122: "non ergo unum de Seraphin, sed carbo quem tulerat de altari, ignitus videlicet sermo Dei atque docrina, abstulit iniquitates prophetae, et peccata mundavit." Cf. ibid., pp. 105ff., 121, and Jerome's *Tractatus de Psalmo CXIX*, ed. Morin, op. cit., III, 2 (1897), p. 227.

77. Basilius, *In Isaiam*, c. VI, PG 30, col. 435. In *In Isaiam*, c. V, ibid., 430A, however, Basil compares the coal with the Second Advent of Christ.

78. Chrysostom, *In Isaiam*, VI, PG 56, col. 73.

79. Chrysostom, *In illud: Vidi Dominum*, VI, 3, PG 56, cols. 138–39. Cf. Franz J. Dölger, in *Antike und Christentum*, 5 (1936), 237, n. 15. See also Chrysostom's *Homilia XLVII*, PG 63, col. 898, where again the priest represents the seraph.

80. Hilarius, *Tractatus in Psalmum CXIX*, PL 9, col. 650A: "Sitque vel devastans carbo vel purgans." Augustinus, *Ennaratio in Psalmum CXIX*, c. 5 PL 37, col. 1601: "Nam extincti carbones mortui dicuntur; ardentes vivi appellantur."

In the Liturgies of Byzantium—"Basil" and "Chrysostom"—the word coal itself is not found. Nevertheless, it is most popular among the Byzantine theologians and interpreters of the liturgy, as "Chrysostom" alludes to it.[81] It here may suffice to quote the Patriarch Germanus of Constantinople (†733) whose exposition on the Mass was well known in Rome because in the late ninth century it had been translated into Latin by Anastasius Bibliothecarius. This translation in its turn has been copied several times in the tenth century. Germanus writes:[82]

> That other image, however, namely the one referring to the seraph holding a coal in his hand, which he has carried from off the altar with the tongs, signifies the priest, who holds *the intelligible coal, Christ,* in the tongs of his hand over the holy altar, and who sanctifies and purifies those that receive it and communicate.

This again is the Syrian interpretation—the hands replacing the seraphic tongs—which perhaps Chrysostom has popularized in Constantinople. Chrysostom's successor in the patriarchal see, Germanus, has the tendency of extolling the priest whose seraphic character he illustrates in the following way:[83]

> Regarding the imitation of the seraphic powers, the priests by their stoles are covered, as it were, with two wings; and with two wings, their lips, they sing the (seraphic) hymn; and they hold *the divine and spiritual coal,* Christ, raising it with the tongs (of their hands) above the altar.

---

81. Brightman, op. cit., 395, 26, where Isaiah 6:7 is quoted when the deacon communicates; cf. Brightman, 103, 18, where the same observance is found in the Syriac liturgy of the Jacobites, deriving probably from the custom to communicate the clergy with the particle signed XC (χριστός) while the laity is communicated with the particle signed NI-KA.

82. "Illud vero quod missus est unus de seraphim et accepit carbonem in manu, quem forcipe tulerat de altari, significat sacerdotem et ipsum tenentem intelligibilem carbonem Christum forcipe manus suae in sancto altari et sanctificantem atque purgantem eos, qui accipiunt et communicant." Germanus, *Historia mystica,* c. 60, ed. S. Pétridès, "Traités liturgiques de Saint Maxime et de Saint Germain traduits par Anastase le Bibliothécaire," *Revue de l'orient chrétien* 10 (1905), 362; cf. PG 98, col. 433 for the interpolated Greek text.

83. Germanus, c. 16, ed. Pétridès, 313: "et presbyteri quidem secundum imitationem seraphicarum virtutum sunt, qui stolis quasi alis cooperti et duabus alis, labiis scilicet, hymnum clamantes retinent divinum et spiritalem carbonem Christum hunc forcipes gratiae in altari ferentes." Cf. PG 98, col. 393, where the text is at variance with the translation of Anastasius. Cf. *supra,* n. 72, for the seraphim as represented by the priests. For the elevation of the host as referred to by Germanus, see Josef A. Jungmann, *Die Stellung Christi im liturgischen Gebet* (Münster, 1925), 213.

Byzantium, as may be mentioned, *en passant*, harbored one of the very few churches dedicated to "St. Isaiah."[84] Moreover, pictorial representations of the angel carrying the live coal to Isaiah are not rare in Byzantine art.[85] They are indeed very common in Egypt, and we are told that in Cairo the scene is frequently depicted in the apses of Coptic churches as well as on the canopies vaulting over the altar.[86] As far as Byzantium is concerned it is worth mentioning that the metaphor was adduced in a curious way by the Metropolitan Eustathius of Thessalonica in an address to Emperor Manuel Comnenus (ca. 1173).[87] The rhetor expands on the radiancy of the imperial diadem. He mentions the traditional two rows of pearls in the diadem, which according to him represent the *logoi*, of the Trinity;[88] he further mentions the fire apparently of a ruby in the diadem which he compares to the incarnation of the Logos represented by the coal of Isaiah. The comparison is as strange as it is interesting. It reminds us of the famous "Orphan": the legendary ruby (*carbo* or *carbunculus*) in the crown of the Western Emperors.[89] Also we may recall that the most caesarean of all mediaeval popes, Boniface VIII, who placed on the top of his extremely high tiara, one ell in length, a *carbo* which is described in the official papal

---

84. Jean Paul Richter, *Quellen der Byzantinischen Kunstgeschichte* (Vienna, 1897), 163. Byzantine theologians allude to the "coal" of Isaiah until the latest times of the Empire; cf. e.g. Theodore of Melitene, *Ethicon*, caps. 10, 16, ed. Angelo Mai, *Nova patrum bibliotheca* 6 (Rome, 1852), 486, 491.

85. See, e.g., the late ninth century Homilies of Gregory of Nazianzen (Paris, Bibl. Nat. MS gr. 510, fol. 67$^v$) in Henri Auguste Omont, *Miniatures des plus anciens manuscrits grecs de la Bibliothèque Nationale du VIe au XIVe siècle* (Paris, 1929), pl. XXV; further, an ivory plaque, now in Orléans, Musée historique, reproduced by Adolph Goldschmidt, *Die byzantinischen Elfenbeinskulpturen* (Berlin, 1930 [Kantorowicz gives 1918]), 2, no. 193, pl. LXX (9th–10th century) and closely related to the Ascension in Petersborough; cf. I, no. 137/138. The Princeton "Index of Christian Art" kindly called my attention not only to the works of art as quoted but also to a Psalter (10th–12th cent.) in the National Library in Athens (MS. 7, fol. 243$^v$), cf. Paul Buberl, *Die Handschriften des Nationalbibliothek Athens* (Athens, 1917), pl. XIX (45). See also the Serbian Psalter in Munich (Staatsbibl. slav. 4, fol. 195$^v$, 14th–15th cent.), J. Strzygowski, *Der serbische Psalter*, pl. XLVIII, fig. 114.

86. See, e.g., C. Stornajoio, *Le miniature della Topografia Cristiana di Cosma Indicopleuste* (Milan, 1908), pl. 37. The paintings in the Coptic churches of Old-Cairo have been mentioned by Anton Baumstark, in *Oriens Christianus*, 4 (1904), 427, but I have not been able to trace any reproduction of these images.

87. Eustathius of Thessalonica, *Oratio ad Manuelem imperatorem*, ed. Wilhelm Regel, *Fontes rerum byzantinarum* (St. Petersburg, 1917), 53, 17ff.; PG 125, col. 968D.

88. "Pearls" is likewise a popular metaphor for the particles of the eucharistic bread; cf. Brinktrine, in the article quoted above, n. 43.

89. Franz Kampers, "Der Waise," *Historisches Jahrbuch* 39 (1918/19), 433–86.

**FIGURE 5.1**  Statue of Pope Boniface VIII by Arnolfo di Cambio (executed ca. 1300), Museo dell'Opera del Duomo, Florence. Wikimedia Commons, public domain. Photo: Divot.

records as well as in the poem of Cardinal Jacopo Stefaneschi, who writes:[90]

... gemmis radiantibus auro Vallatum in gyrum, cui summo in vertice carbo evomit et cubito gemmarum maxima flamma, imposuit capiti ...

Did these *carbones*, the Western imperial and papal, symbolize like the stone in the diadem of the Basileus the "coal" of Isaiah?

---

90. F. X. Seppelt, *Monumenta Coelestiniana. Quellen zur Geschichte des Papstes Coelestin V.* (Paderborn, 1921), 98; Émile Molinier, "Inventaire du trésor du Saint Siège sous Boniface VIII (1295)," *Bibliothèque de l'École des Chartes* 45 (1884), 47–48, 667: "In summitate autem habet unum rubinum grossum." For the history of this ruby see Konrad Burdach, *Vom Mittelalter zur Reformation* (Berlin, 1913–28), II, 1, pp. 423ff.; see also Gerhart Ladner, "Die Statue Bonifaz' VIII und die Entstehung der dreifach gekrönten Tiara," *Römische Quartalschrift* 42 (1934), 48. Percy Ernst Schramm, "Zur Geschichte der päpstlichden Tiara," *Historische Zeitschrift* 152 (1935), 307–12, has indicated the superabundance of cosmic symbolism as represented by the tiara of Boniface VIII (length of an ell, white peacock feathers etc.) so that the *carbo* topping the papal head-gear is indeed likely to refer to the "coal" of Isaiah.

Admittedly, the "coal" as a metaphor of Christ or the host was not a common image of Western stock and trade. This was impossible, since the Vulgate did not translate *carbo* but *calculus*. Thus it is not a coal but a little stone which, in the prayer *Munda os meum* of the Roman Mass is to cleanse the lips of the deacon before he reads the Gospel, a prayer which, by the way, was introduced at a late period, apparently not before 1200.[91]

In a prayer serving a similar purpose, namely to purify the lips of the priest, the verse of Isaiah is quoted at a much earlier time in the Mozarabic Liturgy. Here, however, we find not the Vulgate version but the more archaic translation *carbo*, which is still found in the late *Missale mixtum* of the rite of Toledo.[92] This may have influenced the arts since Western representations of the "coal" of Isaiah, rare altogether, are found comparatively often in the Hispano-Gallican orbit.[93]

To meet with the "coal" in a Roman poem of ca. 1000 A.D. is not surprising. There is no need to construct a theory about the author's knowledge of Byzantine writers, say of the tractates of Germanus. Byzantium, after all, was the great fashion in Rome under the Ottonian

---

91. It first occurs in the *Ordo Romanus XIV*, c. 53, PL 78, col. 1161C, which in the light of the study of Michel Andrieu, "L'Ordinaire de la Chapelle Papale et le Cardinal Jacques Gaétani Stefaneschi," *Ephemerides Liturgicae* 49 (1935), 230–60, may suggest the introduction under Innocent III.

92. Marius Férotin, *Le Liber Ordinum* (Paris, 1904), 20. The prayer, which here appears in the *Ordo Misse omnimode*, is said to have been a work of Julian of Toledo (680–690), cf. PL 96, col. 760. In the *Missale mixtum* (PL 85, col. 113, cf. col. 538–39) it has the same function, but it is spoken on the first Sunday of Advent on which Isaiah 6, 1–10, serves as a Lesson in the Merovingian Lectionary of Schlettstadt, of ca. 700; cf. Morin, *Études, textes, découvertes* (Maredsous and Paris, 1913), 1, p. 441. It is surprising to find, not the reading of the *carbo* which has survived in the masses, but *calculus* as a Sunday Lesson in the *Liber Comicus*, ed. G. Morin, *Anecdota Maredsolana* I (1893), 331. In the *Liber Comicus* we find on the other hand the archaic reading "Ecce tetigi (for tetigit) labia tua," which is found in Hilarius (*supra* n. 73) and Cassiodorus, *In Psalmum CXIX*, PL 70, col. 903D ("abstuli"). The first person, instead of the third, is found also in the Latin translation of Origen's Homily *In Isaiam* I, 4, ed. Baehrens, p. 246, 19; cf. G. Morin, *Anecdota Maredsolana*, III, 3, p. 122, note to line 7.

93. See, e.g., Wilhelm Neuss, *Die katalanischen Bibelillustrationen um die Wende des ersten Jahrtausends und die alt-spanische Buchmalerei* (Bonn and Leipzig, 1922), pl. XXVIII, fig. 90; furthermore a fresco from S. Maria d'Aneu in the Museum of Barcelona, cf. Josep Gudiol, *Els Primitius*, 1 (Barcelona, 1927), fig. 142; further in a fresco on the south wall of the choir in the church of Vich. For the general problem (Spain and Egypt), see Anton Baumstark, "Die karolingisch-romanische Maiestas Domini," *Oriens Christianus* 23 (1927), 242–60. The scene is found also in the Bible of Charles the Bald (Bibl. Nat., MS lat. 1, fol. 130ᵛ), cf. *Dictionnaire d'archéologie chrétien et de liturgie*., cols. 1577ff., s.v. "Isaie," and in a slightly later (9–10th cent.) ivory plaque, now in the Musée Historique at Orléans; cf. Goldschmidt (as n. 80), 2, no. 193, pl. LXX. In the 13th century, the scene is found in a relief on the cathedral of Amiens; cf. G. Durand, *La cathédrale d'Amiens* (1901–3), 3, pl. XXX. Here again I am greatly indebted to the Princeton Index of Christian Art for the detailed information readily given to me.

dynasty. To write one's name in Greek capitals was common among the educated people. Among the Roman nobility and the clergy the Byzantine party was never stronger than in the tenth century when the Basileus, time and again, tried to re-establish his former hold on Rome by supporting anti-popes who were either of Greek stock or friendly to Byzantine plans.[94] After all, the days of the Greek anti-pope Philagathos (John XVI: 997–998), whose name was assiduously recited in the Byzantine diptychs whereas Byzantium deliberately omitted the names of other popes, was only two years back when the poem was written.[95] The best argument for the Greek substratum, however, is offered by the poet himself: He emphasizes that the *Schola Graeca* sang, on that day, the liturgical chants to the Virgin, whom he styles the *Theotocos*, and to Christ, whose name Emmanuel—a designation unusual in the West—was written with big white letters in the upper part of the *Volto santo*. This name is recurrent in the Eastern liturgies . . . [here a few illegible words].

The 18th couplet of the poem makes perfect sense once we have realized the reference to the coal of Isaiah: Near is the artisan who refashions Rome, the gem, by the power of the eucharist, the coal. In the *Allocutio* the poet mentions the baptism; Roma, in her Response, indicates the communion. Moreover, the powerful "coal" effects also an expansion of Rome's pale, Rome's dominion. With this image the poet alludes to a phrase current since Leo the Great and recurrent ever since: what the Roman sword left unconquered religion gained. Christianity has expanded the Roman dominion far beyond the borders of the ancient empire, has carried the Roman fame to peoples whose names have been unknown to the Caesars or, so as to quote the papacaesarean juridical version of Gregory VII, "more lands has conquered the Law of the Roman Pontiffs than that of the Caesars."[96] In short, it is neither penitence all by itself nor "purifying fire" in a vague and general sense by which Rome has been renewed and refashioned. The poet is quite definite in his formulation. It is Isaiah's "coal," the power of the host,

---

94. See P. E. Schramm, "Kaiser, Papst und Basileus in der Zeit der Ottonen," *Historische Zeitschrift* 129 (1924), 424–75; Anton Michel, *Humbert und Kerullarios* 1 (Paderborn, 1924), pp. 11ff.

95. Cf. Michel, 16, n. 7.

96. Gregory VII, *Registrum*, II, 75, ed. Erich Caspar, MGH, Episotolae selectae II, p. 257. For Leo the Great, PL 54, col. 423: "*civitas sacerdotalis et regia . . . latius praesideres religione divina, quam dominatione terrena,*" and ibid., note a, the famous line of Prosper of Aquitaine: "*quidquid (Roma) non possidet armis/Religione tenet.*"

which has effected the second world domination of Rome—a Rome, not of Caesars, but of Apostles, Martyrs, and Pontiffs.

## Lustration and Theophany

Some efforts have been made to link the ritual, observed at the Assumption-Day procession, with antique rites of lustration.[97] The idea is doubtless tempting, nor shall the persistence of antique traits here be denied. The ritual washings of the image at the various stations inevitably would recall the washing of the image of Cybele in the Almo at the annual procession.[98] To believe in a relationship with the *Magna Mater* cult may appear as all the more legitimate as the *Mirabilia urbis Romae* (ca. 1140) mention that the Basilica of S. Maria Maggiore was built on the ground on which formerly a temple of the Great Mother had its place.[99] Moreover, Christ appears in the poem as the *Deus purificans*, and the purification of Rome and the Romans is one of the main topics of the poem. Finally, in a second poem on the Assumption celebrations in Rome (it is directed to Emperor Henry II, Otto's successor) Christ is called "flamen immensus purgans crimina mundi."[100] Hence there is some justification for laying stress on the lustral character of the ceremony. But one will hesitate to assent to the suggestion that the carrying of torches—by that time a common Christian custom—indicates an additional element of lustral magic.[101] We may ask instead whether the Roman *pompa* on August 15th had not an altogether different meaning and whether the lustral elements were not accessories rather than the essence of a performance the nature of which fortunately can be defined quite unambiguously.

The source for the nocturnal celebrations and the Roman torch procession, in fact, is as canonical and legitimate as it could be, and there is no need of seeking hazardous survivals and rudiments of some

---

97. Schneider, Burdach, *locis citatis*; cf. Schramm, *Kaiser, Rom und Renovatio*, I, p. 152, n. 5, reduces these pagan cultural influences. [Here a handwritten addition, the opening of which is difficult to decipher, ends with reference to an article by L. Huebner, ". . . in the Roman Procession" in *Bollettino dell'Associazione internazionale degli studi mediterranei* 6 (1935-36), 1ff.]

98. Georg Wissowa, *Religion und Kultus der Römer* (2nd ed., Munich, 1912), p. 319, n. 7; R. Heberdey, "Δαιτίξ: Ein Beitrag zum ephesischen Artemiscult," *Jahresheft des Österreichischen Archäologischen Instituts in Wien* 7 (1904), 213, n. 10; Otto Gruppe, *Griechische Mythologie und Religionsgeschichte* (Munich, 1906), s.v. "Bad."

99. See the edition of Schramm, op. cit., 2, p. 88, §25: "*Ubi nunc est Sancta Maria ad Praesepe, fuit templum Cybeles.*"

100. MGH, Poetae latini, 5, 468, line 5.

101. Schneider, op. cit., 151.

particular pagan cult. In the Gelasian Sacramentary there is found, in the Mass of Assumption Day, the following prayer:[102]

> Castimoniae pacem mentibus nostris atque corporibus interce- dente sancta Maria propitiatus indulge, ut *veniente sponso* Filio tuo unigenito *accensis lampadibus eius digni praestolamur occursum.*

According to the Mass of that day, the procession is an *occursus accensis lampadibus*, a solemn reception, at the *Adventus* of the divine bridegroom. From the present *Missale Romanum* that prayer has been eliminated, but the oldest layers of the Assumption liturgy make it evident that originally a *Parousia*, an epiphany of Christ, was inseparable from the Virgin's Assumption.[103]

This concept is supported by the second Roman poem on Assumption. These verses represent a paraphrase of a Pseudo-Jeromean letter to Paula and Eustochium, a fabrication of the eighth century, in which the Assumption of St. Mary is broadly discussed.[104] The axis of the poem is formed by Pseudo-Jerome's sentence "Salvator omnium ipse . . . per se totus festivus (Mariam) occurrit et cum gaudio eam secum in throno collocavit." Against it is the *festivus occursus*—in this case of the Lord himself—in which the feast centers.[105]

The Pseudo-Jeromean letter had a wide circulation. It even formed a Lesson of the Office in the Lateran Basilica in which alone by that time the *Antiqua Romani Sedis Consuetudo* was observed. The author of the *Ordo Lateranensis* reports that the canons met with some difficulties at the accomplishment of Vigils on the eve of Assumption because the crown gathering with torches in the Basilica and in front of it was noisy. For this reason the expedient was found to anticipate Vigils by a few hours so that the canons might sing their responsories without disturbance and also listen to the chapters from Pseudo-Jerome's letter which was read as the Lesson on the eve of Assumption Day. The gathering for

---

102. *The Gelasian Sacramentary*, ed. Henry Austin Wilson (Oxford, 1894), 194.

103. The prayer is still found in the *Gregorianum*, cf. PL 78, col. 133, where it belongs to the Vigil of Assumption Day. On the *Adventus* see the author's study, "The 'King's Advent' and the Enigmatic Panels in the Doors of Santa Sabina," *Art Bulletin* 26 (1944) [typescript omits page numbers: they are 207–31]. For the *occursus* of the Virgins [*sic*], see Erik Peterson, "Die Einholung des Kyrios," *Zeitschrift für systematische Theologie* 7 (1930), 682–702.

104. PL 30, cols. 122–42. According to G. Morin, in *Revue bénédictine* 9 (1892), 497 [*sic* for 496—but this reference still does not check out] the letter has been fabricated about 750 A.D., probably in France near Reims. Very many passages of that letter bear upon *occursus* and Epiphany of Christ and Mary.

105. MGH, Poetae latini, 5, 468–69, lines 6–14 ("*Venit totus, ut ille sacer Hieronimus infit. . .*")

the procession thus coincided with the reading of the words "Salvator (Mariam) totus festivus occurrit."[106]

The general concept of the Roman torch procession is obvious. As evidence by three sources (the Mass of that day, the short Assumption poem, and the Lectionary of the Lateran), it was an *occursus*. To be correct, however, the celebration was bifocal. One *occursus* was performed by the people to receive the *Volto santo* and to celebrate the *Parousia* of the Lord. The second *occursus*, at which the procession of the people had the function of a conduct of honor, was performed by the Lord who came to meet his mother, whose Assumption Day was at the same time her "Day of Epiphany."

The antecedents of these performances are well known. Within the Graeco-Roman world, it was a familiar phenomenon to see a deity leave its customary sanctuary once, or even more than once, a year in order to "appear" to the people and dwell for the duration of the festival in another temple. It is a so-called *Epidemy*, a word almost synonymous with Epiphany or Theophany. The ritual observed on the occasion of a journey and of an apparition of a deity was practically always the same: a festival reception, often including a *pompa*, on the part of the people who gathered to conduct the God; hymns soliciting the God to make his appearance; finally the apparition of the God, viz. of the cult image.[107]

None of these elements seems to be missing in the Roman poem. The *Volto santo*, the Emmanuel, is, the "God manifest," whose reception is described in a most picturesque way in the introductory four couplets. *Kletika*, that is hymns or cries inviting the God to appear, which are anything but rare in the *Epiklesis* [Eucharistic prayer] of the Eastern and Hispano-Gallican Masses and which are found in the Roman Mass as well,[108] that is hymns or cries inviting the God to appear, are mentioned *expressis verbis* in the poem:

---

106. *Ordo officiorum Ecclesiae Lateranensis*, ed. Ludwig Fischer (Munich, 1916), 150. Despite the popularity of the Pseudo-Jeromean letter, it does not seem to have served as a Lesson except in the Lateran. Suitbert Bäumer, *Geschichte des Breviers* (Freiburg, 1895), 623–30, does not mention the letter in his list of apocryphal texts which serve as Lessons in the Breviaries.

107. For the *Epidemia*, see Gaston Deschamps and Georges Cousin, "Inscriptions du temple de Zeus Panamaros," *Bulletin de correspondence hellénique* 15 (1891), 178, and in general Christian Pfister, "Epiphanie," in Pauly-Wissowa-Kroll, *Realenzyklopädie der classischen Altertumswissenschaft*, Supplement IV (Stuttgart, 1924), cols. 302ff. §25, and ibid., col. 304, §27.

108. Cf. Petrus Hendrix, "La fête de l'Épiphanie," *Congrès d'histoire du christianiisme: Jubilé Alfred Loisy*, 2 (Paris, 1928), 213–28, at 216–17, who quotes solicitations such as "*Adesto, adesto, Jesu bone pontifex*" in the Mozarabic Liturgy, and "*adesto mysteriis, adesto sacramentis*" in the Roman Missal (Blessing of the Water on Holy Saturday). In the Eastern and Gallican Rites the

> Sollicitemus ob hoc dominum prece, carmine, lingua,
>     Et matrem dominis sollicitemus ob hoc.

That these lines appear at the end of the poem rather than at the beginning is caused by the fact that these *Kletika* are directed also to St. Mary, urging her Epiphany as well. Finally, the apparition proper of the Emmanuel receives a very complete description. "Unde fremit populus?—Nec procul est opifex—En, ubi vultus adest?—Vultus adest domini—Sistitur in solio." These are the various phases of the apparition of the God, a gradual progress towards the climax depicted in an impressive and telling manner.

The reception of the *Volto santo* was but one part of the feast. Christ himself performs an *occursus*, as he comes to meet his mother and to conduct her to heaven. The *parousia* of a God who comes to meet another deity, or a divine ruler, is likewise a ceremony the antecedents of which are found in the Graeco-Roman Antiquity. In the Hadrianic series of *Adventus* (Epiphany) coins, we find among the deities which receive the emperor, not only the personifications of the provinces, but also Sarapis and Osiris. In the arch of Galerius at Salonica, we recognize at the open gates of a temple a deity ready to receive the *Divus* who approaches the city *en grand cortège*. Sometimes the *Divus* would visit at his arrival the shrine of the main deity whose "temple-sharer" or even "throne-sharer" he might be, and offer a libation or a sacrifice.[109] Christian mythology has adopted and "translated" these customs. The Lord, at his *Adventus* in Heaven, was seated as a *synthronos* in the divine throne; and the Lord's Ascension, in its turn, became the model of the Assumption of Mary.[110] According to a later Roman legend, angels transferred the throne of the Saviour to the glaring shrine of the Virgin, while St. Mary herself came to meet her son with a galaxy of angels and saints.[111] The classical version, however, is that the Lord came to meet St. Mary's soul and that "Domino praecedente" angels conducted her

---

*Epiklesis* has the same function, namely to call for the Holy Ghost to appear and transform the elements. See for the various types (*descendat, adesto, emitte, inlabere, infundat*) Hans Lietzmann, *Messe und Herrenmahl* (Bonn, 1926), 93–106.

109. See the author's article quoted above, n. 101.

110. Cf. Friedrich Gerke, "Das Verhältnis von Malerei und Plastik in der theodosianisch-honorianischen Zeit," *Rivista archeologica Cristiana* 12 (1935), 15, who in another connection stresses the fact that the iconographical type of the Theotocos in the throne was modeled after the images of Christ enthroned.

111. Cf. Cecchelli [as n. 23], 316. In this case, St. Mary herself performs an *occursus* to receive her son.

to the throne of Heaven which had been prepared for her "ante mundi constitutionem."[112]

The poem does not mention the Ascension proper nor the Coronation of the Virgin. St. Mary merely appears in the heights as the glorified God-bearer. She, too, becomes manifest and is present in the city; the Roman people, says the poet, is happy because only a very small distance separates the Romans from the Queen of Heaven ("modico discrimine laeti").

The poem, just as the feast, centers in the apparitions first of the Lord, then of Mary. This does not exclude, it rather includes, the lustral character of the ceremonies. Every epiphany of a God has a purifying effect.[113]

The interpretation of the poem as a *parousia*, an Epiphany of both the Lord and the Virgin, explains also the supplication for the emperor at the end of the poem. A similar supplication is found also in the shorter Assumption poem in which Henry II is remembered. The *supplicatio pro imperatore* in this place falls in with the general tradition. When the Gods become manifest, king or emperor becomes manifest too. Such was the custom in the Hellenistic realms, and it survives in Byzantium.[114] In Ottonian Rome this Hellenistic-Eastern subcurrent breaks to the surface once more. This current desiccated definitely in and after the Gregorian Age, when the Roman Pontiff, in taking over the part of the *verus imperator*, was the only one to become manifest at the epiphanies of the celestials.

It is instructive for a full appreciation of the poem to cast a glance at Western and Eastern pictorial representations of the Assumption. Western art in the Gothic period showed a predilection for representing the coronation and inthronization of the Virgin in Heaven. These

---

112. Cf. Gregory of Tours, *De gloria martyrum*, MGH, Scriptores rerum Merovingicarum, 1, 4, p. 493 [passage unlocatable from this citation]. Pseudo-Jerome, Epistola 9, PL 30, col. 130C: ". . . quanto magis credendum est hodierna die militiam coelorum cum suis agminibus festive obviam venisse genitrici Dei, eamque ingenti lumine crcumfulsisse et usque ad thronum olim sibi etiam ante mundi constitutionem paratum, cum laudibus et canticis spiritualibus perduxisse." For the Ascension, not only of the soul, but also of the body of St. Mary, see Anton Baumstark, "Die leibliche Himmelfahrt der allerseligsten Jungfrau und die Lokaltradition von Jerusalem," *Oriens Christianus* 4 (1904), 371–92.

113. There is no need for adducing material, since the Second Coming of the Lord implies the purification of the whole world; see, however, Sophronius, *In occursum Domini*, in PG 88: 3, cols. 3291ff., also cols. 3749ff.

114. See the author's "Epiphany and Byzantine Coronation" [now chapter 3 of the present book].

**FIGURE 5.2**   Koimesis mosaic, Church of Holy Savior in Istanbul, 1320. Wikimedia Commons, CC BY-SA 4.0. Photo: Dosseman.

topics have not been developed in the West before the twelfth century; they were unknown in 1000 A.D. when the poem was written, and they remained completely unknown in the East. Eastern art clung to the very old design of the *Koimesis* which has been adopted by the West during the tenth century but here always betrays its Byzantine origin. The representations of the *Koimesis* show Christ as he appears on earth once more to assist his mother on her deathbed. He comes to meet and to receive her soul which he takes in his arms before handing it over to the care of angelic attendants. Often the *Assunta* appears in the heights as well, in her celestial glory and majesty; the focal point of the *Koimesis* is always the Lord's appearance at the deathbed. The conduct of Mary to Paradise forms as little a subject of Eastern art as her crowning and inthronization.[115]

---

115. Cf. Karl Künstle, *Ikonographie der christlichen Kunst* (Freiburg, 1928), 1, 564ff. See also Marion Lawrence, "Maria Regina," *Art Bulletin* 7 (1925), 156, on the earliest representations

The Crowning of the Virgin takes place in heaven; the *Koimesis* is an occurrence on earth. The religious sentiment of the West, ever since the beginning of the twelfth century and in the age of Gothic mysticism displays an irresistible drift upward, a desire to ascend, a craving after the heavens, away from earth, away from man. The East, as usual much nearer to Graeco-Roman Antiquity, seeks and experiences the break of the divine into the domain of man; it stresses the descent of the heavens to earth, and likes to think of the epiphany of the celestials in this world. This latter is the religious climate of the poem. The *hieros gamos* of the Lord and the Virgin has not yet been removed to a world beyond; it is consummated on earth, and in this case in Rome.[116]

---

of the crowning of the Virgin. The East is familiar, however, with the *Gürtelspende* (St. Mary throwing her belt down from heaven to convince St. Thomas); cf. *Das Handbuch der Malerei vom Berge Athos*, tr. G. Schäfer (Trier, 1855), 279 §396.

116. Cf. Hendrix (as above, n. 108), 227–29. One of the most striking examples for the change in Western attitude is offered by Anton L. Mayer, "Renaissance, Humanismus, und Liturgie," *Jahrbuch für Liturgiewissenschaft* 14 (1938), 166–67, in his interpretation of the early and late forms of the hymn *In dedicatione Ecclesiae* ("*Urbs beata Hierusalem*").

# CHAPTER 6

# Glosses on Late-Medieval State Imagery

The present article evolved through numerous phases. Ralph Giesey reported that "in addition to three drafts meant for publication, there were three drafts in lecture form, much abbreviated." Giesey, who inherited all of these items from his mentor Ernst Kantorowicz along with "two quite thick files of material relevant to 'State Portraits' (Kantorowicz's preferred title for this work) which include dated correspondence revealing that drafts of the lecture predate drafts of the article, related letters and clippings," generously donated all this material to the Kantorowicz archive of the Leo Baeck Institute but unaccountably retrieved it, and since his death everything he mentioned has become unlocatable. What survives is a copy of Giesey's retyped and scanned version of most of the last draft of the article, completed by attachment of the apposite part of the final lecture version. Giesey placed this work online,[1] but it merges notes for his own introduction with notes belonging to Kantorowicz's text without renumbering. Moreover, the production is rife with misprints caused by the use of an optical scanner, a problem compounded by typing

---

1. Ernst H. Kantorowicz, "Glosses on Late-Mediaeval State Imagery," pdfcoffee.com_eka-unpub-glosses-pdf-free%20(6).pdf.

errors and Giesey's shakiness in German. Thus the version offered here is much corrected.

Kantorowicz's article began as a lecture, "Glosses on the State Portrait," delivered at a meeting of the College Art Association in Pittsburgh in January 1956. A few weeks earlier Kantorowicz had written to Leonardo Olschki that it had been a mistake to have accepted the invitation, since he was still in the midst of working on *The King's Two Bodies* and still had many other commitments. Yet he was pleased that the subject "left him interesting things to say."[2] Indeed he was sufficiently satisfied with the lecture to give it again at the Warburg Institute in June 1958 as "Legal Glosses on the State Portrait in the Later Middle Ages." By then he also had transformed the lecture into a more extended article with an alternate title referring to "State Imagery." (It takes little to see that the word "portrait" in the title of the lectures was intended to attract historians of art and that Kantorowicz recognized he had nothing to offer about "portraits" in the conventional sense.) The article, however, was never finished: a few pages remained, as well as the last part of the footnote apparatus. Although the author did intend to complete it—in 1961 he referred to it as "not yet published"[3]—other projects took precedence before he died.

Kantorowicz turned with full energy to Roman and canon law and their respective commentaries in the 1950s. Although he drew on this material most notably in *The King's Two Bodies*, it also provided the substance for several articles, including the present piece, which matured concurrently around 1955 with *The King's Two Bodies*, and an article, "The Sovereignty of the Artist."[4] "State Imagery" treats Frederick II's Capuan gate and descriptions of it by the jurist Lucas de Penna in ways that approximate the same subject in *The King's Two Bodies*; some passages are even duplicated. In addition, "State Imagery" refers to a quotation from Justinian's *Institutes* that appears as well in "The Sovereignty of the Artist." ("Minorum natu non posse maioram adoptare placet: adoptio enim naturem imitatur et pro

---

2. To Leonardo Olschki, December 8, 1955, Olschki Papers, Getty Research Institute, Los Angeles: "Für Ende Januar habe ich dummerweise einen Vortrag in der College Art Association übernommen—'Glosses on the State Portrait'—worin ich den Anteil der Glossatoren, die die Imagines-Gesetze zumal des Codex interpretierten, am Wiederaufkommen des Staatsportraits kurz behandeln will. Friedrich II. gehört mit dem Capuaner Tor natürlich völlig in die Linie der Juristen. Aber es gibt da Interessanteres zu sagen."

3. "The Sovereignty of the Artist: A Note on Legal Maxims and Renaissance Theories of Art," in *De Artibus opuscula XL: Essays in Honor of Erwin Panofsky*, ed. Millard Meiss (New York, 1961), 267–79, here 267, n. 4; reprinted in Kantorowicz, *Selected Studies* (Locust Valley, NY, 1965), 352–65, here 353, n. 4.

4. As previous note.

monstro est, ut maior sit filius quam pater.") Moreover, in "Sovereignty of the Artist" Kantorowicz offers the thesis of "State Imagery" by writing: "we may recall that the laws concerning statues, images, and the decoration of public squares, which are found in considerable numbers in the law books of Justinian, had some effect in so far as they promoted the concept of a profane art."[5] All told it is difficult to tell which of certain similar passages in the three mentioned works preceded the other.

How do edicts from the law books of Justinian and medieval glosses thereupon relate to the emergence of state imagery in public buildings primarily in the early modern period? As customary, Kantorowicz was not aiming to display direct causes but was positing overlaps, in this case "the interrelations between the reappearance of state-official art and the so-called revival of Roman law." He disavows maintaining that the sudden early modern appearance of state imagery in public buildings "was *caused* by the scientific jurisprudence of the glossators of Roman law," but he does wish to say that "the idea of the ruler's omnipresence and his ubiquity in the law courts, and the simple fact that the jurists themselves became—and made others become—conscious of the saintliness of ruler images, should not be dismissed too lightly." He is aware of a chronological gap—that the evidence from "scientific jurisprudence of the glossators" clusters in the thirteenth and fourteenth centuries, whereas it was first in the early modern period that "the image of the ruling prince would be displayed in every assembly hall and court room." Indeed the only chronological correspondence he can adduce between the glossators and state imagery in public buildings is Frederick II's Capuan gate of ca. 1235. But this does not stand in his way.

Discounting the author's indifference to explaining early modern developments, the article is outstanding in its meticulous exposition of how Roman law and its glossators came to attribute "quasi-religious values" to images of the ruler. Kantorowicz's starting point is the fundamental observation that the high-medieval legal glossators "transferred and applied . . . classical knowledge almost directly and with very little qualification to their own surroundings." Consequently these medieval authors discussed such matters as Roman zoning regulations whereby buildings had to be constructed in a straight line for frontage and "public beautification . . . serving for the dignified appearance of a city." Particularly important was the sanctity of imperial statues and images, which were omnipresent in ancient Roman cities. (Commentaries cited examples of the

---

5. Page 353 (267).

crime of changing clothes near a statue of Augustus, and of a woman who was executed for undressing near an image of Domitian; placing one's own statue higher than that of the emperor counted as treason.) Late Roman law also drew equivalences between images of princes and that of saints, thereby reinforcing the rank of the secular. Ruler images in public places were absent in the Middle Ages until the erection of Frederick II's Capuan gate, and thereafter state imagery was fully revived beginning at the start of the sixteenth century.

"Homer" meant one thing to Heinrich Schliemann and another to Babe Ruth or Joe DiMaggio. And "gloss" means one thing to the artist and another to the student of medieval law. Here we will be dealing only with legal glosses, marginal comments made by medieval commentators, chiefly of Roman law, which have importance for the reappearance of state imagery in late medieval and early modern times.

About the reappearance of a more or less official state imagery we are not too well informed. Whereas the student of classics is in a position to acquire without great difficulty a rather sound and full knowledge of the political, legal, and cultural implications of the ruler images in the Hellenistic-Roman world, including Byzantium;[6] and whereas the students of medieval history have taken great strides at evaluating the representations of princes in contemporary miniatures and other works of art,[7] the same cannot be said with regard to the more modern ages: the historians of that period have hardly started to integrate the, so to say, "archaeological" material into their studies in order to secure a more profound understanding of political, constitutional, and

---

6. See, in addition to Kenneth Scott, "The Significance of Statues in Precious Metals in Emperor Worship," *Transactions and Proceedings of the American Philological Association* 62 (1931), 101–23, and Helmut Kruse, *Studien zur offiziellen Geltung des Kaiserbildes im römischen Reich* (Paderborn, 1934), the numerous studies of Andreas Alföldi, Richard Delbrück, H. P. L'Orange and others; for Byzantine, André Grabar, *L'empereur dans l'art byzantin* (Paris, 1936); Ernst Kitzinger, "The Cult of Images in the Age before Iconoclasm," *Dumbarton Oaks Papers* 8 (1954), 83–150; also Kenneth M. Setton, *Christian Attitudes Towards the Emperor in the Fourth Century* (New York, 1941), Chapter III ("Imperial Images"); and Gerhart B. Ladner, "The Concept of the Image in the Greek Fathers and the Byzantine Iconoclastic Controversy," *Dumbarton Oaks Papers* 7 (1953), 1–34, for the age of transition.

7. It would be sufficient to mention here the name of Percy Ernst Schramm, *Die deutschen Kaiser und Könige in Bildern ihrer Zeit* (Leipzig, 1928), and his volumes (with collaborators) on *Herrschaftszeichen und Staatssymbolik* (Stuttgart, 1954–1956); see moreover, also the numerous studies by Josef Deér: "Das Kaiserbild im Kreuz," *Schweitzer Beiträge zur allgemeinen Geschichte* 3 (1955), 48–112, "Ein Doppelbildnis Karls des Grossen," *Wandlungen christlicher Kunst im Mittelalter* (Forschungen zur Kunstgeschichte und christlichen Archäologie 2 (1953), 103–56; and Gerhart B. Ladner, *I ritratti dei papi nell'antichità e nel medioevo* (Vatican City, 1941).

religious history.[8] The brunt of exploring the various aspects of the more modern state imagery, therefore, had to be carried by the art historian who, very legitimately, studied in the first place problems of style and general artistic development. It would be ungrateful, however, and also wholly unjustified to maintain that the students of art history did their best to link the new state portraiture to the new "concepts of governmental authority or royal majesty" significant of the budding or fully blooming absolute monarchies;[9] and if their remarks were based mainly on somewhat casual observations and couched in somewhat vague and general terms which lacked precision, this deficiency reflects unfavorably on the professional historian who has failed to prepare the ground and to consider works of art as sources for his political and constitutional studies. The marriage of history and archaeology, characteristic of classical and medieval studies, has not yet been visualized by the student of the more recent periods.[10]

To cut through the haze of generalities and generalizations, however, is not totally impossible. That, in the later Middle Ages and early Renaissance, the representative ruler image stepped, as it were, out of the concealment of the vellums, visible only to the few and often to the ruler alone, and that it appeared again in the open, in the squares of cities, in assembly halls and court rooms, where it became visible to everyone, implied among indeed very many other things also a legal problem: the Prince apparently represented a power that in the eyes of the law was potentially omnipresent.

It is true, our legal sources—the glosses, commentaries, and opinions (*consilia*) of the medieval interpreters of Roman and to a lesser degree of canon law—do not answer every question we might wish to pose, nor do they solve the whole problem. But at least they open up an avenue towards a sounder understanding of the conditions which favored, by the end of the Middle Ages, the re-emergence of a representative state imagery. It appears, to say the least, worth the effort to focus our attention on the legal aspects of the problem, which indeed exist, and point

---

8. The study of Frances A. Yates, "Elizabeth as Astraea," *Journal of the Warburg and Courtauld Institutes* 10 (1947), 27–82, has shown how rewarding studies in early modern political iconography can be.

9. Marianna Jenkins, *The State Portrait: Its Origin and Evolution* (New York, 1947) certainly did her best to find a link between state portraiture and general history (see, for the quotation, p. 2). See also Harald Keller, "Die Entstehung des Bildnisses am Ende des Hochmittelatlers," *Römisches Jahrbuch für Kunstgeschichte* 3 (1939), 229–356, at 305ff.

10. See the excellent discussion of the problem by Arnaldo Momigliano, "Ancient History and the Antiquarian," *Journal of the Warburg and Courtauld Institutes* 13 (1950), 285–315.

out the interrelations between the reappearance of state-official art and the so-called revival of Roman law. Moreover, the question will have to be raised, even though as yet not satisfactorily answered, whether the stimuli emanating from works of jurisprudents have released any traceable effects, and also whether the later display of the Prince's image in court rooms and assembly halls, which remain customary *mutatis mutandis* until this day, was not perhaps the ultimate outcome of certain legal ideas and implications of which the medieval jurists grew conscious when they began to expound systematically the law books of Justinian in a scientific fashion.

It has often been remarked that the significant features of the works of the glossators, from the twelfth century onwards, was not as much a revival of Roman law—which, especially in Italy, had never been completely obsolete—as it was a revival of professional and scientific jurisprudence.[11] When, at the height of the Struggle of Investiture, the applicability of Roman law to the then raging controversies became manifest, the burden of exploiting individual laws and finally of reinterpreting the whole Roman Corpus fell to the trained jurists, rare though they were prior to the twelfth century and the rise of Bologna.[12] Justinian's codification of Roman law was a scientific, if hastily performed, work of accomplished scholars, and its reinterpretation in the Middle Ages likewise was to become the domain of the scholar, without leaving any chance to the jurisprudential layman. The method developed by the medieval jurists was in fact sired by their classical and post-classical predecessors. It consisted not only of collecting legal parallels from Roman law itself, and often from canon law and the works of other jurisprudents, but also of supporting their arguments by relevant non-legal material extracted from philosophy and poetry, literature, and historical, biblical, patristic, and theological sources.[13] It

---

11. See the balanced judgment of Woldemar Engelmann, *Die Wiedergeburt der Rechtskultur in Italien durch die wissenschaftliche Lehre* (Leipzig, 1938), chapter 1.

12. On this point, see Walter Ullmann, *The Growth of Papal Government in the Middle Ages* (New York, 1955), 368, who rightly refers to Karl Jordan, "Der Kaisergedanke in Ravenna zur Zeit Heinrichs IV.," *Deutsches Archiv* 2 (1938), 85–128 (see the summary, 127–28).

13. *Digest* [henceforth D.] I,8,6,5 quotes Vergil *Aeneid*, III, 303f. The *Glossa ordinaria*, influenced probably by Azo, remarks, "sed falsus testis est . . . et est argumentum quod auctoritates poetarum sunt in causis allegandae et tenendae"; see Erich Genzmer, op. cit. [*sic*: but no work by Genzmer previously cited], 396, n. 189, for Azo's restrictions of poetical testimonies. Others were more lenient. Albericus de Rosate, *Commentarii*, fol. 63ᵛ on that law, n. 2, declares that poets and philosophers should be referred to "deficientibus legibus, sed non necessario, nisi rationem necessarium assignent." He is even more positive when commenting on D.I,5,12,

was this scientific approach of the medieval jurists to their texts, and their effort to make sense despite contradictions, which eventually gave birth to our philologico-historical method. What resulted from this scientific activity was, especially in Italy, a juristic or legal culture which conveyed a peculiar tinge to all learning in the thirteenth and early fourteenth centuries. It was not by chance that in Bologna's heyday jurisprudence not only eclipsed, but also fertilized all other branches of knowledge, that practically all the early humanists had some training in law, and that the new scholarly jurisprudence exercised its influence also on the *humaniora*.

Law, by its very nature, has to consider, in one way or another, almost every range of human life, and no law that we know of was more completely a whole, a "universe" all by itself than Justinian's body of Roman law. Of this universality of the law the medieval jurists were not only fully aware but also proud: "the legal science," wrote Albericus de Rosate, a younger contemporary of Dante, whom he quotes repeatedly, "is commendable because it is more universal than other branches of knowledge. For the other sciences deal with something particular; the legal science, however, deals as it were with all branches of knowledge and above all the liberal arts."[14]

---

n. 2, fol. 48ᵛ, where the last quotes Hippocrates, for he asserts that one quotes also *proverbia antiquorum* and *divinae auctoritates* (see also below, n. 10). For the biblical authorities, see e.g. Andreas of Isernia, *In usus feudorum commentaria*, prael. n. 46 (Naples, 1571), fol. 8: "Item attendendum, quod in hoc opusculo producuntur plerumque authoritates sacrae Scripturae: nam illae allegantur in causis, sicut leges scriptae . . ." In a rather interesting discussion he declares that every reasonable word from any source may be alleged: "Nam rationabile dictum debet movere, sicut lex: quia lex est omne, quod ratione consistit." Therefore St. Paul (1 Cor. 15:33) could quote Menander Comicus. On the whole, however, Andreas of Isernia considered those quotations an embellishment rather than a necessity: "Quando alii authores extranei dant testimonium legi scriptae, fit inde lex pulchrior, non validior, quia lex per se sine eo valida est." It is apparently for fear of more, or of too much, Divine Right that a later English pamphleteer from the revolutionary period declares: "'Tis from the Statute-Book, not the Bible, that we must judge of the Power our Kings are invested withal, and also of our own Obligations, and the measures of our Subjection"; cf. Charles H. McIlwain, *The High Court of Parliament and Its Supremacy* (New Haven, 1910), 99.

14. Albericus de Rosate [*Commentarii in Digestum novum* (Venice, 1585)], on D.39,1, rubr., n. 18, fol. 2ᵛ: "Ex his etiam commendabilis est haec legalis scientia, quia universalior est aliis scientiis. Aliae enim scientiae de aliquo particulari tractant; haec autem de omnibus scientiis, et maxime liberalibus, tractat." Actually, Albericus develops in his prologues, like so many other jurists before him, a full philosophy of law and legal science. It would be rewarding to analyze the philosophical prologues of the works of the jurists in general, and not only that of an individual author. See, for an essay on Baldus, Walter Ullmann, "Baldus's Conception of Law," *Law Quarterly Revue* 58 (1942), 386–99.

Albericus demonstrated with great eloquence in what respect juris-prudence was linked to every knowledge pertaining *ad humanum salute*. He did not conceal his satisfaction when emphasizing that the law referred to poets because the Aedilician Edict regulated the activities poets were referred to by law; or when claiming that even music was within the compass of jurists because the Aedilician Edict regulated the activities of comedians and choruses just as it ordained concerning physicians and medicine.[15] It was in that respect also momentous that that the medieval jurists applied the legal universe of the Justinian law books freely to the conditions of their own time. Moreover, by their method of interrelating the legal problems with almost every bit of classical material accessible to them, they brought classical literature, if in selection, into practical circulation by extracting from it juristic principles and applying those principles to various contingencies of daily life. *Seneca iurista optimus* had a function, a practical function, very different from the moral philosopher who served as a source of general education or of edification.[16] Hence through the work of the glossators many a feature of classical thought and of Antiquity at large became generally valid again, comparable perhaps to a re-activated currency, to the *solidi veterum principium*, which according to a decree in Justin-ian's Code, were to be respected and have full validity throughout the empire.[17]

That attitude held good for the jurists of the thirteenth and fourteenth centuries to a greater extent than for the sixteenth-century savants of the historical school of jurisprudence: Alciati, Cujas, Gotho-fredus. Those great scholars had at their disposal practically all the classical text material now known to us; but what they lacked owing to their historical relativism was the unbiased approach and unsophis-ticated candor of their earlier colleagues who transferred and applied the classical knowledge almost directly and with very little qualifica-tion to their own surroundings—as often as not with a noble disregard

---

15. For Albericus on poetry, see above, n. 8; also on. D.39, 1, rubr. n. 20, fol. 3: "Allegat haec scientia poetas, ut Homerum [with reference to D.18,1,1]. . . et Oratium [with reference to *Glossa ordinaria* v. *non continebuntur* on D.32,52]. For music, Albericus (loc. cit., n. 20) quotes D.21,1,34, and 21,1,1ff.

16. Andreas of Isernia, *In usus feudorum commentaria* 2, 56 (*Quae sunt regalia*), n. 78, fol. 305ᵛ: "Seneca fuit iurista optimus." I may treat the subject separately; see, however, for Sen-eca's influence in a quasi "absolutist" sense, Antonio Marongiu, "Note federiciane," *Studi Me-dievali* 18 (1952), 297ff., also in *Atti del Convegno Internazionale di Studi Federiciani* (Palermo, 1952), 42–43.

17. Code [henceforth C.] 11.11.1.

of the obvious errors they made when, for example, identifying the ancient Roman *sacerdotes* and *pontifices* with the contemporary priests and bishops of the Catholic Church.[18] For all that, however, they were able to detect the fundamental legal principles of Roman law with admirable clarity, and it mattered little that often they detected by some misunderstanding even new principles which made sense only in their own orbit of social stratification—as, for example, the firm belief that every Doctor of Law was a *nobleman*, a *miles*, and every professor who had read law for twenty years ranked with a count.[19] At any rate it will

---

18. The basis of Ulpian's remark in D.1,1,1, when he compared jurisprudents with priests of justice. The mediaeval jurists interpreted that quasi-priesthood of their profession in the sense of Christian priests: like priests of the Church *sacra ministrant et conficunt*, like priests of the Church they handle *sacramenta* ("oaths" in the case of the jurists), and they act like priests *in danda poenitentia*: see Accursius' *Glossa ordinaria* on D.1,1,1, v. Sacerdotes. Gulielmus Durandus, *Rationale divinorum officiorum* (Lyon, 1565), II, 8, 6, fol. 55ᵛ, quite obviously refers to glossators of his time when he explains the Prince's character of *rex et sacerdos* along the lines of Ulpian's comparison: "Quidam etiam dicunt . . . quod [imperator] fit presbyter, iuxta illud [i.e. Ulpiani]: "Cuius merito quis nos sacerdotes appellat." And he adds, "Imperator etiam pontifex dictus est," because in ancient Rome the emperor had this rank (cf. *Decretum*. D.XXI, c. 1, ed. E. Friedberg, *Corpus iuris canonici* [Leipzig, 1879–81] I, 68). Against this equivocation [*sic*] the Renaissance jurists of the historical school objected; see e.g. Guillaume Budé, *Annotationes in Pandectarum libros* (Lyon, 1551) on D.1,1,1, 29–30: "Accursius peracute sane (ut solet plerumque) sacerdotes hoc in loco absolute intelligit . . . , ut ipse inquit poenitentiam dantes." He is, however, less willing to recognize the merits of Accursius when he continues: "Similis est ignorantia Accursii vel seculi potius Accursiani, quae hac aetate riducula est . . . Ubi pontificum Ulpianus minimet de collegio pontificum loquens, a quo ius pontificium apud antiquos dictum, quod Accursius ad nostros pontifices retulit."

19. The basis for that new *militia legum* (*militia litterata* or *doctoralis*), ranking with the *militia armata* of the gentry and the *militia coelestis* of the clergy, is found in C.2,6,7; 2,7,4';2,7,14; also 12,30,1, and 12,15. The doctrine concerning the *militia legum*, developing ever since Placentius and Azo (cf. Hermann Fitting, *Das Castrense peculium in seiner geschichtlichen Entwicklung* [Halle, 1871], p. 543) and "equiparating" the soldiers' pay (*peculium castrense*) with the pay of the civil service and of scholars, is neatly summarized by Baldus, C.2,7,14 (Venice, 1586), fol. 132: "Advocati [including *iurisperti* etc.] militibus aequiparantur, quia per eos tanquam per milites vita et patrimonia hominum defenduntur . . . Nota, quod advocati ita militant in legibus, sicut milites in armis . . ." And his brother Angelus de Ubaldis, on C.2,7,14 (Venice, 1579), fol. 16, adds yet another note when he writes: "ipsi [advocati] militant, ipsi dicunt pugnare pro patria sicut milites armatae militiae." See, for *pugnare pro patria* (Distichs of Cato), Gaines Post, "Two Notes on Nationalism in the Middle Ages," *Traditio* 9 (1953), 281–96. The equation of professors and counts on the basis of C.12, 15 is mentioned already by Andreas of Barletta (who wrote after 1257), *Commentaria super tribus postremis libris Codicis* (Venice, 1601), p. 272: "quod doctor perveniat ad comitis dignitatem, debent in eo octo precipue concurrere . . . Nono, quod docuerit per viginti annos." See further Bartolus on C. proem, *De novo Codice* (Lyon, 1555), n. 10–11 fol. 3, who explains "quod doctoratus est dignitas . . . Fateor tamen quod non est illustris . . . ; sed si legisset per viginti annos tunc esset Comes sacri palatii vel saltem clarissimus." Bartolus himself was *illustris*. See Angelus de Ubaldis on C.9,8,5, n. 4 (v. *virorum illustrium*), fol. 258: "Nota quod omnes consiliarii consistorii princeps intelliguntur illustres. Et ideo, quia Carolus [IV] princeps in suum consiliarium Bartolum assumpsit et *eidem arma donavit*, fecit illustrem." See, for the problem in general, Fitting (as this note, above).

always be most surprising to observe how much classical material had been reasonably and usefully digested in the *Glossa ordinaria* composed by Accursius in the 1230s, and utilized in the works of scholars such as Durandus, Cino da Pistoia, Andreas of Isernia, and Lucas de Penna. It should be emphasized that, as a result also of the work of the glossators, the thirteenth century began, and later centuries on a broader basis continued, to live in an atmosphere of applied—juristically applied—Antiquity which differed from the belletristic reading of classical authors. For the applied Antiquity of the jurists was backed by the authority of the law behind it, and was officially enforced by the individual governments not because it was "antique" but because it was, or was credited to be, the valid law.

In that respect jurisprudence fell in with other branches of knowledge as well, and it fell in with the visual arts which at, or about the same time began to apply and utilize antique models in a new fashion. The thirteenth century (if we disregard Aristotle) had hardly more classical material in store than the preceding centuries. What characterizes the great change in that period is the practical application of "applied Antiquity," and to this change the jurists have contributed, to say the least, their very considerable share.

Art, though certainly a factor of life, was a factor of law only incidentally. In Albericus de Rosate's essay-gloss about the liberal and other arts which were of concern to jurisprudence the arts of painting, sculpture, and architecture do not figure at all. When jurists talked about "art," they meant in the first place their own art as defined in the opening clauses of the Digest: *Ius est ars boni e aequi,* "law is the art of the good and the equitable."[20] This was the meaning of "art" also when, independently of Aristotle's *Physics* and even before that work was generally known, they used a catchword which became so very meaningful and ambiguous to Renaissance artists, *Ars naturam imitatur.*[21] The jurists, of course, did not think of the visual arts, or artistic naturalism or aesthetics. They found the slogan in the Digests and Institutes where it had a perfectly concrete meaning in the law of adoption: You cannot adopt an older person because the legal art, in its law of adoption, *naturam imitatur,* and it would be a monstrosity and a phenomenon

---

20. D.1,1,1, rubr.
21. Aristotle, *Physics,* II, 2, 194a21.

incompatible with nature were the adopting father to be younger than the adopted son.[22]

Art, however, in the sense of the visual arts, came like music or medicine into the purview of legal studies for other reasons: objects of art were often objects of legislation and therewith also of judicial decisions. A man donates a statue to his city. To whom, asks the law—and asks, for example, Odofredus writing in the first half of the thirteenth century—does the statue belong? To every individual citizen? To the body politic of the city? Can the donor take it back again? Can he sell it? Can he pawn it?[23] Or, take the laws on usufruct, the right to use and enjoy the returns of a thing the substance of which does not belong to you.[24] Strange things could form the substance of usufruct—coins, for example, because they could be used as gems or attached to a necklace, might be worn by the usufructor without belonging to him.[25] In that connection, one law discusses also statues and images. "Statues and images may yield usufruct, because they too have some utility when placed in a well-designed spot."[26] To this passage the *Glossa ordinaria* remarked:

> But what returns can there be received from these statues? I answer that everyone has to pay a penny that he may see the statue, as is the case with the lion which is in Florence.[27]

What the glossator, Accursius, refers to is hardly a thirteenth-century precursor of Donatello's Marzocco, the insignia of the people's independent power displayed originally at the column of Mars, but the live lion which the city kept in a pit near the Palazzo dei Podestà, while

---

22. Institutes 1,11.4: "Minorum natu non posse maioram adoptare placet: adoptio enim naturem imitatur et pro monstro est, ut maior sit filius quam pater."

23. See D.41,1,41 and 42,5,29 (= 42.6,14 in mediaeval editions). Odofredus only elaborates in the *Glossa ordinaria* when he says on D.41,1,41, nn. 1–2 (Lyon, 1552]), fol. 47ᵛ: "Aliquis ad ornamentum huius civitatis sua propria pecunia posuit status, id est, statuae non fiunt singulorum civium, sed totius civitatis: unde aliqui non possunt auferre eas, nec etiam ille qui possit: unde sunt universitatis." Also on D.42,5,29, n. 1, fol. 90ᵛ: "Statua in honorem debitoris posita npn venit in venditione honorem eius." Or on D.44,4,14, n. 1, fol. 106: "Statuam in municipio ponens non potest eam repetere. Also D.43,24,11,1, with the notes of Gothofredus (they are found in most editions of the *Corpus iuris civilis* of the 17th and 18th centuries).

24. D.7,1,1.

25. Odofredus on D.7,1,28, v. numismatum, fol. 250ᵛ: "Poteris uti [numismatibus] in gemmis et portare ad pectus vel docorare teipsum," follows *Glossa ordinaria* on this law, v. *usufructus*.

26. D.7,1,41: "Statuae et imaginis usum fructum posse relinqui magis est, quia et ipsae habent aliquam utilitatem, si quo loco opportuno ponantur."

27. *Glossa ordinaria* on D.7,1,41, v. statuae: "Sed quia fructus ex his percipitur? Respondeo quod quilibet daret nummum ut possit videre: ut fit de leone qui est Florentiae."

collecting an admission fee from the visitor.[28] The selection of the Gloss, however, to pay a penny for seeing a statue, is perhaps the earliest evidence of an admission fee imposed for contemplating a work of art.

Building and zoning regulations of Roman law actually began to weigh heavily with the municipal authorities in the thirteenth century, that is, at a time when Western Europe in general entered into its formative period. Two titles in Justinian's Code were relevant for building problems. *De aedificiis privatis* and *De operibus publicis*.[29] It has been pointed out recently to what extent these and other laws of late Antiquity have determined the legislation concerning city-zoning of Italian cities.[30] For example the decree of the Emperor Zeno (d. 491), prescribing a straight line for the frontage of buildings in public streets and containing other regulations as well, was included, by the second half of the thirteenth century, in the statute books of practically all Italian cities, and exercised, through communal by-laws, a permanent influence also in the transalpine countries.[31] The enforcement of Zeno's law, which conveniently summarized earlier prescriptions, avowedly changed the looks of the irregularly built medieval cities, at least in Italy, and helped to shape and form their geometrical squares such as we know them today.[32] This, we may say, was a clear case of "applied Antiquity."

Roman law, in the discussion of the Law of Things, proceeded from the assumption that *res sacrae* and *res publicae* were on equal footing. They were juxtaposed because things belonging to the temples and

---

28. That Accursius had a live lion in mind was certainly the opinion of Angelus de Ubaldis, on D.7,1,41, fol. 177ᵛ: "In eadem glossa ibi, *de Leone*: Ex hoc patet quod datum [donarium] cani vel animali alicuius, non obstante quod ipsum animal non sit capax, tamen pertinet ad dominum, sicut pertinet ad fructuarium animalis, ubi in eo est usufrctus constitutus." For the live lions kept in Florence, see Robert Davidsohn, *Geschichte von Florenz* (4 vols. in 6 parts: Berlin, 1896–1927), IV: 3, 266–67. The Florentines even seem to have bred lions, for on August 16, 1355, Czenko of Lipa, Marshal of the Kingdom of Bohemia, repeats his request to the Florentines to send him two lion cubs: cf. Theodor E. Mommsen, *Italienische Analekten zur Reichsgeschichte des 14. Jahrhunderts* (Stuttgart, 1952), 192, No. 466. Besides, the lion as an insignia of the popular movement in Florence (Marzocco) does not seem to have existed at the time when Accursius wrote.

29. C.8,10 and 11. For the following, see the excellent book of Wolfgang Braunfels, *Mittelalterliche Stadtbaukunst in der Toskana* (Berlin, 1953), who most successfully has utilized the vast material of Italian municipal legislation and law in general for assessing the development of city-zoning in Tuscany and in Northern Italy in general.

30. Braunfels, op. cit., pp. 87ff.

31. C.8,10,12. This compendious constitution represents a collection of city-planning laws dating back to considerably earlier times. Justinian found it practical to refer to this law quite frequently; see, e.g. C.8,10,13, or *Novellae*, 63 and 165.

32. Braunfels, op. cit., pp. 111 and 114.

things belonging to the public sphere—we would say the "state"—were both defined as *res nullius*, things belonging "to none"—that is, to no individual person.[33] To the student of political theory it is well known how important it was that in the course of the thirteenth century a *ius publicum* was consciously recovered, a public law which, if necessary, prevailed over private rights, including those of the king as a private person.[34] The recovery of a "public" sphere affected the arts indirectly. From Roman law there derived the notion of *publicum decus*, "public beautification," referring to columns, statues, precious metals and, in general, works of art serving for the dignified appearance of a city.[35] Those things did not figure among the *res sacrae* of the Church, but among the *res publicae* of the state or the city; they were "profane," since they were merely part of the *ornatus civitatis* and had nothing to do with religious equipment. Before the law, however, *res publicae* and *res sacrae* were on one level and both were equally protected by the government. In that respect, there was no difference between buildings on the Piazza del Duomo and those on the Piazza della Signoria; for, as the jurists would define the principles, Church and Fisc, divine law and public law walk together on equal terms—*paribus passibus ambulant*.[36] Under those conditions the notion of "profane art" began to emerge, an *ars profana*

---

33. Basic is D.1,8,1, rubr.: "quod autem divini iuris est, id nullus in bonis est . . . quae publicae sunt, nullius in bonis esse creduntur, ipsius enim universitatis esse credutntur." Also *Inst.*, 2,1, where the parallelism does not appear quite as clearly as in *Nov.* 7,2,1: "utique cum nec multo differant ab alterutro sacerdotium et imperium, et *res sacrae* a communibus et *publicis*. Cf. C.1,2,23, rubr., or C.7,38,2 ("iuris rei publicae vel iuris templorum"). Roman law, of course, distinguished between *res communes* (air, water, etc.) and *res publicae* belonging to the *universitas*, the body politic. D.50,16,15, warns, it is true, not to mistake things pertaining to any city for things public: "Bona civitatis abusive 'publica' dicta sunt: sola enim ex publica sunt, quae populi Romani sunt." It goes without saying, however, that in the Italian cities, which were quasi sovereign (*civitas sibi princeps*) [Bartolus], things communal were also legally things public; see e.g. Albericus de Rosate on D.1,8,1,§ *Hoc autem*, fol. 62: "et tunc comprehendit non solum Romam sed alias civitates."

34. For the problem, see the brief sketch by Gaines Post, "The Theory of Public Law and the State in the Thirteenth Century," *Seminar* 6 (1948), 42–59; also Peter Riesenberg, *Inalienability of Sovereignty in Medieval Political Thought* (New York, 1956), and, for a few remarks, Kantorowicz, "Mysteries of State," *Harvard Theological Review* 48 (1955), 65–91, at 83–91. In a broader sense, of course, the whole recovery of the notion *patria* belongs to "public law"; see Post, "Two Notes on Nationalism in the Middle Ages," *Traditio* 9 (1953), 281–320, at 281–96.

35. D.42,5,29: "ornandi municipii causa"; D.43,9,2: "ornamenta rei publicae"; C.8,10,6: "publicum decus"; C.8,11,13: "in usu vel ornatu civitatis"; C.8,10,2, forbids the demolition of buildings, lest "publicus deformetur adspectus." Cf. Braunfels, pp. 176ff., also pp. 87–88.

36. Bartolus on C.11,62 (61), 4, n. 1 (Lyon, 1546), fol. 50ᵛ: "ecclesia et fiscus paribus passibus ambulant (reference to C.1,2,23; see above, n. 28); but the expression was used before by Jacques de Révigny (ca. 1270–1280), quoted by Post, "Two Notes," 313, n. 81.

which was "public" and therefore no less sacred than the *ars sacra* of ecclesiastical origin and destination.

In order to preserve the dignified appearance of a city, Roman law prescribed that "no person was permitted to move or remove columns or statues of any material within the same province or from one province to another.[37] This law together with others applied also to private buildings, and it implied at the same time an effort to put a stop to the custom of using existing buildings as quarries.[38] The statues mentioned in that law were apparently private or decorative works of art, they were most certainly not imperial statues because these were protected by other means and no one would have dared to move them anyhow.

We have to recall how rigid the laws were not only against violation or defacement of imperial statues, but also against any acts betraying or suggesting a lack of respect, and therefore punishable under the *lex Julia maiestatis* or other laws as well.[39] It was a lack of respect equaling lese majesty if a governor inscribed his own name on a public work after its completion without mentioning that of the emperor,[40] and every acclamation of a local dignitary had to be preceded by that of the imperial name.[41] By analogy the images were treated in like manner. Justinian decreed that no statue of bronze or other material should ever be set up to the Ostrogothic king alone without being sided by an imperial image which always had to stand on the right.[42] It was likewise high treason if a man placed his statue higher than that of the emperor, a charge leveled under Tiberius against one Granius Marcellus, who was accused also of having removed the head of Augustus from a statue only to have it replaced by a head of Tiberius.[43] Legal cases of that kind are known in too modest a number, and they have been enumerated repeatedly ever since the times of Gothofredus.[44] There was the case of Lucius Ennius

---

37. C.8,10,17.

38. C.8,10,2; 8,11,13.

39. D.48,4; C.9,8.

40. C.8,11(12),10.

41. Procopius, *Bellum Gothicum*, I,6,4. This ceremonial apparently was observed in the tenth century when Dalmatian bishops promised to acclaim the name of the Doge of Venice after those of the Byzantine emperors; see Kantorowicz, *Laudes regiae* (Berkeley, 1946), p. 148, n. 4; cf. 44ff.

42. Procopius, ibid., I,6,5. Cf. Deér, "Das Kaiserbild im Kreuz," (above, n. 2), 101–2.

43. Tacitus, *Annales*, I,74. See, for discussion of the trial, Erich Koestermann, "Die Majestätsprozess unter Tiberius," *Historia* 4 (1955), 72–106, at 83–87.

44. Theodor Mommsen, *Römisches Strafrecht* (Leipzig, 1899), 585, n. 1; Gothofredus, on D.48,4.7.4. Floyd Seyward Lear, *Treason and Related Offenses in Roman and Germanic Law* (Houston, 1955), 26–27 and 121, n. 92.

who was accused of having converted a silver effigy of Tiberius "to promiscuous use," though he was finally acquitted;[45] of the case of a person beating a slave and changing clothes near a statue of Augustus;[46] of a woman who was executed for undressing near an image of Domitian;[47] of a man relieving his bladder near the place where statues and effigies of emperors were located;[48] of persons bearing an amulet coin bearing the emperor's features into a brothel or public convenience;[49] and of the thoughtful slave, mentioned in Seneca's *De beneficiis*, who quickly drew off from his master's finger a ring bearing the engraved portrait of Tiberius when his master grabbed for the *matella*, the chamber-pot.[50]

Quite evidently, imperial legislation had to consider problems related to imperial statues and images. Under the title rubric *De spectaculis*, a law in the Code ordered that in porticoes or other places in municipalities where imperial images were customarily displayed—that is, in legal language, "consecrated"—no malpropre pictures representing actors, charioteers, or disreputable persons were allowed to be shown, though advertising posters of that kind were not forbidden in other places, at the entrance of the circus or in front of the stage of a theater.[51] Another title of the Code is inscribed *De statuis et imaginibus*.[52] Here the legislating emperors advised the provincial governors how the imperial statues or images were to be exhibited, as was usual, on festal days: the governor himself had to be present, the statues should not be adored; and the governor's presence should grace the day, the locality and the memory of the emperors, who, after all, were present in their images and should live, says the Theodosian Code, in the hearts and minds of those attending.[53] The laws dealt further with penalties for putting up statues of governors with the emperor's permission, and they prohibited the collection of money for erecting statues to governors and any other person, so as to be able to preclude abuses and oppression.[54] And, needless

45. Tacitus, *Annales*, III, 70; cf. Koestermann, op. cit., 105.
46. Suetonius, *Tiberius*, 58.
47. Cassius Dio, *Historia Romana*, LXVII, 12,2.
48. Scriptores Historia Augustae, *Caracalla*, V,7.
49. Suetonius, *Tiberius*, 58.
50. Seneca, *De beneficiis*, III,26, 1–2.
51. C.11,41,4.
52. [left blank]
53. *Codex Theodosianus*, 15,4,1.
54. C.1,2r,3–4 concerning collections. For the senatorial or imperial permission to put up statues, see D.43,9,2, with the remarks of Gothofredus; cf. Mommsen, *Römisches Strafrecht*, I³, 452, n. 1. The permission which he decorated with his own image, was given ipso facto to any private person who built or repaired some *opus publicum*. The permission of the magistracies

to say, the *lex Julia maiestatis* made it high treason to mutilate or even tamper with imperial statues, whereas it was not considered a crime to repair them, to hurt them by some misfortune, or even destroy them if they were not yet consecrated, that is, dedicated for official use.[55]

An important aspect of the problem of imperial images is mentioned under the title *De his qui ad statuas confugiunt*, that is, on those who flee for sanctuary to the statues of the emperors.[56] The law, issued in 386, is found already in the Theodosian Code and it was referred to quite often in the Digest.[57] The intention of that law was limited though: it only meant to stop certain abuses of the right of asylum granted by the imperial images. Its importance, however, should be sought chiefly in the imperial right of asylum itself which, by the fourth century, had been extended also to the churches and which later glossators tried to extend also to the priest carrying the Corpus Christi.[58] We visualize a budding competition between the images of the emperor and the holy images of Christ and the saints, a competition which became a prominent factor during the iconoclastic controversy in Byzantium, especially when, in

---

was needed anyhow insofar as the statue was erected on public ground; cf. D.35,1,14, and also Mommsen, 449.

55. D.48,4,5–7; C.9,8, does not deal with images.

56. C.1.25.

57. *Codex Theodosianus*, 9,44,1; D.1,6,2; 1,12,1,1; 21,1,17,12; 21,1,19,1; 47,10,38; 47,11,5; 48,19,28,7.

58. D.47,10,38: "ne quis imaginem imperatoris in invidiam alterius portaret" (that is, dodging the right of asylum by showing, e.g., a coin displaying the emperor's image); Accursius, on that law, thinks of some little statue of the emperor carried by a person: "Portabam quandam statuam principis . . . quia timebam Titium, qui me volebat occidere." For the right of asylum, see now Luke Wenger, "Asylrecht," *Reallexikon für Antike und Christentum*, I, 836ff., esp. 840ff. Imperial legislation concerning the right of asylum of all churches does not, however, antedate the fifth century; see also Mommsen, *Römisches Strafrecht*, 458ff. For the extension of the right of asylum, see, e.g. Angelus de Ubaldis, on D.1,6,2, n. 3. fol. 16. The *Additio*: Adde quod sicut is qui confugit ad statuam principis, est tutus, quia ibi capi non potest . . . Adde quod idem est in is qui confugit ad sacerdotum deferentem corpus Christi, ut inde capi non possit." This argument is found also in Ludovicus Romanus, *Singularia*, 339 (*Singularia omnium clarissimorum Doctorum*, ed. Gabriel Sarayna [Lyon, 1560], p. 97), who refers to an event in Urbino where the malefactor was captured although he embraced a priest carrying the *Corpus Christi* because the *Glossa ordinaria* on *Decretum*, C.XIII, q.2, c.30, v. *in patibulis*, declares "Ecclesia et non corpus Christi protegit malefactorem." The reason was that, otherwise, a person who had taken communion could claim that he could not be captured—an argument, by the way, which was not too different from that of the Roman jurist denying protection to a fugitive on the grounds that he was carrying a coin or an amulet displaying the emperor's image. Other canonists, however, did not share that opinion (Hostiensis, Guido de Baysio, and others) "quia si hoc ecclesiae concessum est propter Christum, a fortiori concedi debet sacerdoti proper Christum" (according to Felinus Sandeus, a fifteenth-century decretalist and auditor of the Rota).

the course of the sixth century, the images of Christ began to dislodge the imperial images from their former place of honor.[59]

The imperial statues and images, if anything, belonged to the *res publicae*, they were certainly not among the *res privatae*. This argument referred also to other statues erected by imperial permission in public places: it would have been an act of contempt of the emperor himself to mutilate or remove what had imperial approval. This would have been true also with regard to purely ornamental statues and columns placed in public squares of the cities to which the law refers quite frequently—an ornamentation, by the way, which was not at all customary in medieval cities.[60] Finally there should be mentioned the laws *De falsa moneta*; for to falsify money *vultu principum signata* and displaying the *aeternales vultus* of the emperors who guaranteed the right weight of the coins, was likewise a sacrilege—not to mention the fact that the coin-image of Caesar was, as it were, hallowed by the Gospels.[61]

If we add to all these laws the numerous references to funerary monuments, we realize that in fact a quite substantial amount of legislation about statues and images was embedded in Justinian's law-books. At any rate, it was enough to make the medieval jurists conscious of the legal importance of imagery and to make them as it were, image-conscious in general and in a fashion which formerly existed only with regard to holy images. Ruler image, after all, had for centuries been confined to miniatures in manuscripts and certainly did not serve the *decus publicum*, public embellishment. Hence, the only parallel known to the jurists was ecclesiastical imagery—the pictures of Christ, the Virgin

---

59. See above, n. 1, the studies of Grabar, Kitzinger, Ladner. See also William H. Worrell, *The Coptic Manuscripts in the Freer Collection* (New York, 1923), 375–76, for a sermon in which the indwelling forces of an imperial image are claimed also, and with greater justification from the preacher's point of view, for an image of the Virgin; see, for the date (probably ninth or tenth century), Kitzinger, 101, n. 59.

60. Braunfels, pp. 116ff.

61. C.9,2r,2; *Codex Theodosianus*, 9,21,3,9. Tampering with the imperial picture made falsification *eo ipso* a crime of majesty, a connection which Jacques Cujas, *Observationes et emendationes*, XIX, 25 (*Opera* [Prato, 1836], I, 864–65) stresses by referring to the *lex Julia* on statues and images (D.48,4,6). Cf. Pauli, *Sententiae*, 5,25,1 (*Fontes iuris Romani Antejustiniani*, ed. Salvatore Riccobono et al. [Florence, 1940], 410: "qui . . . vultuve principum signatam monetam praeter adulterinam reprobaverit." Cf. *Codex Theodosianus*, 9, 22 and Cassiodorus, *Variae*, VII, according to whom Theodoric the Great wrote: "monetae debet integritas quaeri, ubi et vultus noster imprimtur. Quidnam erit tutum, si in nostra peccetur effigie? Sit mundum, quod ad formam nostrae serenitatis addicitur." *Glossa ordinaria* on C.11,11,3, v. *aeternales vultus*: "id est principis, cuius est ibi imago . . . quia imperium semper durat." The *Glossa ordinaria* on C.11,11, rubr., alludes to the evangelical *Cuius est imago etc.*, and Bartolus on C.11,11, rubr., n. 3, fol. 37v, refers to it.

and the saints. Now, however, there was recovered by the new scientific jurisprudence, though at first only intellectually, a whole new orbit of secular art; for the jurists were compelled to recognize that in their authoritative texts the images of Christian emperors were deemed hardly less sacred and hardly less powerfully charged with invisible *virtutes* than the sacred images themselves.[62]

It should not be forgotten, however, that not only Roman law but canon law dealt with images. In the *Decretum Gratiani* (ca. 1130) we find the two famous chapters taken from Gregory the Great, the first being a warning against the violation of images and any form of iconoclasm, since the picture served for the education of the illiterate; and the other a warning against any form of exaggerated worship of images and against mistaking them for "gods."[63] These excerpts were later repeated in a decretal of Gregory X, published during the Second Council of Lyon (1272) and incorporated in the *Liber Sextus* of Boniface VIII, in which once more the extravagant adoration of pictures was forbidden.[64] The decrees of Trent finally rejected the assumption that the Deity or even divine virtues were dwelling in the images which had their peculiar value only in a commemorative and educational sense.[65] In order to interpret those laws of the Church, however, the glossators referred to the laws about statues in the Digest and Code,[66] or drew the obvious conclusion that offending the majesty of God was an even greater crime than offending the imperial majesty, and that therefore the *lex Julia maiestatis* was valid also with regard to God.[67] On the other hand, the civilians referred to the canonistic texts so that also in this respect "divine law and public law walked *pari passu*."

A source of puzzlement was the word "consecrated" in connection with works of profane art, that is, the *statuae et imagines consecratae* which were mentioned in the law books of Justinian.[68] While an anointing of the holy images was completely foreign to the Roman rite proper,

---

62. Among the Western Fathers of the Church, St. Ambrose was not at all averse to the imperial images (cf. Setton, *Christian Attitude*, p. 205), and the jurists referred to his remarks quite frequently.

63. *De consecratione*, D.3,cc 27–28: Friedberg, *Corpus iuris canonici*, I, 1360.

64. *Liber Sextus*, I, 16, 2, ed. Friedberg, II, 986.

65. Cf. Hubert Jedin, "Entstehung und Tragweite des Trienter Dekrets über die Bilderverehrung," *Theologische Quartalschrift*, 116, 404–29, at 423ff.

66. See, e.g. Joannes Andreae's *Glossa ordinaria* on *Lib. Sext.*, I,16,2, v. *in terram*, quoting C.1,8, and v. *ultrix*, quoting C.1,25 and D.48,19,28,7.

67. *Glossa ordinaria* on X 5,26,2, v. *blasphemiam*.

68. [left blank]

it was nevertheless practiced in the West sporadically outside of Rome, for example in Arles and in some English churches; but a blessing of the images at the time of their dedication was, of course, quite common, and the Pontifical of Durandus (late thirteenth century), which eventually became almost authoritative during the later Middle Ages, contained quite a number of elaborate benedictions for the dedication of images of the Holy Virgin and the saints.[69] Nothing seems more natural than the procedure of the civilians who tried to understand and interpret the word *consecratae* in the sense of ecclesiastical consecration. Andreas of Barletta, writing some time after 1257, apparently thought of holy and perhaps of processional images rather than of profane ones when, glossing on *De spectaculis*, he explained that no pantomimic jesters "who made a laughing-stock of their body" were to be admitted to, or base pictures to be displayed in, a place "where images are consecrated or introduced with great solemnity." For, said he, no unworthy persons should have a stay in a worthy place, just as the tombs of the apostles and martyrs should not serve as burial places for others.[70] Albericus de Rosate, when glossing on *De statuis*, offered a long discussion about the etiquette to be observed when holy images in churches were greeted.[71] Angelus de Ubaldis, when discussing the usufruct of statues, thinks in the first place of images of the Holy Virgin or any other saint placed in a private location, which worked miracles, "as I have seen it repeatedly in my city (Perugia)," and to which many gifts were made; but that usufruct does not belong to the private owner, but to God, since the gifts were made in contemplation of the immortal God.[72] To be sure, when talking about usufruct in connection with statues or images Angelus de Ubaldis discusses also the signboard of a pharmacist's shop which may yield usufruct by attracting customers; however, the first thing that occurred to him was a holy image.

Likewise, Lucas de Penna, writing in the middle of the fourteenth century, interpreted the coin images of imperial *solidi* by referring to the famous words of Gregory the Great, saying that *ob reverentiam* of those represented images should be venerated, since they were quasi the books

---

69. Anointings of pictures were anything but common in the West; cf. Philipp Hofmeister, *Die heiligen Öle in der morgen- und abendländischen Kirche* (Würzburg, 1948), 213–14. See for the benedictions of images, Michel Andrieu, *Le Pontifical romain au moyen-âge* (Vatican City, 1938–41), II, 15,17, 80, 204, and, for the Durandus *Pontifical*, III, 525ff.

70. [this and following notes up to 83 left blank]

71.

72.

of the illiterate.[73] On the other hand, Andreas of Isernia (d. 1316) interpreted the law according to which intercourse with the *augusta* or any princess of the imperial house was a crime of lese majesty by a simple reference to the images: if the defilement of a consecrated statue representing the Prince was punishable on account of *laesa maistatas*, how much more so the defilement of a consecrated human being, the queen, who at her marriage, was "consecrated" and blessed to be one body with the king. Also Andreas of Isernia would ask whether it was heresy to break the images of Christ and the saints, and he would answer that it was not necessarily heresy, but that it was certainly a crime punishable under the *lex Julia*, since the holy images were consecrated no less than the images mentioned by the *lex Julia*.[74] We may think of a thirteenth-century miniature depicting the Laocoön: because Laocoön was said to be a priest of Poseidon, he and his two sons were shown in priestly garbs of the Roman Church, and with tonsures.[75]

The arguments were running in a circle. The tendency, however, towards expanding imperial images through ecclesiastical images, and vice versa, is very obvious in connection with the right of asylum granted by the imperial images. In the early thirteenth century Azo of Bologna, who exercised an almost permanent influence on the interpreters of Roman law, compared the asylum of statues to the asylum granted "by the supreme king's statue or image, that is, the Church of Almighty God" (*per summi regis statuam vel imaginem, id est omnipotentis Dei ecclesiam*).[76] In a similar sense the glossators interpreted the right of asylum of statues actually quite correctly, since the Church asylum was indeed next of kin to, perhaps even derived from, that of the imperial statues. What matters here is that the jurists customarily "equiparated" the images of saints and the images of princes, reduced both to one denominator, and treated them as equals. That is, they merged, as was their custom anyway, the sacred with the secular, thereby raising the secular to the rank of the sacred.

One of the first things the glossators would try to explain was the difference between imperial statues and imperial images, and for that purpose they referred practically always to the definition of Azo, who

---

73.

74. [Kantorowicz writes in *King's Two Bodies*, p. 111, n. 72: "Andreas of Isernia, *In usus feudorum*, on *De statutis et consuetudinibus*, n. 28, fol. 135ᵛ, refers to the parallelism between images of kings and images of saints or of Christ."]

75. [One would really like to have the source here . . .]

76.

declared that "in a statue nothing exists that would not represent a man's effigy, whereas in an image, being merely a painting, there may be many parts which do not represent the limbs of a man."[77] Azo, of course, and the other jurists of that age would hardly have had an opportunity to see any imperial statues. On the basis of Justinian's law-books, however, they would argue that *if* an emperor put up his own statue, collections should not be made to raise the money for that purpose, or that *if* a person wished to erect a statue, he needed the emperor's permission.[78] Azo, of course, did not say or even imply that princes around 1200 were doing those things. But the potential "*If*" of the law-books and the glossators—"*If* an emperor put up his image"—may have had the effect of a stimulus inviting princes to do so. And certainly there was *one* prince on whom the juristic stimuli were not wasted: the Emperor Frederick II.

The production of the artistic movement at the court of Frederick II—the triumphal gate of Capua, the sculptures in or near the palaces, the picture in the palace hall in Naples, the design of the augustales—reflect the stimuli emanating from the new scientific jurisprudence and may be called a first re-translation of Roman law influence into reality.[79] This re-translation of law into practice was not restricted to art. Frederick's law-book, the *Liber augustalis* was teeming with Roman law; so was the exuberant language written by his clerks.[80] If Frederick II publicly celebrated his *dies natalis*, his natural birthday—a most unusual celebration during the Middle Ages, when only the birthdays of Christ, the Virgin and John the Baptist were honored—this was done not for reasons of sentimentality. Frederick merely followed Roman law, which classed the emperor's birthday among the *feriae publicae* on which the law courts were not in session.[81] Innovations such as these would hardly have startled the jurists, who, after all, inspired them. Startling, however, were the famous sculptures of the Capuan gate, which attracted the attention of many a visitor in the thirteenth and fourteenth centuries and thereafter, and they challenged also the wits of a famous jurist.

Lucas de Penna commented on *De spectaculis*, the law ordaining that in porticoes and other places where imperial statues were customarily displayed or "consecrated," pictures of lewd persons should not be

---

77.
78.
79.
80.
81.

**FIGURE 6.1** A nineteenth-century drawing of the triumphal arch of Frederick II at Capua.

shown.[82] He assumed rather significantly that the law meant locations where not only the consecrated statues of the emperors were placed, but where the emperor might frequently show himself in person.[83] For, argued the jurist, a picture or image is placed *pro simulatione vel fictione*, "in that it represents the figure of truth of a certain thing," as one would say that the delegate [judge or officer] is the image of the delegating power."[84] In other words, the statues of the Emperor stand vicariously for his person. He then defined the difference between statues and images by referring to Azo,[85] and pointed out that also according to canon law it was a crime of lese majesty to violate statues or break the image of the Crucified and the icons of saints.[86] Further, he defined the word *porticus* of Justinian's Code as a site where there is, so to say, a *porta* a

82.
83.
84.
85.
86.

gate, or something having the aspect of a gate.[87] With that definition
in mind, he finally essayed to interpret the word *consecrare*: "That is,
to set up the consecrated statues or place them in a *porta* a gateway, as
in the gateway of the city of Capua, where the statue of the Emperor
Frederick has been put up, truly Caesar in human cunning and craft,
and in some respects Augustus had he not been an enemy and rebel of
the Church."[88] Though Lucas de Penna finds the verse inscriptions of
the gate insipid, he quotes them nevertheless and gives even a vague
description of other figures of the gate before drawing the conclusion

> On the basis of such works [as the Capuan gate] royal statues may
> be called "consecrated"; or else, should kings be deficient in justice,
> "they might be called "execrated" rather than "consecrated."[89]

The jurist may have been mistaken in assuming that the concept of
"consecrated" statues of the emperor must refer to the times when the
Roman princes still were idolaters, since according to Catholic faith
imperial images were not consecrated, although everything connected
with the emperor was called "sacred," and emperors, like priests, were
anointed—that is "consecrated."[90] He grasped, however, that the display of the emperor's image in the portico, in the *porta* of Capua, was
in harmony with C.11,41,4: *in publicis porticibus . . . , quibus nostrae solent
imagines consecrari*, and we may wonder if his suggestion was intended to
make some specific point. The Capuan gate had no antecedents during
the Middle Ages; its design was not repeated until two centuries later
when Alfonso of Aragon's gate at Castel Nuovo, in Naples (fig. 6.2), was
avowedly inspired, as the original design shows, by the imperial gateway
in neighboring Capua; and the purpose of the imperial gate is not at
all obvious.[91]

Perhaps we should recall the fact that one of the most famous porticoes of Italy, the Loggia dei Lanzi in Florence, met in the 1350s with
the resistance of the Florentine *popolo* for a reason disclosed by Matteo
Villani: "that a loggia befitted a tyrant and not a people" (*che loggia si*

---

87.

88. "*Consecrari, id est, consecratas apponio, vel in porta collocari, ut in porta civitatis Capuae, ubi
apposita statua Frederici Imperatoris vere in humanis vertutiis aut astutiis Caesaris et in quibusdam
Augusti, nisi quia hostis et rebellis ecclesie.*"; Lucas de Penna (Lyon, 1582) on C.11,40,4. p. 446.

89. Ibid., "*Ex his operibus possent dici regales statuae consecrari; alias cessante in regibus
iustita, dicendi sunt potius execrari quam consecrari.*"

90. [Kantorowicz expands on the Capuan gate in *King's Two Bodies*, p. 111, with n. 72,
providing further bibliography.]

91.

**FIGURE 6.2** Alfonso of Aragon's Gate, Castel Nuovo, Naples. Wikimedia Commons, CC BY-SA 4.0. Photo: Marco Ober.

*convenia a tiranno e non a popolo*).[92] The antithesis of "tyranny" and "free community" in this connection is not self-evident, but it may become meaningful through Luca da Penna's combination of the *publici porticus* of the law and the Capuan gate, whose sculptures were felt to have a menacing character, *ad metum transeuntium*, as a thirteenth-century author put it.[93]

However that may be, Frederick II's *porta Capua* was the first, and perhaps even a unique expression of the unalloyed Spirit of Jurisprudence which, by that time, was strong enough to influence artistic enterprise and was as yet not burdened and buried by that heavy overlay of other intellectual currents which became effective a century later. The juristic purity of the monument may account also for the straightforwardness of the bridge-gate itself showing, as it did, the marble statue of the emperor enthroned, the big female head which cannot

92.
93.

easily be interpreted except as a representation of the *Iusticia Caesaris* and the two philosopher busts which Lucas de Penna first designated as imperial "judges."[94]

Straightforward was also the purpose of the monument: Emperor, Justice, and Judges protect, as the verse inscriptions proclaim, the entrance into the kingdom and its *concordia*, promising security to those of good will and punishment to all transgressors of the law. They protect—let it be noted—a bridge which traditionally would be protected by a "bridge saint," by some "consecrated" images of Christ or a local saint.[95] The very fact that the emperor put up his own "consecrated" image in the bridge-portico on the frontier of the realm indicates whence the wind was blowing; and it is significant too, that the Guelphic visitor around 1300 re-translated the completely profane imagery of the Capuan gate into Christian terms, maintaining that the emperor's image signified Christ, while the gate itself signified man's entrance into the kingdom of heaven.[96]

Of "equiparation" in the jurists' sense of the word there is plenty, and it is moving both hither and thither. The copying of Antiquity was secondary and incidental only. It certainly was lacking any romantic features; for what counted was the advice and suggestions of the law-books and the law interpreters. The law was "antique"; hence in the case of the law Antiquity penetrated into daily life. That may hold true also for the thirteenth-century heads, allegedly of Frederick II, which in recent years have been mushrooming from Italian soil.[97] Though none of them represents Frederick II, these sculptures may still have served as a *decus publicum* in the sense of the jurists, as a public embellishment so often discussed in the laws, even if we know nothing about the place in which they may have been erected. Finally, to the judicial sphere there belonged also the picture in the palace of Naples showing Frederick II enthroned as the *justus judex*; to his side, though a step lower, his logothetes Petrus de Vinea; and in the foreground the parties—a forerunner, as far as can be judged from the scanty description, of the later imagery of "Examples of Justice" which became popular in the later Middle Ages.[98]

---

94. [Lucas de Penna: "hinc et hinc imagines erant duorum iudicium"—cited in Kantorowicz, *King's Two Bodies*, 111, n. 72]

95.

96.

97.

98.

[Footnote indications in the prepared text end here, with the exception of some notes supplied by the present editor.]

However that may be, the development of a monumental art which was profane, and at least at one prominent point—at Capua—took over the functions of ecclesiastical imagery, should not be severed from Roman law and the glosses of the jurists, who customarily equiparated holy images and secular images, or transferred, as it were, the *virtutes* dwelling in holy images to those of the secular rulers. In a way, this merging of the two orbits of imagery, ecclesiastical and profane, renewed some of the problems of early pre-iconoclastic Byzantium where competition between imperial images and images of Christ and the saints led to the great movement against ecclesiastical art. It is true, of course, that the bitterness of the eighth-century struggles about the images was rarely reached in modern times, but we do prick up our ears when we read the arguments with which, in Elizabethan England, the Catholic scholar Nicolas Sanders defends the images of Christ, the Virgin Mary, and the saints against the attacks of John Jewel. Why, asks Sanders, if the images of Christ are to be destroyed, are the images of rulers to be respected? "Breake if you dare the image of the Queenes Maiestie or the Armes of the realme."[99] It is clear that the ruler image has achieved quasi-religious values which can be compared only with those attributed by Roman law and the glossators to imperial images.

This influence becomes quite manifest in sixteenth-century France, where, until the French Revolution, the kings alone and exclusively were entitled to be honored by the public display of a statue in a public square. Accordingly, Joys Buysson, a jurist of the French crown, in a speech before the dead [*sic*] Henry IV in 1594, could remark quite plainly that "the statues of the French kings were *tenues comme sainctes*" and could attribute to them the right of asylum.[100] A new age was dawning in which, as in antiquity, the image of the ruling prince would be displayed again in every assembly hall and court room.

Therefore, and before concluding this scrappy paper [perhaps the author meant this term only for the lecture version], yet another item has to be considered. In antiquity, the images had the function to make

---

99. [Nicolas Sanders, *A Treatise of the Images of Christ, and of His Saints* (Louvain, 1567), f. 109ʳ⁻ᵛ. Kantorowicz cites the same passage in *King's Two Bodies*, p. 427, n. 371, where he acknowledges his source as Frances Yates, "Queen Elizabeth as Astraea" (as above, n. 8).]

100. [Joys Buysson, *Remonstrances faictes à Nantes en l'an MDXCIV en la présence du deffunt Henri IV* (Paris, 1610): i.e., the publication of 1610 referred to the king as dead; he was not dead in 1594.]

the Prince as omnipresent as he claimed to be; for they represented vicariously the absent emperor. The idea of the omnipresence of the imperial or royal power re-appeared in another form in the thirteenth century when the feudal government was superseded by the new centralized administration through royal officers.

English jurists, ever since the sixteenth century, discussed the legal ubiquity of the king. "His majesty, in the eyes of the law, is always present in all his courts."[101] This maxim, needless to say, had a very long history. The Roman emperors of course claimed omnipresence, and since the Prince could not be everywhere in his person, his presence was vicariously indicated by the images placed in assembly halls, court rooms, market places, theatres, etc. The imperial omnipresence reappeared in the thirteenth century when the new centralized administration through imperial vicars replaced the old feudal government. Frederick II called his governors and high officers "images of our person" and proclaimed time and time again that he, who could not be present everywhere *personaliter*, was nevertheless everywhere present *potentialiter* through his officers.[102] Around 1300, in the France of Philip the Fair, it became the custom to signify the royal presence by hoisting the king's coat-of-arms wherever the *garda regis*, the royal jurisdiction, was to be manifested. Only in relatively modern times did the monogram flourish of the prince ("E.R.II") take over some of the functions of the coat-of-arms, though the flourish was artistically used as early as the fifteenth century.

On the other hand, however, in the later Middle Ages it became customary to decorate the courtrooms and council halls with so-called Justice-Images—allegorical or historical scenes recalling the working of Justice, or a representation of the crucifixion. That the ruling Prince should have been represented was not the general custom; however, in the hall of his palace in Naples, Frederick II had his picture displayed as the supreme judge sitting in court. By the late sixteenth century, however, we find some indications for replacing historical or religious Justice-imagery by portraits of the ruler. De la Roche Flavin, councilor of both the French king and the Parlement of Paris (the highest law court) and later at Toulouse, describes the chambers of the Supreme Court.[103] In the great Audience Chamber, he says, there is no image of the king

---

101. [William Blackstone, *Commentaries on the Laws of England* (London, 1765), I, 270; cited in *King's Two Bodies*, 5, n. 6.]

102. [Parallel passage in *King's Two Bodies*, 142.]

103. [Bernard de la Roche Flavin, *Treize livres des Parlements de France* (Geneva, 1621).]

because over the royal throne or over the seat of the Chief Justice is the image of the Crucified "in order to refrain by the commemoration of things holy the all too active spirits." And this, says he, was done after the model of the ancient Roman tribunals where, according to Cicero, the images of Castor and Pollux were displayed. However, the portraits of the kings were displayed in the *Salle des Procureurs*, where the parties met; and the same was true in Aix, Toulouse, and other places. And de la Roche Flavin contemplates in that connection that originally "the introduction and usage of those images was a privilege of the Gods." By and by, however, this privilege slipped from the imperial images to those of Christ and the Saints, until it returned—with a new aura of holiness—back again to the rulers of the modern monarchies.

It would be a quite impermissible exaggeration to maintain that this whole development was *caused* by the scientific jurisprudence of the glossators of Roman law. However, the perpetual juxtaposition of images of saints and images (or insignia) of Princes, the idea of the ruler's omnipresence and his ubiquity in the law courts, and the simple fact that the jurists themselves became—and made others become— conscious of the saintliness of ruler images, should not be dismissed too lightly. And therefore, when the art historian tries to trace the de- velopment of the modern state portrait, he should not forget that in addition to numerous other factors there should be taken into account also the legal "Glosses on State Imagery."

# CHAPTER 7

# The Dukes of Burgundy and the Italian Renaissance

Whereas most of the works in this collection originated as lectures and then were turned into articles, the present piece is a straightforward lecture. Its pedigree is well attested. Kantorowicz engaged in the research on which it is based in Brussels, Berlin, numerous Italian cities, and Paris in the years between 1936 and 1938 with the aim of writing a book on the Valois Dukes of Burgundy and particularly Charles the Bold.[1] But in February 1938 when it became clear that he would be forced to leave Germany, he put aside this plan in favor of preparing a number of lectures to be given in England and America in order to make a living and seek potential employment. Thereafter he never returned to the book project, only salvaging pieces of what evidently was much preparatory work for two lectures. He gave one of these at the Courtauld Institute in London early in 1939; this then became an article "The Este Portrait by Roger van der Weyden," published in 1940 in the *Journal of the Warburg and Courtauld Institutes*. He wrote the other lecture, "Charles the Bold and the Italian Renaissance," in late 1938 or early 1939, but it has never been published until now. He delivered it as a guest speaker at Yale in March

---

1. For details, Robert E. Lerner, *Ernst Kantorowicz: A Life* (Princeton, 2017), 198–200.

1939 and again in Berkeley in 1940. Then he retrieved it in November 1960 as a talk given on the occasion of an exhibition of Flemish art in Detroit. The typescript of the Detroit version provides the basis of what is offered here.

Without ever specifying it in either of his Burgundy pieces, Kantorowicz's project was clearly conceived as an alternative to Johan Huizinga's classic, *The Autumn of the Middle Ages*. The reference to "Lancelots, unicorns, and palfreys" at the opening of the lecture is an implicit evocation of Huizinga, and the clearest proof that Kantorowicz worked with notes from Huizinga before him resides in his mention of three composers, "Binchois, Dufay, and Ockeghem"—names taken directly from *The Autumn of the Middle Ages*. (Kantorowicz himself was never interested in music—he ostentatiously shunned it.) A pointed contrast to Huizinga lies in both method and argument. Whereas Huizinga suffused himself in literary sources—poems, chronicles, manuals—Kantorowicz traveled from one archive to another looking for documents. In terms of argument, Kantorowicz's alternative to Huizinga can be seen immediately in the title of this lecture, "Charles the Bold and the Italian Renaissance": Huizinga portrayed the culture of Burgundy as late medieval, whereas Kantorowicz disagreed in regard to the reign of Duke Charles (1467–1477). His argument is that Charles dreamed of greatly expanding his realm to match the Carolingian "Middle Kingdom." This led him to seek alliances with Italian princes, which in turn led to the presence of a large number of Italians at his court who were representatives of "Italian thought and culture." According to Kantorowicz, "under their influence Charles became, so to speak, a prince of the contemporary Italian Renaissance."

Kantorowicz's advancement of a governing thesis is unusual for him, and rare as well is its presentation with a minimum of superfluous erudition. Although the original lecture was written in Europe, it displays fluent English, raising the possibility that it was touched up. The text often lacks distinct paragraph structure, partially no doubt because of the lecture format and also because much of it consists of extended examples. Nevertheless, it still offers some of Kantorowicz's most accessible reading because of its clarity and often witty phrasings: Flemish masters engaged in "enlarged miniature painting"; "cultures rooted in the most different soils and souls"; the introduction of "a certain amount of Italianità." For texture there is: "even in his military camp there would be found the choirboys who received daily a dish of raw beef at his table, just like the heralds, in order to keep their voices clear." One great frustration, however, exists: there is no documentation. Because we know that the author had spent many months of work in archives in Brussels and throughout the length and breadth of Italy and can infer that he was drawing on documents he had found in these locations, specific details elude us. Perhaps someone may wish to track down Kantorowicz's sources from their use in the text, but this might necessitate a renewed trip to the archives. (But not the Neapolitan archives, which were destroyed in the Second World War.)

Much has been said and written about the problem of cultural relations and artistic interchange between Flanders and Italy during the fifteenth century; and the fascination emanating from that problem is easily understood. It always appeared as a most remarkable and even slightly disquieting fact that in fifteenth-century Europe two centers of art and culture so different from one another and so important as those of Flanders and of Renaissance Italy could have co-existed side by side.

In Italy we visualize a high idealism, nourished by classical and Christian doctrines, encouraged by the remnants of classical art, and invigorated by the dogma of a direct Roman ancestry to the Italians of those days. The Italian Renaissance was consciously revolutionary by its intention of restoring the Roman past, and it derived its impetus from its romano-classical and cesaro-Christian garb.

On the Burgundian side of the fence (if we accept the term "Burgundian" to encompass the intellectual and artistic life at the court of the Dukes of Burgundy and Flanders) we visualize a very different myth. Within the court circles, the nobility was ready to make the romanticism of chivalry, of *chansons de geste*, and fairy tales a reality of life—to live in the imaginary world of Lancelots and Merlins, of white unicorns, white palfreys, and unredeemed ladies, flowering like the ornaments of the contemporary Arras tapestries which we may admire at the Musée Cluny and in the Cloisters of the Metropolitan Museum. But we have to recognize also the modest and slightly puritan religious feelings related to the *devotio moderna* of the Flemish people and well-to-do citizens; furthermore, the strong sense for a contemplative naturalism and realism of detail on the part of the Flemish artists. In their, so to say, enlarged miniature painting they still performed an art illustrating the word [*sic*—but probably should be "world"] rather than an art ambitious to create, by means of huge frescoes and baffling sculpture, the ideals of a glorious past anew.

Yet, even though these two cultures rooted in the most different soils and souls, and developed almost independently of each other, Europe was too small to keep them completely apart and to preclude any contact between North and South.

To be sure, there always was a certain amount of interchange, and we know that since about the middle of the Quattrocento Italians began to take great interest in the Flemish-Burgundian world. Burgundian customs became popular in Italy. Italian writers began to praise Flemish painters, styling Jan van Eyck a prince of painters. Flemish artists worked in Milan, Urbino, and other places, and their technic [sic] as well as their artistic conceptions or their predilections for *intérieurs* such as studies and merchant offices began to influence Italian painters.

There exists also the other side of the same problem. The Bishop of Tournai Guillaume Filastre, the second Chancellor of the Order of the Golden Fleece, had his tomb made in the workshop of the Della Robbia. Moreover, as has been pointed out time and time again, there were Italian merchant colonies in various Flemish cities, particularly in Bruges, which had been of importance to the exchange not only of money and goods but also of objects of art and artistic industry. And at Bruges, the Florentine banking house of Medici kept a permanent agent—Angelo Tani and Tommaso Portinari are the ones best known.

In short, interchange and mutual influence were certainly not lacking around 1450. All these, however, were more or less casual relations. A more or less purposeful unlocking of the Netherlands to the Italians belongs to a slightly later period. And fortunately the epistolary material, letters scattered about in Italian and other archives and as yet only fragmentarily exploited, permits us to disclose some of the channels through which the new Italian mentality passed to the North.

What I therefore propose to show are the circumstances under which the Burgundian court and its society came, for a certain time, under the influence of Italian elements, especially in the time of Charles the Bold, whereby the political constellations were effective as a highly important stimulant. In fact, the increase of Italian influence in Flanders and Burgundy cannot be separated from both the political background and the personal impulses of the Dukes.

Political relations between Burgundy-Flanders and Italy were insignificant before 1450. By that time, however, things changed. The scattered possessions of the Dukes—Flanders with Holland, Zeeland, Brabant, Hainaut, Luxemburg in the North, and the duchy of Burgundy with Franche Comté in the South—began to grow closer and closer together. By the usual means of territorial policy: marriage, inheritance, claims, and conquests, the scattered possessions were rounded out to

form a state. And with the consolidation of this new buffer-state between France and Germany, which rose to the rank of a first-rate European power, a new mirage began to rise: the mirage of a revival of
that ancient Carolingian middle-empire of Lotharingia, the result of
the partition of the treaty of Verdun in 843.

Lotharingia, in the ninth century, was combined with both Italy and
the imperial dignity; and although Lotharingia was blotted out from
the European map after less than thirty years, the existence of that
middle-empire had not fallen into oblivion. Poems, such as the epic
*Girart de Roussillon* which glorified a Lotharingian empire, were eagerly
read at the Burgundian court, where the mirage of Lotharingia's revival
began to influence quite seriously the political plans of Philip the Good
and especially of Charles the Bold.

Philip the Good, although the one who first rediscovered the Lotharingia idea, was an imperialist of the old mediaeval fashion; that is, his
imperialism was restricted to rounding out his territories, whereas his
more far-reaching ambitions focused on the old-fashioned and good
mediaeval idea of a crusade.

In fact, it was the fall Constantinople, in 1453, that first brought
Philip the Good into touch with the Italian courts. In the almost legendary "Feast of the Pheasant" at Lille (fig. 7.1) in 1454, he took the
cross against the Turk and, in setting himself up as the leader of the crusade, he succeeded in outdoing his two feudal lords, the Holy Roman
Emperor and the King of France, the two traditional commanders-in-
chief of crusaders in former centuries.

**FIGURE 7.1**    *Vow of the Pheasant* (Philip the Good and Isabella at the Feast of the Pheasant in Lille
in 1454), anonymous, sixteenth century. Rijksmuseum, Amsterdam.

Now Burgundy had taken their place. Philip appeared as the champion of Christendom, *le grand duc d'Occident*, negotiated endlessly with Enea Silvio Piccolomini, later Pope Pius II, dealt with Italian princes and the Republic of Venice, tried to enter into some opaque alliances in Italy, and sent, in 1459, a marvelously equipped Burgundian delegation to the Council of Mantova, where deliberations were carried on about the crusade, while Burgundian ships were already cruising the Black Sea. Although Philip's crusade never came off, his plans at least had one result: Burgundy manifested herself to the Italian princes as the most important European power, [while] Philip himself was thought of, especially in Italy, as a possible successor to the imperial throne.

Philip the Good had hardly ever aspired to the imperial rank, nor did his Lotharingian plans carry him so far away from reality as to prompt him to aspire to a reunion of his dominions with Italy, which had belonged to his Lotharingian predecessors in the ninth century. It is true, Philip aspired at his own elevation to the rank of king—be it of Lotharingia, Flanders, or Burgundy. But he merely wished to rid himself of his feudal ties which made him dependent on both the Emperor and the King of France, and to achieve the legal recognition of a sovereignty which in fact he held.

Philip of Burgundy had never been really eccentric in his political aiming, passionate and vehement though he was in his domestic affairs. His countries enjoyed peace for some thirty years, and during that period he as well as his subjects grew rich. He was styled the *good Duke* even during his lifetime and was admired by the world as the model gentleman of his century. The distinction of his appearance, unforgettable through the art of Roger van der Weyden (fig. 7.2) was indeed hardly to be matched.

He was the founder of the Order of the Golden Fleece, then and for many centuries thereafter the most distinguished Chivalric Order in Christendom. And Philip was also the creator of the solemn and stylized grandezza of his court—a punctilio of ceremonies which we are used to call the "Spanish Style" though in fact it was received by the Habsburg dynasties of Spain and Austria in a very legitimate way from Burgundy.

This high credit Philip the Good passed on to his son, Charles Count of Charolais, together with whom he is shown in a drawing of the *Recueil d'Arras* fashioned by Roger (fig. 7.3).

**FIGURE 7.2**    Philip the Good, Duke of Burgundy, after Roger van der Weyden, ca. 1450, Groeninge-museum, Bruges. Photo: Wikimedia Commons.

In 1463, Philip the Good, then a broken man of ill health, resigned the government and placed it, four years before his death, in the hands of Charles.

Charles the Bold was much more problematic a character than his father had been. There is something strange about him. He must have been quite cheerful in his youth and certainly very attractive at the time when he was painted by Roger van der Weyden. We learn, however, from his courtiers and his physicians that with advancing age (he died at the age of forty-four) he grew more and more irritable. Some undefinable grief, a sudden melancholy, would at times overwhelm him; and from those depressions he would turn to almost feverish activity. These qualities explain also that he so frequently was carried off and away by the abundance of his often most ingenious political ideas which he might quickly abandon or to which he might stick stubbornly.

**FIGURE 7.3** Philip the Good and his son Charles the Bold, from the Recueil d'Arras, mid-sixteenth century. Arras, Saint-Vaast Abbey Media Library—266 (CGM 1136, inv. 1839), fol. 61r.

The fact that he loved arts and literature does not disagree with this character. Of the four temperaments, that of the "Melancholic" was always said to be that of the artist, and Charles himself felt much like an artist. His handwriting—a clear, wide, lavish hand, artificial and stylized as hands then were—seems to betray his artistic inclinations. Above all, however, he was a musician, devoted to the ancient Dutch music which then came near to its apogee, owing to masters such as Binchois, Dufay, and Ockeghem. Charles himself was a composer of motets which occasionally were performed in cathedrals, and even in his military camp there would be found the choirboys who received daily a dish of raw beef at his table, just like the heralds, in order to keep their voices clear. Olivier de la Marche, his Lord Chamberlain, mentions that the Duke loved music which was *la récréation de tous cueurs tristes et désolés*, and something of this Saul-like pathos seems to be preserved in a miniature of a Paris manuscript.

**FIGURE 7.4**  Louis XI of France, from the Recueil d'Arras, mid-sixteenth century. Arras, Saint-Vaast Abbey Media Library—266 (CGM 1136, inv. 1839), fol. 7r.

For all his restlessness and vacillations, however, there was one feeling in him that may be called constant: his hatred of Louis XI of France, who is handsomely depicted in the *Receuil d'Arras* (fig. 7.4).

Although himself a Valois, Charles declined to be called a Frenchman, and frequently preferred to use the English language (his second wife being Margaret of York), or claimed to be Portuguese, which his mother was. And he loved the Italian language, which he mastered perfectly. One of the few presents which Louis XI in his later days (less handsome than in his youth according to a painting in a private collection by an unknown painter; fig. 7.5), made to his cousin Charles was a Charlemagne manuscript *in lingua et littera italiana*, because he knew that Charles was *in tuto dato* (in every respect devoted) *alli costumi, modi et governi italiani*. Indeed, with regard to his wishes and predilections we might ask whether Charles was not intellectually of the kin of the princes of the Italian Renaissance.

**FIGURE 7.5**    Louis XI of France by Jacob de Littemont (attr.), ca. 1469. Photo: Wikimedia Commons.

His policy was universal and encompassed in fact all of Europe. He, too, was fascinated by the idea of a revived Lotharingian empire. Negotiations with pope and emperor were in progress about his elevation to the rank of King of the Romans. These plans failing he tried to secure the imperial succession by marrying off his daughter Mary to Maximilian of Habsburg, the emperor's son. At a diet in Dijon, Charles made some allusions to Burgundy's great past as a kingdom bordering upon Italy. And an alliance with Savoy which he then concluded, established in fact a Burgundian sphere of influence from Flanders to the Mediterranean and to Northern Italy.

Vague as these plans were, they reveal the drift of his ambitions. From his father's somewhat old-fashioned feudal traditions Charles changed to plans of a far greater scale. He was spell-bound by the idea that a royal or imperial title would carry him from Burgundian affairs to the mastery of Europe and to a Caesar-like fame. And his hatred of France prompted him to venture upon political entanglements which in fact covered almost the whole of Western Europe.

Charles' great contest with Louis XI of France passed hastily through many phases. It finally culminated in the great scheme of encircling France. With this object in mind, Charles renewed the old Burgundian alliance with England. Having married in 1463 Margaret of York, he made the cause of the White Rose his own and promised to Edward IV the Crown of France. He then entered into an agreement with Aragon, the neighbor of France and therefore, as well as for many other reasons, her age-old enemy. To this alliance Castile was added, the famous marriage between Ferdinand of Aragon and Isabella of Castile taking place in 1469. Here begins that joyful combination of Spain and Burgundian ideals. Charles the Bold, the Aragonese ally in the Pyrenees, became almost automatically the ally of the Aragonese in Naples, France's irreconcilable foe ever since the Sicilian Vespers of 1282 and later on as the result of the expulsion of the French Anjous from the Kingdom of Naples (1464). Charles' treaty with Ferrante of Naples, in 1469, and his alliance with Savoy resulted perforce in his becoming entangled with the affairs of the Italian states. With Venice a treaty was signed under the pretext of a new crusade against the Turks. Milan, the traditional supporter of France, finally had to yield to pressure from the East (Venice) and West (Savoy) and joined the Burgundian party. Smaller powers such as the Este in Ferrara or the Gonzaga in Mantova, were at least on friendly terms with Burgundy at a time when the Peninsula was split in a Burgundian and a French faction, parties which, so to speak, replaced the old factions of Guelfs and Ghibellines.

Only Florence, that is, Lorenzo de' Medici, kept out of the magic circle of Burgundian dealings, only to fall prey to France at a later date. Lorenzo did not trust Charles the Bold, and nothing can prove his feelings better than the advice given to his agent in Bruges not to lend Charles more money than at most 6,000 pounds. Lorenzo, after all, was not only a clever statesman; he was a good banker, too.

At any rate, it was Charles' political friendship with Italian sovereigns and states that started a new phase of cultural interchange. The intensity of earlier relations increased, and the correspondences make it quite clear that not this or that painter, nor this or that or that conception or invention alone brought about the acceleration of Italo-Burgundian relations, but rather the fact that simply the compound of men in the Duke's field-camp, at his dinner table, and at his court in general began to change. In former days, Burgundian and Flemish noblemen and a sprinkling of German princes from the Lower Rhine (such as the Duke of Cleves, so well-known from Roger's painting; fig. 7.6) formed the retinue of the Duke.

**FIGURE 7.6**    John I, Duke of Cleves. Sixteenth-century copy (1584) of fifteenth-century original from the workshop of Roger van der Weyden, from ca. 1490. Photo credit: © RMN-Grand Palais/ Art Resource, NY.

Now, however, the ducal court was swamped with Italians. Italians became Charles' attendants, officers, and advisors. the Flemish-Burgundian atmosphere was pervaded by a current of Italian air, and the colorful Burgundian dreams of chivalry and crusading exploits were superseded by an Italian appreciation of power as such.

To begin with, all the Italian sovereigns allied with Burgundy found it necessary to keep permanent ambassadors at the ducal court. Nothing like that was known in the time of Philip the Good though diplomatic communication and embassies for special purposes of course always existed. At Charles' court, however, the Italian ambassadors became almost the Duke's personal attendants who followed him wherever his armies marched, careful observers and reporters of all facts and rumors of interest. We find their traces everywhere in the Duke's military camp and in the Duke's tent, in the accounts of the ducal kitchen registering accurately the expenses for their meals at the ducal table, and in the accounts of the ducal *Chambre des Comptes*. Vice versa, the ambassadors reported back to their masters about conversations with the Duke who, as they pointed out, spoke Italian fluently and would often find a quick answer by quoting an Italian proverb.

These ambassadors were highly cultured and educated men. This was certainly true in the case of the Venetian ambassador, Bernardo Bembo, who remained for four years at the Burgundian court. It may be that Bembo's greatest achievement was the procreation of his most famous son Pietro, later cardinal, the author of the *Asolani* and immortal through Castiglione's *Cortegiano*. But Bernardo Bembo, scion of one of the great Senatorial families of the Laguna, was himself well known as one of the leading men of Quattrocento humanism. Though a representative of Venetian humanism, his name remained connected with those of the Florentine Platonists: Lorenzo de' Medici, Marsilio Ficino, Cristoforo Landino, Angelo Poliziano, and others. Ficino dedicated three works to him; Poliziano honored him with a poem; Poggio, also his friend, presented him with a Cicero Codex. Bembo participated at that famous convivium when the crème of the Florentine Platonists gathered to celebrate Plato's birthday.

At any rate, Bernardo Bembo was the exponent of the most advanced Florentine-Venetian humanism, and he could not have failed to convey some of that atmosphere to the ducal court. His successor, after 1474, was Antonio Morosini, bearer of a great name, though otherwise not very important. A most scholarly man, however, was the ambassador of Naples, Francesco Bertini, Bishop of Capaccio, who for more than five years was the almost permanent companion of Charles the Bold and who, though barely forty, acted as the doyen of the *corps diplomatique* accredited to the ducal court.

Francesco Bertini was a representative of what he called curial humanism, a humanism after the fashion of Pope Pius II. He had spent his earlier years in the suites of high princes of the Church: of the Cardinal of Portugal, the Cardinal of Ravenna, and finally the Cardinal of Pavia, Jacopo Amannati detto Piccolomini, so called because being a close friend of Enea Silvio—Pius II—the pope not only created him a cardinal but also adopted him. Through the Cardinal of Ravenna Bertini became acquainted with the circle of humanists at Ferrara, and in connection with an embassy to England he got in touch with Thomas Bekyston, one of the promoters of early English humanism. Then, when recommended to and taking up service with King Ferrante of Naples, who gave him the bishopric of Capaccio, he came into the orbit of Giovanni Pontano, the greatest humanist of the South. Although today barely known, Francesco Bertini must have been considered a celebrity by his contemporaries, since the Florentine Vespasiano de Bisticci devoted to him one of his biographical sketches in his book on the *Uomini illustri* of the fifteenth century. Bertini died in his early forties in the Netherlands. His successor as the envoy of Naples was Giovanni Palomaro, whose personality would be of little interest to us were it not for a rather handsome medal of his which was cut during his sojourn at the Burgundian court, and had not the artist been a compatriot of his, Giovanni Candida.

Giovanni Candida came to the Netherlands not as has often been assumed as the envoy of Naples. Being a partisan of the Angevine kings of Naples, he resented the accession of the Aragonese: he left the kingdom and offered his services to the Burgundian Duke in 1472. Candida, whom a contemporary styled *summus et orator et historicus*, seems to have known Giovanni Pontano, the head of the humanist movement in the South, and was a great admirer of Platina and of Flavio Biondo, the historian. He himself wrote a short history of Naples and Sicily from Greek and Roman times to his own days. At any rate, he was eminently qualified to become the private secretary of Charles the Bold, who used him also as a diplomatic agent and sent him, time and time again, to negotiate at the Italian courts.

In addition to that, however, Candida was called *sculptoriae artis atque plastes hac aetate consummatissimus*, "a most consummate sculptor of that age." He was in fact one of the best medalists of that time although he used his talent not professionally to make a living. But he used his talent socially all the more extensively, leaving us interesting medals of the Duke and his courtiers and officers. A medal of Anthony of Burgundy, the Grand Bâtard, the Duke's half-brother may display here his style (fig. 7.7)

This medal is interesting in so far as we have at our disposal yet another one. A few years before Candida came to the ducal court, the Florentine Niccolò Spinelli worked for Charles the Bold and engraved a seal for him. But he also cut a medal of Anthony of Burgundy. Candida's effort to reproduce the Grand Bâtard *a l'antica* is obvious, while the Spinelli medal as well as a portrait at Chantilly (fig. 7.8) show the somber prince in Burgundian dress.

Candida was not the only Italian secretary and counselor of Charles the Bold. We find in that position also a Master Guido Brunori and

**FIGURE 7.7**   Anthony of Burgundy, medal by Giovanni Candida, ca. 1472–1480. National Gallery of Art, Washington, DC.

one Anselmino da Prato and above all a South-Italian from Troia, Salvatore Clarici. Our interest in Clarici, who was dispatched quite often on diplomatic missions, has a special reason, for his brother, Matteo de Clarici, was the physician in ordinary to Charles the Bold. The fact is significant all by itself. The physicians of Philip the Good had been Franciscan—Roland Lescrivain and the surgeon Jacques Candel in addition to others. Now the Italians took over also in this respect. There are many dispatches of Italian ambassadors to the ducal court which show how great was the Duke's confidence in his doctor, and how great the indiscretion of Matteo de Clarici. Later there was another Italian physician in care of the Duke, Angelo Cato, whose name will come up immediately in other connections.

   In addition to Italian men of letters, ambassadors accredited to the ducal court and the Italian secretaries, political agents, and physicians, Italian soldiers came to the North in great numbers. Charles the Bold,

**FIGURE 7.8**  Portrait of Anthony of Burgundy by Hans Memling (1467–1470). Gemäldegalerie, Dresden.

though in vain, sought to secure the services of the most renowned of all Italian Condottieri then living: Bartolomeo Colleoni (fig. 7.9).

He was to become commander-in-chief of Charles' troops. But the Duke's request, conveyed to Colleoni by Giovanni Candida, stirred up so much anxiety and uneasiness all over Italy that the [Venetian] Signoria refused to allow Colleoni to take service with Burgundy.

In his place a South-Italian, the count of Campobasso, a relative of Giovanni Candida, became the commander of the ducal army, a man ill-famed in later days because he deserted the Burgundian cause on the eve of the battle of Nancy in which Charles was killed. With Campobasso scores of Italian officers were enrolled—among them Jacopo Galeota whose features have been transmitted through a medal cut by Giovanni Candida—and thousands of Italian knights and soldiers were enlisted. We should not forget that the Duke, for many years, had his daily conferences with his Italian commander and his Italian officers. His strange predilection for the Italian soldiery went so far (as is shown

**FIGURE 7.9**    Statue of Bartolomeo Colleoni by Andrea del Verrocchio. Wikimedia Commons, CC BY-SA 4.0. Photo: Didier Descouens.

by one of Charles's orders of battle) that of his four army-corps he put three under the command of Italians, and that of his eight military captaincies no less than four were held by Italians.

One of these higher commanders was an Italian prince, James of Savoy, Charles' lieutenant general in Burgundy. A second Savoy prince—known from a painting in the style of Roger van der Weyden and clearly emulating Roger's picture of Philip the Good—was Philip of Savoy (Ph. Sabaudiae dux). He was governor in the Netherlands and knight of the Golden Fleece since 1468. The presence of these and other Italian princes was of course particularly important in view of the cultural exchanges.

In 1475, Don Federigo of Aragon, son of the King of Naples, very handsomely sculptured by the Sienese medalist Francesco di Giorgio, arrived at the Burgundian court as a suitor for Mary of Burgundy, Charles' daughter. He did not succeed as a suitor, since Charles had more imperial plans for her, but he stayed for a year with the Duke whose favorite he became, taking even command of one of the four ducal army-sections then ready to fight the Swiss. This young prince, himself a man of education, was attached in close friendship to Lorenzo de' Medici. One of Lorenzo's letters to Don Federigo was in fact a whole treatise on the development of Italian poetry, preceding the *Raccolta Aragonese*, a collection of specimens of Italian poetry, and showing clearly the high intellectual level of their friendship.

The prince of Naples came to Charles with a large and noble retinue. One of his attendants was Eligio Colenzio, then a well-known and quite celebrated poet and humanist. Colenzio was not the founder but one of the first members of the Accademia Pontaniana in Naples. Later he became a close friend of Sannazaro, who was younger than he and whose *Arcadia* ushered in a new style of poetry and ideal of life. In Rome, he became the continuator of the tradition of Pomponius Laetus and the latter's Academy, and became a friend too of Giovio, Pietro Bembo, and Castiglione.

Another celebrity was Angelo Cato, philosopher and astrologer, who at the same time acted as Don Federigo's physician, and later became the physician of Charles the Bold. In fact, the medal by an artist of the Neapolitan school has the inscription *Angelus Cato Supinas phylosophus et medicus*. But he was also a patron of historical writers, among others of Philippe de Commynes, who dedicated his great work to Angelo Cato, by that time archbishop of Vienne.

Charles the Bold was obviously ambitious to draw Italian princes to his court; for in addition to the Savoy princes and Don Federigo we find others as well. In his last year he invited most fervently the young Sforza Maria, son of the Duke of Milan, whose alliance with Burgundy was no longer reliable. At an earlier date, in 1469, a younger son of the Marquis of Mantova, Rodolfo Gonzaga, went to the Netherlands to stay with the Duke. There is no need to indicate the fame of the house of Gonzaga. When Rodolfo left for Burgundy, Mantegna was already working on the frescoes in the palace of Mantova; and in his famous picture of the Gonzaga family in the *Camera degli sposi* we can identify Rodolfo standing, one arm akimbo, in front of the column to the right (fig. 7.10).

This young prince too came to Brussels with not too mean a cortège, and his parents may have considered his equipment quite brilliant. But the letters of Rodolfo, who wrote home very regularly every fortnight, prove the luxury in the Netherlands to have been much more extravagant than his parents had imagined. For no sooner had he arrived in

**FIGURE 7.10**   Detail from the "Court Wall" of the Bridal Chamber in Mantua by Andrea Mantegna (1465–1474).

Brussels than he complained how expensive life was in Flanders and that his monthly allowance had to be increased at least fivefold if he wished to live up to the standard expected of his princely position. The Marquis of Mantova granted the money and sent the amount with the messenger of another Italian prince then living at Brussels and serving with Charles the Bold, Francesco d'Este.

It may have been Francesco d'Este who put in a word with the Marquis of Mantova in favor of his younger cousin Rodolfo, an illegitimate son of one of the most celebrated princes of the Italian Renaissance, Lionello d'Este (best known from the Pisanello portrait in Bergamo [fig. 7.11] and Pisanello's medal [fig. 7.12]).

Francesco had been living for a long time at the Burgundian court. He actually had shared for many years household and teachers with Charles, then still Count of Charolais, so that the Este prince was an intimate friend of the Duke. We find him mentioned quite often in connection with court celebration. He was occasionally sent in diplomatic business to Italy, and became in his later years captain and governor in Artois and in the Netherlands.

But Francesco d'Este had other claims than these for wider recognition. For Roger van der Weyden's portrait of a nobleman, holding a

**FIGURE 7.11**   Portrait of Lionello d'Este, Marquis of Ferrara, by Pisanello (ca. 1444). Bergamo, Accademia Carrara. Photo: The Yorck Project (2002) 10.000 Meisterwerke der Malerei.

**FIGURE 7.12**   Pisanello, obverse of a bronze coin of Ferrara showing Leonello d'Este, about 1441. Hood Museum of Art, Dartmouth: Roger Arvid Anderson Collection—250th Anniversary Gift, 1769–2019; 2016.64.11.

small hammer in his hand (in the Metropolitan Museum), represents without any doubt the young Este (fig. 7.13).[2]

   This identification is ascertained in the first place by the reverse side of the panel itself, where we find the Este coat-of-arms and the name FRANCISQUE, which together with the initials twice repeated M.E. cannot have other meaning than *Marchio Estensis Franciscus* or *Marquis d'Este Francisque* (fig. 7.14). Moreover, the frenchified form of his name used by the painter was used by the young Este himself whose letters are always signed *Francisque*.)

   The identity of the sitter was furthermore clarified when I chanced upon a Roman fifteenth-century manuscript containing miniature medallions of all members of the Este family in 1476; and among them was one medallion representing Francesco, *fratello naturale de quello Niccolò de Lionello; e stà in Borgogna*. It is a profile likeness. But the hair covering the forehead, ears and neck with untidy fringes, the long aquiline nose, the protruding lower lip, then the costume: the upright collar and the golden chain encircling the neck—all these details correspond with the Roger portrait.

---

2. [Kantorowicz developed this argument in a separate publication: "The Este Portrait by Roger van der Weyden," *Journal of the Warburg and Courtauld Institutes* 3 (1939–40): 165–80; reprinted in Kantorowicz, *Selected Studies* (Locust Valley, NY, 1965), 366–80.]

**FIGURE 7.13** Portrait of Francesco d'Este by Roger van der Weyden (ca. 1460). The Metropolitan Museum of Art, New York.

**FIGURE 7.14** Reverse of portrait of Francesco d'Este by Roger van der Weyden (ca. 1460). The Metropolitan Museum of Art, New York.

Let me conclude this short survey of the Italians at the Burgundian court and add a few words so as to give some finishing touches to the image of Charles the Bold.

The political relations between Burgundy-Flanders and the Italian states, the permanent ambassadors of the Italian sovereigns, the Italian poets and humanists, secretaries and physicians, the Italian officers and soldiers of the Burgundian army, the Italian engravers working for the court, the Italian princes in attendance to Charles, perhaps also the Italian merchant colony at Bruges: they all must be recognized as agents introducing a certain amount of Italianità, of Italian thought and culture, learning and working, which at that time began to penetrate into the Netherlands. The Flemish-Burgundian courtly society in those years was intermingled with Italians, and the court's romantic display of medieval chivalry was blended with classical ideas imported from Italy.

When we compare, for example, the medals showing the portrait of Philip the Good with those cut for his son, we notice immediately the great change that has taken place—the change of an ideal. The medal of Philip the Good is Burgundian, or if you prefer another expression, it is Gothic and beautiful in its realistic truthfulness. And then the medal of Charles the Bold by Giovanni Candida! Costume, i.e. nakedness except for laurel crown, and even sense of spacing, are Italian or "classical"—not realistic, but idealizing (fig. 7.15). They represent, no more nor less, than simply another species of rulership, another kind of human, and therefore also of political ideal.

**FIGURE 7.15**   Giovanni Candida (Italian, ca. 1445/1450–ca. 1498/1499). Charles the Bold, Duke of Burgundy (b. 1433; r. 1467–1477), ca. 1474. Copper alloy, cast. The Frick Collection, New York; gift of Stephen K. and Janie Woo Scher, 2021. Image © The Frick Collection.

It has been mentioned that Charles the Bold, in his political ambitions, had changed from feudal traditions to a sphere of a more Roman, and Romanly conceived, imperialism. And the medals seem to justify that analysis. There can be no doubt but that Charles deliberately made his contributions to the new spirit which was neither Flemish nor French, but which came from Italy. If we try to visualize the Duke, surrounded not only by Flemish, Burgundian, and German courtiers, but also by princes of Savoy, Naples, Mantova, Ferrara, by Italian men of letters and humanists, then we cannot be surprised to find a strong touch of humanist rhetoric in his allocutions to Flemish diets or to find these addresses abounding in allusions to Rome and quotations from Livy—very different from the jovial and straightforward fashion which Philip the Good preferred when addressing his subjects.

One of Charles' attendants tells us that the Duke, after having worshiped in his youth Lancelot and King Arthur, abandoned the fairyland chivalry in his later years and that, every evening for two hours, he made one of his courtiers read to him "the grand histories of Rome, because in listening to the exploits of the Romans he took the greatest pleasure." It is on record that Giovanni Candida had to read to the Duke, when convalescent, *"de Tito-Livio un pezo."* In fact Charles had ordered the works of ancient authors to be newly translated into French for personal use, such as Livy and Curtius Rufus, Valerius Maximus and, apart from others, Vegetius, the writer on Roman warfare and military history. These authors were certainly not without influence on his own actions. His fateful predilection for employing Italian soldiers; his efforts to persuade Colleoni to become commander-in-chief of his troops; his enrolling minor Italian condottieri simply because they were Italians, seems to be a result of his eager reading of Vegetius. He may have believed that the Renaissance descendants of the ancient Romans were trained in Roman warfare ever since antiquity and were the natural heirs of the art of Pompey and Caesar. It was a new romanticism which Charles nourished while dropping the romantic ideal of mediaeval chivalry.

Justus van Ghent, working in Urbino for Federigo of Montefeltro, painted Charles as King Solomon, thus portraying him as the wise prince of his century (fig. 7.16).

Charles may have liked this biblical allegorical allusion though he may have preferred other ones. "He aspired—wrote one of his translators of Roman historians—to play the part of one of the heroes whose portraits were placed constantly before his eyes by the translations." And, says another one, "he disliked novels and pleasant stories, and enjoyed merely the Roman histories and the exploits of Caesar, Pompey, Hannibal, Alexander, and of other great and noble men he wanted to follow and rival."

The Burgundian masters of tapestries knew better how to flatter Charles when representing him in the guise of the classical heroes of the past. A tapestry in the Palazzo Doria in Rome shows Charles the Bold as young Alexander on his Bucephalus greeting Philip of Macedonia or Burgundy and the Queen-Duchess Olympia-Isabella. And the tapestries at Berne, made before 1475, show Caesar himself in the costume and attitude of Charles ready to cross the Rubicon. This homage of the artists would probably have pleased Charles the Bold. To follow the great warriors and conquerors of the world and to emulate their exploits was one of the driving impulses of his political designs. And with this desire he inhaled the sweetest and strongest of all Renaissance poisons: the thirst for fame and glory. "It was—writes Philip de

**FIGURE 7.16**   Charles the Bold as Solomon by Justus van Ghent, ca. 1474, Urbino Galleria Nazionale. Photo: Wikimedia Commons/Shakko Kitsune.

Commines—his thirst for glory that above all things impelled him to perpetual wars. He wished to resemble those ancient princes, who were so much renowned after their death." It no longer was the colorful splendor of Burgundian chivalry; it was the universal fame and the laurel of Caesars that Charles longed for. And in this longing the doctrines and princes of the Italian Renaissance were his teachers.

# CHAPTER 8

# Humanities and History

In the winter of 1943, a group of about twenty Berkeley faculty members in humanistic fields organized a "Committee on Humanities" and wrote brief statements responding to the question: "What do we expect that humanities study will induce in students' minds?" The collection, titled "Aims of the Humanities," was then circulated in "dittoed" form. The fields represented were art, English literature, foreign languages, and history. "History" was taken by George Guttridge, who specialized in eighteenth-century English history. Guttridge's piece was only two paragraphs long. Ernst Kantorowicz evidently did not consider it sufficient and accordingly wrote a longer piece on the same subject. As he informed his friend Lucy von Wangenheim, "I at least could stress the point that history conveys a sort of vicarious experience which is a substitute for the lacking experience we can gather in Kansas City or Columbus."

Most likely the ultimate goal of the committee was to bring out "Aims of the Humanities" as a published pamphlet. But if so, that never happened. Indeed, Kantorowicz's own piece appears to be broken off at the end. Still, it is the nearest we have to his "historian's credo."

Humanities, and education in general, is the knowledge of man and human society as well as of man in human society. This knowledge, from the Eleatic philosophers to John Dewey, has successfully resisted any efforts of being boiled down to formulas, rules or laws which can be memorized or are comparable in any respect to the stabilized laws of science. To acquire the knowledge of man and human society, and of man *in* human society, there is normally only one way practicable, that of experience. Experience of man and human society is acquired, to-day, only to a relatively small degree through personal observation. Our *knowledge of fellow citizens* is limited, our selection perforce casual, and the number of human types from which we may gather experience is nei-ther enough to represent our "cosmos" comprehensive, nor is it always representative of the highest human qualities. The *knowledge of society* gained by personal experience rarely extends beyond the borders of our own country—and not even these boundaries are always reached. If we account for these differences, we realize the importance of the humani-ties. *The humanities must be considered the irreplaceable medium through which the knowledge of man and human society can be extended beyond the boundaries of personal observation.*

The humanities, when reestablished at the end of the Middle Ages in the 13th and 14th centuries, took effect as an antidote against medieval theology, that is the knowledge not of the *variety* of man and human society but of God and of a unified type of man and of a unified society. Humanities, today, are an antidote to "political theology," a pseudo-theology of the state which is likewise not interested in the variety of man and of human society, but is interested, almost exclusively, in es-tablishing a uniform type of man (Nordic Nazi) and a uniform pattern of human society (New Order—NSDAP "Vaterland"). Modern political theology considers the knowledge of, and the respect to, other types of man and other patterns of society undesirable and "unpatriotic." The humanities are tolerated within modern political theology in a similar way as they were within mediaeval theology as a quarry from which evi-dence for the desired one-type man and one-pattern society is collected.

The humanities take effect against self-centeredness and the tenden-cies to make mind "narrow" in the sense indicated. The humanities are the medium to extend our knowledge of man and human society to all times and all regions and thus carry us beyond the boundaries of our casual dwelling places and of the particular epoch to which we are bound, and they teach us to respect others even though these others may be not only different from us but sometimes even more loveable and attractive than we are. The humanities convey this knowledge in various forms, above all in what here may be called "images," that is in cyphers and metaphors of human and social conditions and forms of being which symbolize or stand for a sum total or elicit a compound of associations referring to man and human society (*persons* such as Alexander, Augustus, or Washington; forms of *society* such as Greek polis, religious sects, monastic orders; or human relations such as Alexander and Aristotle, Caesar and Brutus, Christ and Pilate).

"Images" of man, human relations, and human society in the past and in remote countries are transmitted in the most concentrated form by works of art: painting, sculpture, architecture, music, and poetry, and with due alterations by philosophy. The greater the artist, the more telling but also the more concentrated and inexhaustible is the "image." Not every person has access to the knowledge of man and society through the medium of works of art, and indeed few of us have access equally to all species of art. Also, a certain amount of training is the indispensable preliminary condition for approaching art. Few human beings are in a position to gather knowledge of man, of human relations and of human society from a Greek statue or vase, a Roman sarcophagus or a Byzantine mosaic or a wall painting in the Sistine, from the music of Palestrina or Bach, from the philosophy of Descartes or Kant, unless they are prepared and trained to see and hear and read adequately. This training of eye, ear, and our reactions must not be, but usually would be, connected, one way or other, with history. Without a certain amount of historical knowledge, works of art today, and for reasons not here to be discussed, are likely to remain mute.

This does not imply that history is merely an auxiliary to the other branches of humanities. History transmits those "images" which have been called "knowledge of man and human society in shorthand," in a form which is more easily accessible and available to a greater number of people than is the case with reference to arts. The way to history is open, more or less, to everybody, also to those who do not feel like an artist. History confers on us the knowledge of man and human society in a form which is broader and less esoteric or concentrated than the form represented by the arts, and the quantity as well as the variety of human and social images as transmitted by history is probably greater, more detailed and more specific than in the same case when transmitted through arts. Moreover, as far as society is concerned—and man *in* society—history is in a position to offer syntheses which the other branches of the humanities would offer only in exceptional cases. This is true with reference to constitutional or legal history as well as to cultural or biographical accounts. History, therefore, always was and still is the main gateway through which most people are led to a knowledge of man and human society.

Furthermore, history is the gateway to the understanding of evolution both of man in society and of society in itself. The work of art, except for epical poetry, does not account for the category of time; it presents the absolute in a certain moment whereas history presents also the relative within time and with the process of development. History discloses the intellectual, political, economical, social and other branches, movements and changes, and thereby makes us conscious also of the world and the epoch in which we live. It is the instrument, the sextant, to ascertain the position of man's ship in the past and in the present. This instrument cannot be replaced by other branches of the humanities which call in history as an auxiliary. History, which in turn calls in art, philosophy, philology, (and so forth) as auxiliaries, is an independent study and a humanist branch of knowledge in its own right. A superficial knowledge of history from Adam to Adolf as distributed by those branches of the humanities which make history menial as an auxiliary, is of little help and is almost liable to do harm, unless this applied history is continuously controlled and revised and brought into line with the results of the investigation of the professional historian. History cannot be replaced by other disciplines as little as history pretends to replace other branches of humanities. But history indeed is one of the most comprehensive of the humanistic disciplines and a reservoir which at least should be able to receive most of the other branches of the humanities.

The main task of history, therefore, is (1) to provide an adequate assortment of "images" of man and of human society, and (2) of making us conscious of the various ways and trends of evolution. One of the great dangers in this country, as far as education is concerned, is the poorness of the assortment of images which the students have at their disposal. The knowledge of man and society as transmitted through the symbols, metaphors and images of Scripture, of Greek mythology, of Roman mythology of the state, of historical narrations and of fairy tales is, on the whole, acquired by the student not before he enters the university, where he learns elementary things in the classroom which he should have been acquainted with in the nursery. The poorness of the normal student's stock of images and metaphors is appalling. Furthermore, the lack of thinking in terms of evolution—in terms of what things really mean and where they come from—is likewise arrested. From this deficiency, the redress of which is one of the tasks of history, the other branches of humanities are bound to suffer. Students are not trained, for instance, to think etymologically, and the sense for semantics is, on the whole, underdeveloped. That words have history and a meaning which changes is practically unknown to students, probably because they are not taught to think in those terms. They are helpless when hearing a new word which is not borrowed from the horizon of their daily needs. They are ignorant not only of the derivation but even of the fact that a word, an institution, a style or a custom derives from anywhere at all.

# CHAPTER 9

# Postage Stamps and the Historian

No copy of this talk exists in the Kantorowicz archive of the Leo Baeck Institute. It was obtained by Kantorowicz's Boswell, Ralph Giesey, and rescued only in the form of a retyped version made by Giesey that he placed on his website. (Since Giesey's website no longer exists, the present publication is now the second rescue.) Giesey probably obtained his copy directly from the author, for he does not mention it as having ever been in the Kantorowicz papers. The text refers to original page numbers in square brackets, and since these amount to thirteen pages (a large number for a short lecture), Giesey most likely was working from the copy read for a lecture. (Kantorowicz used reduced-size pages for his lecture texts so that he could produce them casually from out of his vest pocket).

Giesey indicated that the lecture was given at the annual dinner of the History Graduate Students' Association in June 1949, meaning that this was a Phi Alpha Theta dinner. The Greek letters are those of a history students' honor society, consisting of both undergraduates and graduate students. For undergraduates the minimum requirement was a 3.1 grade point average, for graduates a 3.5 average. The bar was not high, and such end-of-year annual meetings, held in a preferred local restaurant, were occasions of relaxed conviviality. History faculty members were free to attend, and in 1949 a considerable number were present. Since Kantorowicz did not drive an automobile, someone was appointed to pick him up and bring him back home. It would be good to know whether the talk in June was delivered toward the beginning or the end of the month, for June 14, 1949, was the fateful day when he delivered an impassioned speech at a meeting of the Berkeley Academic Senate protesting the California Board of Regents' plan to impose a faculty loyalty oath.

"Postage Stamps and the Historian" was meant to be a lighthearted talk, and the audience must have been delighted by the straight-faced whimsical introduction. (After referring to a stamp celebrating "the Centennial of the American Poultry Industry," the speaker observed that widely circulating stamps "could appear very global—or oval"; he was referring subtly to hens laying eggs.) Yet it also offered a demonstration of how one might carry out an assignment that Kantorowicz himself set in his spring term "Historical Methods" seminar, namely to show "the value of X for the study of history."[1] The goal was to have students see how they might draw on the widest variety of sources for historical research, as, for example, "law," "theology," "philology," "art," "poetry," and even "ecology" and "technology." In 1948 Kantorowicz offered "numismatics" as a possible topic, but nobody volunteered for it. In 1949 someone did take on "numismatics," and in 1950 he offered the topic "postage stamps as a source," although it is unknown whether anyone accepted this assignment.

The Phi Alpha Theta lecture demonstrated how one could employ mundane source material for historiography with panache (although whether the audience understood the meaning of "pagan henotheism" cannot be told). The evening's project was to demonstrate how both postage stamps and coins could be issued as instruments of propaganda. Since Kantorowicz viewed stamps as "gummed paper coinage," he concentrated on numismatics and showed in a masterful *tour d'horizon* how coins first became instruments of propaganda during the era of the Roman Empire and then again during the French Revolutionary and Napoleonic periods. For him numismatic propaganda was driven by the combined themes of empire and mission. As for contemporary American postage stamps, although commemorative issues always aimed at propaganda of one sort or another, paramount was the theme of American mission. All told, in Kantorowicz's words: "stamps are a very important instrument for the spread of political

---

1. For a full treatment of this seminar see Robert E. Lerner, "Ernst Kantorowicz's 'Methods Course' at Berkeley, 1948–1950," in *Mythen, Körper, Bilder: Ernst Kantorowicz zwischen Historismus und Erneuerung der Geisteswissenschaften*, ed. Lucas Burkart et al. (Göttingen, 2015), 310–28.

ideas and of political propaganda whenever Empire Idea and idea of mission are combined."

Numismatics had long held a particular fascination for Kantorow-icz. As early as his biography of Frederick II of 1927 he commented in detail on the significance of the emperor's gold coinage and chose Frederick's gold "Augustale" for the frontispiece of his book. Then, in his "supplementary volume" to the biography of 1931, he presented a full-length excursus on the subject. Subsequently the first chapter of his book *Laudes regiae* (a chapter first written in German in 1936 but ulti-mately published in the English book in 1946) treated coins. And then he gave the paper included in this book, "Roman Coins and Christian Rites," to a Bay Area group in April 1948.

The Phi Alpha Theta talk carries over two examples already offered in *Laudes regiae*: a coin of Louis XIV announcing *Per me reges regnant*—"Kings rule through me"; and the assertion that "a Duke of Artois allowed his coins to exclaim *Ego sum Deus*—"I (the coin) am your God." It can now be said that the second example is mistaken. The legend on the obverse of this coin reads EGO SUM DE, and the reverse ROBERTI; thus if read alone the EGO SUM DE must mean EGO SUM DE[NARIUS]—"I am a *denier*" (a small silver coin), or if taken together with the reverse it reads (un-grammatically) EGO SUM DE ROBERTI ("I am of Robert").[2] Neverthe-less, it is surely true that an American nickel struck from 1920 until 1938 showed with unconscious irony a nearly extinct buffalo with the inscrip-tion "E pluribus unum."

I am far from being a professional after-dinner speaker, nor do I find it humorous and funny at all to be set to work tonight instead of being allowed to enjoy peacefully my wine and listen to the performance of one of my rhetorically far better equipped colleagues.

I did not even know how to start a table-talk, and I had to turn to mediaeval manuals of rhetoric for advice. They were not very satisfac-tory. Jerome and Alcuin suggested to introduce a speech by a so-called ship-metaphor. The speaker should compare himself and oration with a ship ready to leave the safe harbor and to dare winds and waves of a rough rude sea. But my rather limited nautical vocabulary did not per-mit me to consider this suggestion.

---

2. J. D. Brady, "'Ego sum Deus': A Mistaken Legend of Artois," *Museum Notes* (*American Numismatic Society*) 21 (1976): 153–59.

Another manual recommended to start with a praise of the predecessor's speech. Now the last after-dinner speaker I heard at a Phi Alpha Theta dinner was Mr. Guttridge;[3] his speech, as all of you would admit, was beyond praise, so I cannot praise it.

A third suggestion was to compare banqueters with flowers. I rather liked that idea. I found it suitable and nice to think of Mr. Bolton,[4] our chairman eternal and beyond time, in terms of the queen of the flowers, the rose; and of Mr. Hicks,[5] our chairman within time, logically as primrose—unless Mr. Guttridge would claim for himself this flower so important and dear to Disraeli and therewith to Queen Victoria and the English historian. Also I like to think of my room-mate Van[6] in classical terms as another "hyakinthos," a hyacinth or crocus, or of Mr. Kerner[7] as a violet, modestly hidden away in the cold southwestern corner of Wheeler 30. It would have been natural to compare Mr. Palm[8] with a Phoenix and Mr. Hammond[9] with an exotic Bancroft Yucca. Kinnaird[10] should be given the choice of some Scotch emblem, broom or thistle, leaving to punch-happy Larry Harper[11] of course the snapdragon.

As I said, I liked the idea, and I might have carried it through had my knowledge of Botany been more perfect than it is, and had that flowery comparison led me to the few remarks which I wanted to drop—a few remarks on "Postage Stamps and the Historian."

I assume that all of us had and have the same experience: whenever we buy postage stamps, we get a new type, especially in the 3¢ class,

---

3. George H. Guttridge, born in England, historian of modern England.

4. Herbert E. Bolton, historian of the southwestern borderlands of the US. He had served for twenty-two years as the chairman of the Berkeley history department and was age seventy-nine at the time of Kantorowicz's talk.

5. John D. Hicks, then chair of the Berkeley history department and a leading American historian (*Populist Revolt*, 1931).

6. J. J. Van Nostrand, ancient historian. ("Room-mate" must mean that he shared an office with Kantorowicz.)

7. Robert J. Kerner, historian of Russia and Eastern Europe. The characterization of him as a shrinking violet was ironic, for Kerner was very outgoing and outspoken. Many in the audience must have known that Kantorowicz was being slyly malicious, for Kerner had tried to block his advancement in Berkeley at every step.

8. Franklin C. Palm, historian of France and modern Europe. ("Phoenix" here puns on a plant—the "phoenix palm.")

9. George P. Hammond, historian of Latin America and then director of the Bancroft Library, hence "Bancroft Yucca."

10. Lawrence Kinnaird, historian of the southwestern US and California. (Kinnaird is a Scottish name.)

11. Lawrence A. Harper, specialist in the economic and legal history of the United States, and faculty adviser to Phi Alpha Theta. (His drinking habits are otherwise unrecorded.)

showing an image both beautiful and instructive. Last year's heron of "Everglades National Park," overcutting with its bill the map of Florida (fig. 9.1), seems to tell you where to hibernate when you wish to escape the icy Californian winter.

But, within the ornithological sphere I felt—in my capacity as a cook—more attracted by last year's large brown stamp displaying a well-sized hen which represented (I should say: in a very dignified fashion) the "Centennial of the American Poultry Industry, 1848–1948" (fig. 9.2).

This centennial seemed to indicate that the art of laying eggs successfully was invented in 1848; and in my other capacity—as historian—I realized that this revolutionary invention should probably be connected with the March Revolution, since March is the right time for laying eggs anyhow. Moreover, this Poultry Centennial stamp no doubt should be viewed together with the handsome purple stamp of the same year, indicating together with the portraits of three ladies, "100 Years of Progress of Women, 1848–1948" (fig. 9.3).

I find it difficult to imagine that the historian of 2548 would miss the missing link between the art of laying eggs and the Progress of Women; and, of course, that colleague of 2548 will be a bad historian

**FIGURE 9.1**  Everglades National Park three-cent stamp, 1947 issue, commemorating the dedication of the park. National Postal Museum.

**FIGURE 9.2**   The three-cent "chicken stamp" commemorating the centennial of the American poultry industry, 1948.

**FIGURE 9.3**   The "Progress of Women" three-cent stamp, marking one hundred years of progress, featuring portraits of the women's suffrage leaders Elizabeth Cady Stanton, Carrie Chapman Catt, and Lucretia Mott.

if he overlooks the obvious inner connection of those brown eggs and progressive women, on the one hand, with the *Communist Manifesto* of 1848 on the other, which has not received a memorial stamp. The *Communist Manifesto* leads us of course to Sutter's Mill as depicted on the "California Gold Centennial, 1848–1948" stamps (fig. 9.4)—all the more since Marx, in 1851, discusses very seriously economic implications of the Californian gold findings. I do not know to what extent the device "Forward" of the Wisconsin Centennial stamp of 1948 (fig. 9.5) may have stimulated the events a hundred years ago, but I should not like to exclude the possibility that Wisconsin's "Forward" is causally responsible for the Berlin Socialist Newspaper, the *Vorwärts*. At any rate, it is fascinating to think that in 2548 so much new light should be shed, by our postage stamps, on the events of 1848. It will appear very global—or oval.

We ourselves, however, are contemporaries; we still know that those stamps reflect unrelated facts. This lack of interrelatedness, however, is not true regarding other modern postage stamps. For some time, I faithfully sponged and glued Miss Juliette Gordon Low, "Founder of

**FIGURE 9.4**    The three-cent "California Gold Centennial" stamp, 1948.

**FIGURE 9.5**    The three-cent "Wisconsin Centennial 1848–1948" stamp.

the Girl Scouts of the U.S.A." to my envelopes (fig. 9.6) until recently I received at the post-office a far more interesting stamp. It shows, on green ground, and in full frontality, a Puerto Rican with his broad-rimed straw hat. The inscription reads: "First Gubernatorial Election in Puerto Rico: Inauguration Jan. 2, 1949." In his right hand, the Puerto Rican holds a cogwheel; in his left, an urn with the telling inscription "BALLOT" (fig. 9.7).

Now we begin to move on historically safer ground than hitherto. This Puerto Rican "ballot" stamp, it is true, records a historical event; but it is also political propaganda. This stamp may travel to Bulgaria, Titonia,[12] Hungary, to any country beyond or between the iron curtain; it may reach such countries as have not yet been reeducated, Germany and Austria, or Spain and Argentina. And in that case the square-inch of gummed green paper carries a message to those abroad, a message saying that the principle of free and secret elections and of self-government—in short, the whole compound of political ideas and of *Weltanschauung* as described by the ballot urn—have been given by the U.S. to Puerto Rico. We should not forget that the word "ballot" ranks very highly in

---

12. Referring to former Yugoslavia, then governed by Josip Broz Tito.

**FIGURE 9.6**    Commemorative three-cent stamp, 1948, of Juliette Gordon Low, founder of the Girl Scouts of America.

**FIGURE 9.7**    Stamp commemorating the first free election for governor of Puerto Rico as a US territory, 1949.

our political vocabulary and in our Post-War Propaganda. It has been dinned into the ears of the Post-War Continentals. It is like a magical power or promise. "Saint Ballot" one might call it or compare it to the Roman functional deities: *Pax Romana, Concordia, Fides,* and similar virtues—that is Ballot with a capital B and "she."

Now the historian is not only entitled to, he is obliged to raise the question concerning the sources: where does that political propaganda on postage stamps derive from? What are the fore-runners? Is it a new invention? Is there a tradition? Is it now only by transference, by applying an old idea to a new material?

It is well-known, though not often realized that our postage stamps are nothing but the replacement of coins. Our oldest stamps of the 1840s, as every philatelist would know, betray that original connection of coin and stamp very clearly. Those early value-symbols are round like coins, though pressed in a quadrangle or square piece of paper. This pattern is found in practically all the issues of German States before 1870 (fig. 9.8). It has been preserved with tenacity in England. And in this country the 1¢ and 3¢ embossments on envelopes not only are

**FIGURE 9.8**   Saxon postage stamp, 1863.

**FIGURE 9.9**   1854 "George Washington" postage stamp.

round, but they show the relatively high relief of coin-images and coin-inscriptions (fig 9.8). This, by and large, was the customary type before the modern fancy and propaganda imagery got hold of our gummed paper coinage.

Once we have recognized the connection of stamp and coin it is relatively easy to ascertain the ancestors of our propaganda stamps which proclaim to the world the Western political concepts. The stamp propaganda is a coin propaganda by transference. However, the problem is not quite as simple as that. For in history there are only two periods in which coins propagated political ideas: the Roman Empire period and the High Renaissance and Classicistic era.

The Greek coins, beautiful as they are, were mythological or what we may call "heraldic." They heralded the god or gods protecting the city, or showed insignia of the gods; but they did not refer, or very rarely, to historical-political events; they were not narrative, nor were they related to any contemporary happening.

This was hardly different regarding early Roman coinage. But in the last century of the Republic when Rome had become an Empire—even a missionary Empire—and had a distinct message to convey to the world, the coins began to refer to actual events and, what is more important, to interpret them in an official manner. A coin, bearing the inscription of "Ides of March," showed the Phrygian felt cap, the liberty cap, flanked by two daggers (fig. 9.10). It was issued

FIGURE 9.10   "The Ides of March." Silver denarius (reverse), struck by Marcus Iunius Brutus, 43/42 BCE. American Numismatic Society, 1947.2.575.

by the murderers of Caesar—Brutus, Cassius and the others—and it offered a very telling interpretation of Caesar's assassination from the point of view of his adversaries: it meant freedom recovered.

During the following centuries the Roman emperors developed in their coinage their whole political program, giving at the same time the imperial interpretation of the events. Finally, in the fourth century, the coins reflected the struggle between pagan henotheism and Christian monotheism. But once the new religion had secured the victory, the coin propaganda of their world stopped; it referred to things beyond time and space rather than to events in time. And during the Middle Ages the coinage showed hardly any more than almost unintelligible monograms, signs, and lettering. With very few exceptions they did not allude to contemporary events.

Heraldic coinage, though far better executed than before, prevailed also in the Renaissance. However, medallions were issued quite frequently to commemorate current events—in Italy as well as in France, Germany, and England. A medallion, e.g., of Henry VIII, showing an inscription in the three biblical languages—Hebrew, Greek, and Roman—manifests the king's ecclesial-political program hardly less distinctly than the text of the "Act of Supremacy" itself (fig. 9.11).

Allusions to contemporary events became more frequent in the coinage of the late sixteenth and seventeenth centuries, and by the time of Louis XIV, it becomes actually feasible to write history again on the basis of numismatic evidence. The Peace of Münster, e.g., is commemorated by Louis XIV. He is in the attire of Hercules standing on a Hydra while the inscription expounds *ERIT HERCULE MAIOR*. The threat of the Turks is interpreted by the amusing inscription, "Joshua stopped the Sun, Louis stopped the Moon," i.e. the Half-Moon, the Turks. And in a similar fashion the other evidence of that eventful reign is recorded on coins.

The idea of using coins propagandistically climaxed in modern times, in the age of the French Revolution. Between 1789 and 1815 literally hundreds of different coins and medallions were issued in France. They were genuine proclamations to the world, expounding not only the political philosophy of *Liberté, Égalité, Fraternité*, but heralding also the victories and inner achievements of Republic, Consulate, and Empire (fig. 9.12). Here, that is, during the classicism of the Napoleonic era, we find the greatest proximity to Roman coin propaganda which modern Europe has so far produced. There was, once more, that combination of Empire and Mission.

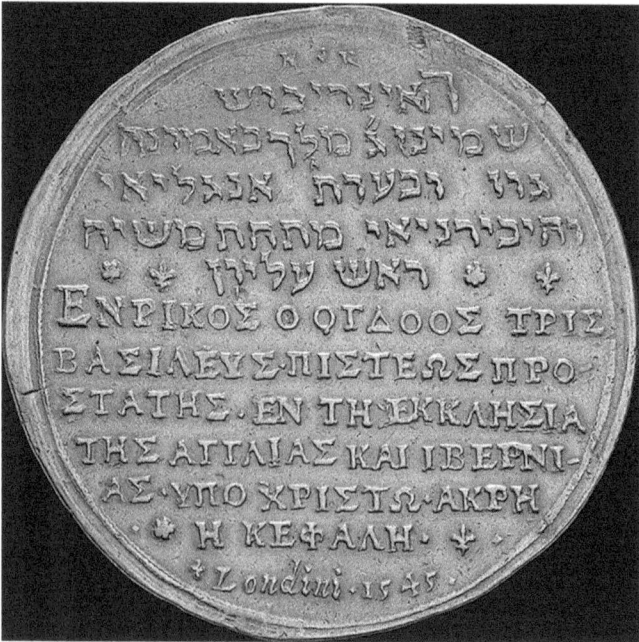

FIGURE 9.11A AND 9.11B   Medal of Henry VIII in profile with Latin inscription ("Henry VIII, King of England, France, and Ireland, defender of the faith . . .") on the obverse and, on the reverse, the same text in Hebrew (to be read backwards) and Greek, 1547. The British Museum, M.6802.

**FIGURE 9.12**  French Revolution coin issue from the First Republic, dated 1793.

The dynastic legitimism of the nineteenth century fell back again on the heraldic display of ruler images and coats of arms, or of national symbols. Narratives, usually of a dynastic pattern, are not lacking completely, but those motives are rare. And since the coins no longer told a continuous story comparable to our comic strips, people did not bother to look very much at the money they used and spent. The coins lost their propaganda value, as this value was not utilized and lay fallow.

This modern blindness may explain the fact that the grossest emblematic cynicisms could pass almost without being noticed. Such involuntary ambiguities had happened before. A Duke of Artois allowed his coins to exclaim *Ego sum Deus*—"I (the coin) am your God"—and Louis XIV was probably correct when issuing coins which announced *Per me reges regnant*—"Kings rule through me" (fig. 9.13). But unsurpassed, in a way, is our nickel preceding the Monticello type. Here we find on the obverse the device "Liberty" symbolized, of all possibilities, by the head of a Red Indian. And the reverse puts, as it were, the dot on the "I." It shows a buffalo with the inscription *E pluribus unum*—"from millions of buffalos one single *buffalino* is left." The coin passes daily through our fingers (fig. 9.14). But how many of you—to be honest—have ever noticed the paradoxes of this coin?

In other words, we no longer look carefully enough at the coins as to recommend them a means of propaganda. Moreover, since 1914 coined currency hardly ever travels abroad. Hence, in our age of currency

**FIGURES 9.13A AND 9.13B**     Coin issue of Louis XIV. Obverse displays the king holding a scepter; reverse displays personified Justice holding a sword and scales. The legend reads "PER ME REGES REGNANT," which means (as Kantorowicz did not either recognize or acknowledge) "kings reign through justice." Dijon, 1645.

**FIGURE 9.14**     Indian head / buffalo nickel, with legend on reverse reading "E pluribus unum." 1935.

**FIGURE 9.15**  The three-cent "Joseph Pulitzer" stamp, 1947.

**FIGURE 9.16**  "These Immortal Chaplains . . ." three-cent stamp, 1948.

restrictions all over the world the colorful little scraps of gummed paper have taken over the role of the mute, yet eloquent, propaganda formerly spread by metal coins. Also the colorful appearance of the stamps may attract our attention more easily than coins; and their propaganda value is certainly high.

For don't let us forget that the Puerto Rican "Ballot" stamp is not an isolated document. The Pulitzer Stamp of 1947, with the inscription, "Our Republic and its press will rise or fall together" (fig. 9.15) announces this country's political creed just as distinctly as the Puerto Rican stamp: Freedom of the Press and Freedom at the polls belong together.

Add to these the stamp of "These Immortal Chaplains" with the inscription "Interfaith in Action," implying "freedom of religion" (fig. 9.16); take the Indian Centennial of "The Five Civilized Indian Tribes of Oklahoma, 1848–1948" (fig. 9.17), perhaps together with the stamp for Dr. George Washington Carver (fig. 9.18) and you add the idea of racial freedom.

Or, the 1946 Smithsonian Institute stamp inscribed, "For the Increase and Diffusion of Knowledge among Men," which proclaims the progress and freedom of scientific research (fig. 9.19). These stamps

**FIGURE 9.17**    Commemorative three-cent stamp honoring the five "civilized" Indian tribes residing in Oklahoma, 1948.

**FIGURE 9.18**    George Washington Carver three-cent stamp honoring the scientist, botanist, educator, and inventor on the fifth anniversary of his death, 1948.

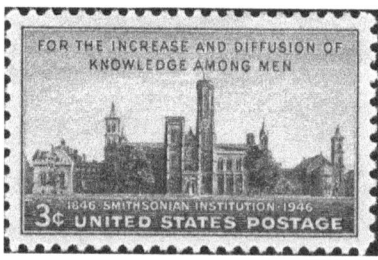

**FIGURE 9.19**    Smithsonian Institution centennial stamp, 1946.

cover the basic principles of life in this country which are summed up by the Abraham Lincoln stamp bearing the message "That government of the people, by the people, and for the people shall not perish from the earth" (fig. 9.20).

**FIGURE 9.20**    "Gettysburg Address" stamp, 1948.

**FIGURE 9.21**    Vatican City airmail stamp, depicting angels carrying the Holy House of Loreto, 1947.

I do not want to discuss the propaganda stamps of other countries—for instance the airmail stamps of Vatican City showing the Holy Angels carrying the House of Loreto (fig. 9.21) or the Austrian (fig. 9.22) and Swiss (fig. 9.23) stamps which remind us of ads of travel agencies.

The main problem may have been clarified: that stamps are a very important instrument for the spread of political ideas and of political propaganda whenever Empire Idea and idea of mission are combined; further that the postage stamps successfully continue a tradition which has been started by the Roman Empire; finally that stamps are a very interesting and most valuable source of information for the historian.

**FIGURE 9.22**    Austrian stamp featuring the Abbey of Melk, 1947.

**FIGURE 9.23**    Swiss stamp in the "Swiss Landscapes" series, 1948.

Let me therefore conclude with an appeal—not one *pro domo*, but an appeal for the sake of the modern European historian and the American historian: that some rich donor provide this university with the necessary funds for establishing an *Institute of Philatelic Studies*.

# Index

Note: Page numbers in *italics* refer to illustrative matter.